# THE OTHER SIDE
# OF NOTHING

## ALSO BY BRAD WARNER

*Don't Be a Jerk*

*Hardcore Zen*

*It Came from Beyond Zen*

*Letters to a Dead Friend about Zen*

*Sex, Sin, and Zen*

*Sit Down and Shut Up*

*There Is No God and He Is Always with You*

*Zen Wrapped in Karma Dipped in Chocolate*

# THE OTHER SIDE OF NOTHING

## The Zen Ethics of Time, Space, and Being

## BRAD WARNER

New World Library
Novato, California

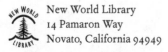

New World Library
14 Pamaron Way
Novato, California 94949

Text design by Tona Pearce Myers

Library of Congress Cataloging-in-Publication Data

Names: Warner, Brad, author.
Title: The other side of nothing : the Zen ethics of time, space, and being / Brad
  Warner.
Description: Novato : New World Library, 2022. | Summary: "A longtime
  practitioner of Zen Buddhism discusses how the Zen concept of nonduality
  — the essential unity of all things — forms the basis of Buddhist ethics. The
  author describes key Buddhist doctrines such as the Four Noble Truths and
  the Eightfold Path, showing their relevance to modern problems" -- Provided
  by publisher.
Identifiers: LCCN 2021062819 (print) | LCCN 2021062820 (ebook) |
  ISBN 9781608688043 (paperback) | ISBN 9781608688050 (epub)
Subjects: LCSH: Buddhist ethics. | Spiritual life--Zen Buddhism. | Zen
  Buddhism.
Classification: LCC BJ1289 .W37 2022 (print) | LCC BJ1289 (ebook) | DDC
  294.3/5--dc23/eng/20220201
LC record available at https://lccn.loc.gov/2021062819
LC ebook record available at https://lccn.loc.gov/2021062820

First printing, May 2022
ISBN 978-1-60868-804-3
Ebook ISBN 978-1-60868-805-0
Printed in Canada on 100% postconsumer-waste recycled paper

 New World Library is proud to be a Gold Certified Environmentally Responsible Publisher. Publisher certification awarded by Green Press Initiative.

10   9   8   7   6   5   4   3   2

# CONTENTS

# INTRODUCTION

You ARE NOT reading this book.

I know some of you will read that statement and say, "If you're going to start off like that, then I'm really *not* going to read this book!" Which is fine. Not every book is for everyone.

But I'm serious. You are not reading this book. Right now. You're not.

There is no "you" who could be reading this book. "You" is a fictional character. Language forces us to refer to this fictional character constantly, and so we have come to believe it really exists. In trying to describe how you do not exist, I am going to have to frame things in terms of "you." In fact, I referred to another fictional character just now when I said "I am going to have to frame things." I am not writing this book either. So there!

This philosophical outlook is what they call nondualism. There is no you. There is no me. There is just one undivided nondual something of which you and I are aspects.

Anyway, let's say you have a friend. Your friend's birthday is coming up, and you want to buy her a nice present. So you focus on the mental picture you have of your friend. Using this mental picture, you can make some guesses about what she might want to receive for her birthday. But no matter how well you know your friend, you can never be completely certain what she wants. Even if she tells you what she wants, she might change her mind. Or she might get that thing and then later on realize she really didn't want it after all.

You also carry a mental image of yourself. If you pay attention to this image, you'll discover that it is only slightly easier to predict what you might want for your own birthday than it is to predict what your friend might want for hers. That's what I have discovered after doing nearly forty years of Zen Buddhist meditation practice, and I don't think I'm all that different from anyone else.

Just like my friend might guess wrongly about what she wants for her birthday, I have often made the wrong guesses about what I want — not only for my birthday but about what I want from life in general.

When I say that you and I do not exist, I'm not saying that all the things we put into a conceptual box called "me" — our feelings, our memories, our opinions, our bodies, and so on — do not exist. What I am saying is that the conceptual box we put those things in is a fiction.

But most of us become slaves to that fiction. We spend a tremendous amount of time and effort defending our box against other boxes, or comparing our box to other boxes and feeling alternately proud or inadequate. Or worse, making our box fight with other boxes. We worry about what might happen to our box in the future. Or we suffer guilt about what our box did in the past. And we are terrified of the unavoidable day when our box will break down and crumble into pieces that can never be put back together again.

When I say that you and I do not exist, what I mean is that all our anxiety about our conceptual box is a big waste of time. Not only is it a big waste of time, but humanity's collective concern over our conceptual boxes is the root cause of all human misery. We are making ourselves and others suffer needlessly over nothing. And we have the ability to end that suffering right now.

This is a book about how to do that. It's about ethics and how ethics relates to nondualism. It is based on the teachings and traditions of a group of people collectively known as Zen Buddhists. Zen Buddhists, for the most part, do not like to call themselves "Zen

Buddhists," by the way. But some of us call ourselves that grudgingly because other people insist on calling us that.

That's because Zen Buddhism is not a religion or a belief system. It's a set of practices that have been refined over the course of 2,500 years of research and development. None of these practices is considered to be so holy and sacred that it can never be improved on with further research and development. In fact, for any given Zen Buddhist practice there may be other practices from other traditions that are just as good and can be used in its place.

Having said that, though, I think there is value in studying a tradition that has such a long track record and has been put to such good use by so many people in such a wide variety of cultures, eras, and social settings. I think there are a lot of good reasons to trust the Zen Buddhist tradition, especially since its founder, the historical Buddha, encouraged us not to trust the practices he recommended until we had tried them out for ourselves.

In this book I intend to explain exactly why the Zen Buddhist tradition says that you and I do not exist, and why it says things will be so much better for all of us once we understand that thoroughly. I will also try to explain the various practices the Zen Buddhists have come up with for thoroughly developing the understanding that you and I don't exist. I'll also be talking about why the fact that you and I don't exist is a good reason to stop treating each other as badly as we humans tend to do.

I am not trying to convert you into a Zen Buddhist. If you like what you read in this book, try it out for yourself. If you don't like it, that's cool too.

This world is in a sorry state right now. We can't keep pointing fingers at others and saying that if only others did the right thing the world would be better. There are no others. We have to do it ourselves. Evil only comes into being when we create it. We are the problem, and we are the solution.

Let's get to work.

# 1. THE MUSIC OF THE UNIVERSE

You ARE THE universe, but you keep punching yourself in the face. So stop doing that. That's all there is to say.

The End

... OK. I'll explain a bit more.

I didn't mean to write this book. I wanted to write a book about ethics — specifically, Buddhist ethics. But in addition to writing about Buddhist ethics, I ended up writing a lot about Buddhist ideas about the structure of reality — what some folks call nonduality. This is the notion that we are not individual beings but components of an infinite reality that is just one single entity.

As I've been writing, I have been struggling to find a way to explain how these two themes interact. Every time I write about Buddhist ethics, I encounter the Buddhist idea of nonduality. These concepts are inseparable — like the Buddhists say, everything in the universe is inseparable from everything else. Which is what *nonduality* means.

While writing this book I've also had to take a hard look at myself and my own history. I've had to think about why this connection between ethics and nonduality makes perfect sense to me and yet is so difficult to explain. And I've had to consider how I feel about what Buddhism has to say on the subject.

I've been studying and practicing Zen Buddhism for most of my life, starting when I was about eighteen years old, which was — *ugh!* — almost forty years ago. I've written a bunch of books about Zen. I've lectured about Zen and led Zen retreats all over the world. I've been ordained as a Zen Buddhist monk. And I'm still working on figuring all this stuff out.

But this book is not just for Buddhists. It's for anyone interested in the truth about life, and how understanding that truth makes it obvious that we ought to treat each other nice. Even though this book is not just for Buddhists or for experts in Zen, I am not going to dumb things down for an imaginary audience of stupid people. I believe in you, dear reader! If I can understand this stuff, anybody can.

And since this book isn't just for Buddhists, maybe I should take a little time here to try to define *Zen Buddhism*. Everyone's heard the word *Zen* before, usually as a synonym for chilling out. But the online urban dictionaries are wrong! Zen does not mean chilling out. It's the Japanese pronunciation of the Sanskrit word *dhyana*, which means "meditation."

Historically speaking, the Zen form of Buddhism is a kind of back-to-basics movement. The historical Buddha spent most of his life teaching meditation to all types of people, without distinction — women and men, high caste and low caste, old and young, advanced and beginner, people of every race he encountered. That was his thing: teaching people to meditate. He wasn't into rituals or belief systems, and he certainly wasn't trying to start a religion with himself as the deity. He never claimed to be anything more than a human being.

After the historical Buddha died, meditation fell by the wayside. It began to be practiced only as a sort of ritual, and even then usually just by people who locked themselves away in monasteries. But a few centuries later certain Buddhists wanted to get back to the more basic form of what the Buddha had taught. They dropped most of the dogmas and rituals and started teaching meditation to everyone. Those were the Zen Buddhists, literally the "meditation Buddhists." So Zen Buddhists are Buddhists whose main thing is meditation.

Zen Buddhism is not a set of beliefs and dogmas. Rather, it's a way to learn to clearly see what reality actually is, beyond all dogmas and beliefs.

Kodo Sawaki, one of my Zen teacher's teachers, puts it like this in his book *Commentary on the Song of Awakening*: "The aim of the practice of Buddhism is to make us discover true reality. It immediately awakens a pressing need to know what it's like.... Due to the very fact that we are human beings, it's impossible for us to see the true nature of reality.... Here, all is illusion. In everything in the world there exists nothing besides illusions.... To discover the true nature of reality is to embrace the panorama of the universe in a single glance. When we have a vision like this, we have comprehended the teachings of the Buddha."

We can't see the true nature of reality, but we can discover it. Zen teachers say a lot of contradictory things.

Have you ever watched the TV show *Ancient Aliens* on the History Channel? It's one of my favorite programs. First they show you some ancient human artifact, like the pyramids or the statues on Easter Island. Then they tell you how mainstream archaeologists think they were made. Then a guy named Giorgio Tsoukalos, who has crazy hair, tells you it was actually built by aliens. It's terrific fun to watch.

There's a popular meme in which Tsoukalos says, "I'm not saying it was aliens. But it was aliens." He never actually said that, but what he says on the show often amounts to that. Zen teachers say things that sound like "I'm not saying it was aliens, but it was aliens" a lot. The Diamond Sutra, for example, one of the foundational texts of Zen, is full of statements like "What the Buddha says is the perfection of wisdom is no perfection of wisdom, thus it is called the perfection of wisdom" and "Beings are all spoken of by the Buddha as no beings, thus they are called beings." It's crazy! Yet there is a very good reason why they say stuff like that. It's because no explanation can ever match the reality it's trying to describe. But you have to describe things anyway.

A contemporary Zen teacher named Shohaku Okumura Roshi explained the Zen Buddhist outlook on the nature of ourselves and our relation to the universe by saying, "A musical performance does not exist before each musician plays his or her role. A musical performance exists only while the players perform their particular roles in concert with each of the other players' efforts, so that all roles are expressed as one integrated whole." This is from an article Okumura Roshi wrote about Zen Master Eihei Dogen's essay "Zenki."* The

---

*   In issue 34 of *Dharma Eye*, the journal of the Soto Zen Buddhist organization.

word *Zenki* is usually translated as "All Functions." I translated it as "the Whole Shebang" in my book *Letters to a Dead Friend about Zen*.

Okumura Roshi is saying that we are each part of the Whole Shebang that is life, the universe, and everything. That's true. And yet the Whole Shebang doesn't exist apart from us. In one sense, God created us. In another sense we are continuously creating God. I know *God* is a dirty word to some people — including lots of Buddhists. But I'm gonna use that dirty word a lot. I apologize.

That quote from Okumura Roshi was really useful in helping me to see why Buddhists are so concerned with both nonduality and ethics. Acting ethically is how we, the musicians contributing to this performance called the universe, avoid hitting bum notes and screwing up the performance. Acting unethically is how we make the symphony of life into something ugly, confused, and cacophonous rather than something beautiful and deeply moving.

Yet somehow we miss the fact that we are — metaphorically speaking — musicians contributing to a vast and infinite universal symphony. Okumura Roshi has something to say about that too: "There is therefore no way to determine if... the entirety of interdependent origination [of the universe,]... or a musical performance, always exist as the absolute 'Oneness' that includes all beings. It is also not possible to say that the entirety is only one and that the individual parts are many. We cannot say oneness and multiplicity are different and we cannot say they are the same."

In other words, he's not saying it's aliens, but... He adds, "There is no way to grasp this reality... with our discriminating, conceptual way of thinking."

The nature of time and of reality may offer us a clue as to why we cannot grasp this oneness. The physicist Carlo Rovelli, who studies the nature of time, used another musical metaphor in a lecture called "The Physics and the Philosophy of Time."* In this lecture he said:

---

* Available on YouTube!

St. Augustine [in his] pages about the nature of time in his book *The Confessions* says, "When I listen to music I get a meaning from a musical phrase, but I never listen to the phrase. I listen to one note at a time." If I listen to one note, how do I know about the previous notes? Well, of course I know because I remember them, but if I remember them... the meaning comes from the notes playing now and the memories of the previous ones. So it's all in the present and it can only be the present together because there is memory. But it's more than that because since the brain is designed by evolution to use memory to anticipate for a purpose, because it is designed to try to get somewhere. That's how living evolution designed our behavior.

The nature of reality and of time hide the truth of universal oneness from us. And yet they make it apparent too, if we know how to look. I'm not saying it was aliens, but...

My first Zen teacher's teacher, a guy named Kobun Chino Otogawa Roshi, said something similar in his book *Embracing Mind*. "Maybe a good example is music. There are strings. If no one touches them, you may imagine there is rich music going on, or complete music is going on, and you are just picking out the sounds of music when you touch the strings. But what is happening is that, by themselves, the strings don't have any music, the instrument doesn't have any music. Only when the musician touches the strings does music appear. In the same way, complete communication among everything is happening when Buddha nature takes form."

If there is no way to grasp this oneness, as Okumura Roshi said, then why do the Buddhists insist that it's so?

Well, notice that Okumura Roshi doesn't say there's no way at all to grasp oneness. He says that there is no way to grasp it *with our discriminating, conceptual way of thinking. Grasp* is a problematic word too. It implies that I can take hold of something, possess it, make it my own. This understanding of universal oneness is not like that. It's not something we can own.

Yet we can meet it. We can encounter it. In moments of quiet stillness it appears and makes itself available. It leans in and says hello to us, then hides again. Sadly, though, most of us never get quiet enough to notice this. As the French philosopher Blaise Pascal famously said, "All of humanity's problems stem from man's inability to sit quietly in a room alone." It's a shame that simply being quiet is so difficult for us.

It's a shame because, when we are very, very quiet, sometimes we can perceive the symphony of life as a whole. In that way, even while we experience only one note at a time — ourselves — we can know for certain that the whole of the symphony exists. And we can come to understand that the whole of the symphony is nothing without the one note that is this present moment, this present body, this present mind. It's the thing you call "me." Which, by the way, is exactly the same thing I call "me." You cannot exist without the entire universe, and the entire universe cannot exist without you.

The mind that discriminates, that can tell hot from cold, that can tell poop from chocolate, is a valuable thing. I'm glad to have those abilities. They've served me well! And yet there is no way for the mind that divides the universe into self and other to ever come to see the universe undivided. As long as we keep trying to perceive the undivided universe as an object, we will always fail.

In his book *I Am That*, Nisargadatta Maharaj, teacher of the Advaita Vedanta form of Hinduism, said, "The obstruction preventing complete perception is that, although you might prepare yourself to accept the thesis that everything in the universe is illusory, in this illusoriness you fail to include yourself!"

Reading this helped me get a handle on one of the biggest problems in understanding all this universal oneness stuff. Even after all my years of Zen practice, and even after all the experiences I've had around it, I still keep falling into the trap of trying to experience oneness as something apart from myself. But that makes no logical sense! Any universal oneness that fails to include me isn't oneness at all. As long as I take myself to be the subject and universal oneness to be the object, I'll never get it.

In this book I hope to take you along on my own journey of trying to understand exactly how the Buddhist ethical teachings relate to the practice of meditation and to the philosophy of nondualism. The relationship has become clearer to me over the years, and it's quite simple.

Let me give you the bottom line, which I gave you right at the beginning when I told you to stop punching yourself in the face. Here it is again in a bit more detail.

Because I am everyone and everything in the universe, it makes no sense at all to act unethically. To act unethically is effectively the same as punching myself in the face. Anything unethical I do to someone or something else, I am really only doing to myself. What's more, anything unethical I do to someone or something else, I am really doing to the entire universe.

The problem is that it's hard to see this fact clearly when you're just starting out on this path. And so, in order to get yourself used to it, you are taught to start acting like an enlightened person long before you ever get to anything like "enlightenment." Which means you're taught to pay very close attention to matters of ethics. That's how you learn to stop punching yourself in the face.

This seems very simple to me now. But in nearly forty years of working with it, it's still not easy to practice. I still fail at it all the time. I'll also try to address that in this book.

So here we go.

# 2. WHAT AM I DOING HERE?, PART 1

LET'S BACKPEDAL A little and start with the easy stuff.

At the San Francisco Zen Center they do a thing called a "Way Seeking Mind Talk." This is where students at the center who are not yet teachers of Zen, and who may not have any desire ever to become teachers of Zen, give a public talk about how and why they got into Zen practice.

The term *way seeking mind* comes from an ancient Japanese Zen teacher named Dogen. Dogen taught a style of Zen that emphasized a practice called *shikantaza*, which means "just sitting." The *just* in "just sitting" isn't like the *just* in "just sitting around." It's stronger than that. The Chinese character used to represent it was originally an image of a hammer striking a nail. It means to do nothing else but *just* sit, to put your whole body and mind into the simple act of sitting still with absolutely no goal in mind. It's harder than you might think.

Dogen was born in 1200 CE as the illegitimate son of a Japanese aristocrat. When he was only two years old, his father was killed by a political rival, and when he was seven his mother died. Losing the most important people in his life at such a young age turned Dogen into a very introspective little fellow. In order to try to understand the meaning of life, Dogen became a Buddhist monk when he was just twelve years old.

The form of Buddhism that Dogen first studied was called Tendai. Tendai Buddhists do lots of rituals and study the old sutras diligently. So young Dogen became very well versed in Buddhist philosophy and history. But he had a question. He noticed that the sutras said we are all perfect just as we are. Why, then, do all these rituals and practice meditation? None of the Tendai monks or teachers he asked could answer him. But one of his teachers recommended he try asking the folks at a temple dedicated to a form of Buddhism that had only recently been imported from China to Japan — Zen Buddhism.

Dogen found that the Zen Buddhists were much more direct and practical than the Tendai Buddhists, so he joined their order. Still, he had his question. When Dogen was in his early twenties he traveled to China in search of the answer.

After a couple of years in China, Dogen met a teacher named Tendo Nyojo, which is how Japanese people pronounce his name (*Tientong Ryujing* is how you say his name in Chinese). Tendo Nyojo said that the purpose of zazen wasn't to reach enlightenment, as Dogen previously had been taught. He said that *zazen itself was enlightenment* — whether or not it felt like it. Dogen liked that and became a formal student of Tendo Nyojo. After studying with him for a while, Dogen experienced what he called "dropping off body and mind." Tendo Nyojo gave Dogen what they call "dharma transmission," which meant that Tendo Nyojo believed Dogen was ready to teach Zen on his own. Dogen returned to Japan and began writing about and teaching Zen in his native country.

In his writings, Dogen frequently used the word *bodaishin*, which translates into something like "enlightenment mind" or "enlightenment heart." And he talked a lot about *hotsu bodaishin*, "establishing the enlightenment mind." Sometimes this is translated as "establishing the mind that seeks the Way." The "way" in question is the Buddhist way.

One of the many weird things Dogen said is that we know we are people who are "it" because we have a desire to know "it." The "it" he speaks about is the unnamable something that is the ground of all being and nonbeing, the source of life, the universe, and everything. It's the Whole Shebang that I referred to in the first chapter. We are all people who are "it," whether or not we consciously acknowledge that fact.

Anyway, in the little Zen group I established in Akron, Ohio, a few years ago when I moved back there for a little while, we stole the San Francisco Zen Center's idea of having students give talks. But I thought that calling it a "Way Seeking Mind Talk" was too pretentious. I didn't think we'd ever be able to get some of the unsavory characters who sat with us to give a talk with a title like that. So I called our version "What Am I Doing Here?" The person giving the talk didn't have to convince us that she or he had established anything as grand and glorious as a "Way Seeking Mind." They just had to tell us what led them to start sitting and staring at walls with us.

Here's my "What Am I Doing Here?" talk.

Some of you may have read my first book, *Hardcore Zen*. I'm sure I'll end up repeating some of the stories I told in that book. But that book is now sixteen years old. In some countries that book would be old enough to drink beer! I tell those same old stories differently now, so don't worry.

My intention here is not to write an autobiography, which would be boring to both you, dear reader, and me as well. Rather, I want to answer for you and for myself the question of how and why I got into Zen, because it's important to the rest of what I want to say here.

For as long as I can remember, I've been interested in two questions. What is this life I am living? And how can I live that life ethically?

I would seem — at least to myself — to be a very unlikely type of person to get into something like Zen Buddhism. I don't come from a religious family. I never styled myself as a "spiritual person" like so many people do. I have never owned a pair of Birkenstock sandals or any patchouli incense. I play bass in a punk rock band. I was one of the main cast of a movie called *Zombie Bounty Hunter*

*M.D.* And I worked for a long time for a Japanese company that made movies about giant monsters smashing downtown Tokyo.

Here's what I can remember about how my interest in Zen got started.

As I said, my family was not religious. I don't mean they were a bunch of raging atheists or anything like that. They just didn't care about religion one way or the other. We never went to church or to a synagogue or even to a Buddhist temple, for that matter. We were vaguely Protestant. But only in the sense that we were not Catholic or Jewish, and those were the only other choices in rural Ohio, where I started out my life. We had a Bible at home, but I never saw anyone read it.

So I didn't grow up with any sort of spiritual framework with which to understand my experience of life. I didn't think of myself as an embodied spirit destined for either heaven or hell like lots of people in Ohio did and still do. All I knew was that I was here in this place. But what this place was, I had no idea. And who I was, I had no idea either.

It struck me as odd that no one else I knew seemed to notice the awesome strangeness of simply being alive. They all appeared to take it for granted that this place, this planet Earth, existed, and they just kind of went on from there. They were interested in football games, or Dungeons and Dragons, or parties, or smoking weed, or whatever else they were into. But they didn't seem interested in the incredible mystery of this life, this place, this state of being.

I don't know how reliable my memories of my childhood are. But I distinctly remember being deeply interested in trying to figure out what this life and this world were from a very early age. I didn't quite know how to frame my questions. And, in any case, there didn't seem to be anyone around of whom I could ask these kinds of questions. At least and not have them think I was some kind of weirdo.

The only way of understanding the world I lived in that I was ever really exposed to was the standard materialistic outlook. I couldn't have articulated this outlook when I was a child, and I can barely articulate it now. But I'll try. The basic idea was that I was a machine made out of meat. I was taught that matter was real and that everything else was unreal or at least not as real as matter. I understood that my experiential sense of my own existence was just an artifact of electrical and chemical energy and movement in my brain. I understood that I was born on a certain day and would die on another day. I understood that there was no grand purpose to anything. Evolution was a purely random process, a series of accidents. I was the product of haphazard chance, nothing more. I understood that the whole universe was basically dead, apart from people and animals and plants. I understood that for the brief time I was alive the best I could hope for was to have a little fun and make some money.

This was a thoroughly depressing way to conceive of the world. It was especially depressing for a wimpy kid like me who wasn't good at sports or math or pretty much anything that school or society rewards you for. I didn't see much hope for my future if my only chance for happiness depended on competing in the materialistic rat race.

I hated that worldview. But I knew that religious people didn't see things that way. So I wondered if maybe religious people could be right. And if so, which ones?

When I was seven years old, my dad accepted a job in Nairobi, Kenya. Up until then I had lived in Wadsworth, Ohio. Wadsworth was a nondescript suburb of Akron, which itself was a nondescript satellite city to Cleveland. In those days, Akron was the Rubber Capital of the World, the home of most of the world's biggest tire manufacturers. The whole city stank like a giant tire fire, and everything for miles around Akron was covered in a layer of black carbon dust. My dad worked for Firestone Tire and Rubber. The dads of almost everybody I knew worked for one of the tire companies or for a company that supplied stuff to the tire companies. Some of their moms did too.

Wadsworth, however, was just far enough away from Akron that it was not smelly. There was a quaint gazebo in the center of town, and a Ben Franklin five-and-dime store around the corner from the gazebo, where they sold plastic dinosaurs for ten cents. We kept our meat in a meat locker downtown. The entire downtown was just two cross streets with a soda fountain called Weireth's and a little A&P grocery store. Not a supermarket, mind you. A grocery store that was barely the size of the produce department in a supermarket.

At one edge of town was the Grandview Park swimming pool, which looked like a giant water tank with the top sawn off. The concrete locker rooms below the pool smelled of piss and mold, and you could buy Good & Plenty candy at the snack bar. There was a Blue Tip match factory at another edge of town, and an apple orchard at yet another edge, where you could pick your own apples. I could ride my bike from one end of Wadsworth to the other in about fifteen minutes.

You could hardly find two places more different from each other than Wadsworth, Ohio, and Nairobi, Kenya. We lived in Kenya for almost four years, and those were four of the most formative years of my young life. I barely remember living in Ohio before we moved to Nairobi. So most of my earliest childhood memories have Africa as their backdrop.

We lived in a nice part of Nairobi called Kileleshwa. It wasn't exactly the Beverly Hills of Nairobi, but it was better than a lot of areas of the city. Firestone made sure their employees lived in decent places, even if it wasn't luxurious by US standards. Our house in Nairobi wasn't much different from our home in Wadsworth. It was one story just like our place in Wadsworth and had a four-foot-tall bamboo fence around it. There was a gate, but not a very impressive one. I could climb over it when I was nine years old.

Today's helicopter parents would be horrified not just that I played by myself outside all the time, but that I played by myself outside *in Africa*. I remember walking through the woods near where we lived looking for wild chameleons in the trees. Lions, leopards, rhinos, elephants, wildebeests, and all sorts of other exotic creatures roam free in that part of East Africa, but they stay away from Nairobi, so they weren't a real concern. We were told to keep an eye out for black mambas, a very poisonous species of snake that was known to attack without provocation. But I never saw one myself. Anyway, those snakes were the most dangerous animal on the loose in my neighborhood in Nairobi.

The major language in Kenya is English, but it's British English. I remember when I first got there, some kid I met told me he owned a torch. I was so excited! This kid owned a torch! I begged him to show it to me. When he brought it out I was majorly disappointed to see it was just a flashlight.

Our neighborhood was a mixture of foreigners and Africans. There was an American family next door, and a Canadian family down the street, both with boys my age. But my closest friends when I lived in Nairobi were the Kashangaki family. Their father was from Tanzania and their mom was from New York City. They were a large family with three boys, James, Thomas, and David, who were all close to me in age. I hung out with Thomas the most. I remember him as Tommy, but I discovered him on Facebook much later in life and found out that he doesn't go by Tommy anymore. Sometime after my family left Kenya, he moved to the States and became an aerospace scientist. He even got on the shortlist for becoming an astronaut, though he never actually went into space.

And of course, one other thing that was very different between Wadsworth, Ohio, and Nairobi, Kenya, was that Wadsworth was made up of mostly white people and Nairobi mostly Black people. Not many white Americans have the experience of standing out in a crowd simply because they're white. But I did, both when my family lived in Kenya and later when I lived in Japan. I think it changed the way I look at lots of racial issues.

In Kenya I was exposed to a lot more religions than I would have been if we'd stayed in Ohio. Contrary to various Obama-era internet rumors, Kenya is not a Muslim country. The majority religion in Kenya is Christianity. The other religions I was most aware of when we lived in Kenya were Hinduism and Sikhism. I'm sure there must have been Muslims too, but I didn't really notice them.

My dad had a good friend who was Indian and a Hindu. I remember eating my first samosas in Kenya and falling in love with Indian food. I also noticed the Hindu religious iconography, probably from seeing it in Indian restaurants and Indian-owned shops as well as in the home of my dad's friend. The idea that God might be a weird-looking blue guy with six arms was absolutely fascinating.

I was eleven when we moved back to Wadsworth, back to the gazebo and the apple orchards, with no black mambas waiting to pounce. But my outlook on life had been irrevocably changed by those years in Africa. I could never be a normal American kid anymore. Not that I made much effort to be. But it would have been impossible even if I'd tried.

Sometime in my teens, my need to figure out what life was all about got turned up a notch. Or maybe ten notches. Two of my mother's sisters — my aunts — started showing signs of Huntington's disease, a genetic condition that had killed my grandmother on my mom's side. Huntington's disease is often described as like having Parkinson's, Lou Gehrig's disease, and Alzheimer's all at once. It's really, really bad.

When I was in high school, my parents sat me down and told me that Huntington's disease was genetic and that if it turned out my mom had it, then I had a 50 percent chance of developing it myself. It usually strikes between your midthirties and midforties. By the time I was a junior in high school, it was clear that my mom did have the disease, although at the time her symptoms were barely noticeable. Knowing that I might be rendered fully incapacitated, if not dead, in about ten or fifteen years gave my quest to understand the nature of life, the universe, and everything a tremendous urgency.

So I went to some churches and even watched a few religious TV shows. But there was nothing there for me. I sincerely wanted to be able to believe in Jesus Christ and His Good News, but it was presented so badly at the churches I visited that I couldn't. The religious TV shows were even worse! Sure, I had doubts about the materialistic view of the world, but I couldn't believe in a God that would create a place where people had one chance to figure out that they ought to believe in Jesus or they'd be sent to hell for eternity. That made no sense.

When I left Wadsworth to attend Kent State University, I immediately started trying to take any class I could about Eastern religions. I wondered if the Hindus I'd encountered in Kenya had anything better to offer than what I'd heard at those churches. The Hare Krishnas were based on a sect of Hinduism, and they had a presence on campus. They hosted cooking classes, which were obviously intended to try to convert you to their religion. I loved the food and I was happy to hear what they had to say about their beliefs. But nothing they said was very convincing.

Just like the Christians I'd encountered, the Hare Krishnas seemed to have a tremendous fear of science. Even though I could not accept the entirety of the materialistic worldview, I knew that the theory of evolution made good sense. I couldn't accept it when Christians tried to prove that evolution wasn't true. The Hare Krishnas also hated the theory of evolution and tried to prove it wrong. Plus, they didn't even believe that men had landed on the moon. That was probably the last straw for me.

I found out about this belief of theirs sometime just after the *Challenger* disaster. That was when I witnessed a lecture by a Hare Krishna teacher who explained that the Apollo 11 astronauts had actually mistakenly landed not on the moon but on a different planet, which he even named, though I can't recall the word. Apparently their scriptures say that lots of demigods live on the moon and have parties there and stuff and that therefore the barren airless rock that Neil Armstrong set foot on couldn't possibly be the moon.

So I wasn't about to join the Hare Krishnas, even though I kept on eating their samosas. But I was aware that there were other forms of Hinduism — partly from my experiences in Kenya but mostly because the Hare Krishnas denounced those other forms of Hinduism so often. They called those other Hindus "impersonalists" because they did not believe that God was a person, whereas the Hare Krishnas knew for certain that God was a person, and that his name was Krishna.

I wanted to find some of these Hindu impersonalists and see what they had to say. It seemed like it might be a lot more interesting than the Hare Krishna version of things. But there were no Hindu impersonalists hanging out on the Kent State University campus in those days. Not that I could find, anyhow.

Back then I didn't know what form of Hinduism I was looking for, but now I do. What I was searching for is called neo-Advaita, and it's a part of the Advaita Vedanta tradition. *Advaita* means "nondualistic" and *Vedanta* means "the end of the vedas." The vedas are the sacred scriptures of Hinduism, including books like the Bhagavad Gita that the Hare Krishnas always sold at their cooking classes. I bought one from them, and I still have it. It's not the most reliable translation, but it is one of the most colorfully illustrated ones.

If I'd been a little smarter and more diligent, I might have figured out that I was into Advaita Vedanta when I was eighteen instead of figuring it out in my fifties. Life might have been completely different if I'd just done a little bit more research, or if I'd stumbled across Alan Watts's book about Advaita Vedanta titled *The Book: On the Taboo Against Knowing Who You Are*. But I didn't.

It's weird to me that I missed something so obvious and easy to figure out. Then again, I missed a lot of things that were obvious and easy to figure out. The story of my life is that I miss the most obvious things. This, by the way, is one of the main ideas in Zen Buddhism — that we miss the most obvious things.

I was probably kind of distracted at that time, anyway. I was heavily into music in those days. Being into music was another thing that does not run in my family yet was very important to me. I started playing guitar when I was fourteen. The summer before I enrolled at KSU I joined the hardcore punk band Zero Defex as their bass player. In those days I thought maybe the answer to the meaning of life might be found in punk rock. Punk was rock music with a purpose, a meaning. Zero Defex had a song called "Drop the A-Bomb on Me." It was an eighteen-second rant against nuclear proliferation. All our songs meant something, either politically or socially. We were a band that could not be content singing songs about sex and partying.

Meanwhile, back at KSU, I took classes in Western philosophy. Some of them were interesting, but I felt like Western philosophy was never going to help me find the answers I was looking for. I kept scanning the KSU catalog for anything remotely related to Hinduism. But there was nothing on offer.

Then, around my third or fourth semester at KSU, I spotted a class in the catalog called Zen Buddhism. It wasn't offered by the philosophy department. Rather, it was part of what KSU called the "Experimental College." The Experimental College offered classes in weird stuff like parapsychology and existential basket weaving. And Zen Buddhism. You didn't get college credit for these classes because, obviously, what university would give you college credit for studying something as crazy and out-there as parapsychology, existential basket weaving, or Zen Buddhism?

Obviously I'm being sarcastic. But apparently that was Kent State's view of Zen Buddhism in the early eighties. It seems absurd to me now that they wouldn't give you credit for studying a legitimate branch of one of the world's oldest, most well-established, and most important religions. Ironically, the one class I took at KSU that had the most influence on my subsequent career does not even appear on my transcripts.

That class literally changed my life.

# 3. WHAT AM I DOING HERE?, PART 2

DONGSHAN LIANGJIE, WHO is known as Tozan Ryokai in Japan (because that's how Japanese people pronounce the Chinese characters in his name), first got into Zen when he heard a line from the Heart Sutra. The Heart Sutra is a very short piece — the whole thing fits on a single page, unlike most sutras, which are hundreds or thousands of pages long. One of the lines of the Heart Sutra says, "No eyes, no ears, no nose, no tongue, no body, no mind."

When ten-year-old Tozan heard a Zen teacher chanting that line, he touched his face and said, "You just said that I have no eyes, ears, nose, tongue, body, and mind. But I can clearly feel my own eyes, ears, nose, tongue, and body, and I experience these things through my mind."

The Zen teacher was impressed. Not many people question Zen teachers so directly. But the teacher didn't know how to answer. He told Tozan to continue his studies with other teachers who might be able to help.

You might wonder why Tozan didn't just decide that the Heart Sutra was a load of crap because it said things that clearly were not true. But Tozan was also aware that the Heart Sutra was a respected piece of literature and that it was considered one of the most profound teachings in all of Buddhism. Buddhism was an important philosophy to a whole lot of people in many different countries. Clearly people got something important out of that sutra. Tozan decided to try to find out what that something was. Many years later Tozan went on to become one of the founding teachers in the lineage of Zen that I practice.

I imagine that Tozan's experience of first hearing the Heart Sutra must have been something like mine. So instead of telling you what happened to Tozan, let me tell you about what happened to me.

My instructor for the Zen Buddhism class I took at Kent State was a skinny, funny white guy named Tim McCarthy. Absolutely no one's idea of a typical Zen master.

I should stop here and explain why I mentioned that he was a white guy. This was the early 1980s. At that point it was pretty unusual to encounter a teacher of Zen Buddhism who was not Japanese, Korean, Chinese, or from some other country in Asia. Non-Asian Buddhist teachers were a new thing back then. I'm not sure who was the first person outside Asia to become a Buddhist teacher. But the first place I am aware of that started ordaining non-Asian Buddhist teachers on a regular basis was the San Francisco Zen Center (SFZC), and they didn't start doing it until the end of the 1960s. If they were not the very first to ordain non-Asian Buddhist teachers, they were certainly among the first.

SFZC was established by a guy named Shunryu Suzuki Roshi. *Roshi*, by the way, is a term than means something like "respected elder teacher." It's not an official designation of rank. It's just something that we in the Zen tradition call teachers that we respect. It's not something you'd ever call yourself, though. Calling yourself "Roshi" is a little like calling yourself something like "the world's greatest lover." If someone else calls you that it makes sense. If you call yourself that, you just sound ridiculous.

Suzuki Roshi had been sent from Japan in 1959 to head up a little temple in San Francisco called Soko-ji. No one expected him to do anything much more than minister to a few Japanese expats living in San Francisco. But by the early sixties, Zen was becoming a hip thing to read about, especially among the beatniks. A few of those beatniks realized there was an actual Zen temple in their city and decided to go check it out.

It must have been kind of weird for those guys to go to a temple that clearly was intended to be a gathering space for Japanese people. They must have felt like total outsiders. But Suzuki welcomed them. What's more, he was impressed that, unlike a lot of the Japanese members of the congregation, these young people were interested in actually doing zazen, the meditation practice in Zen Buddhism. In Japan Zen Buddhism is one of the most popular religions. Yet very few Japanese people meditate, even if they consider themselves Zen Buddhists.

After a while, there were so many of these non-Japanese folks at Soko-ji that they decided to set up a new place down the road and call it the San Francisco Zen Center. Soko-ji is still there, by the way. But these days it's dwarfed by what was once its baby brother, the San Francisco Zen Center.

By the 1970s, SFZC was starting to ordain some of those former beatniks as monks on a fairly regular basis. After a while a few other Zen centers sprang up in other cities, and they started ordaining people too. Pretty soon there were dozens of non-Asian Zen Buddhist monks. My first teacher was one of them.

In the early eighties there might have been, at most, a few hundred non-Asian Zen Buddhist monks in America as well as a few dozen in Europe, and maybe a handful in other places like South America, Australia, and elsewhere outside Asia. But they were still a rarity. For me to actually encounter one of them in northeast Ohio, of all places, was pretty surprising. I remember being a little suspicious the first day of class that a white guy could possibly know anything about Zen Buddhism.

That first day, Tim read to us his teacher Kobun Chino Otogawa Roshi's translation of the Heart Sutra, which I'll tell you about a little later. Kobun had been brought over to the US in 1967 at the request of Shunryu Suzuki, whose non-Japanese congregation had grown too large to be served by Suzuki alone.

Kobun was an interesting character. He was full of contradictions. Suzuki Roshi brought Kobun to the States because Kobun was such a master at Zen ceremonies. Sometimes people are surprised at how formalized and ceremonial Zen Buddhism can get. Yet although Kobun was really good at this formal, ceremonial stuff, by all accounts the man himself was very laid back and not at all the kind of uptight guy you'd expect a master of Zen ceremonial forms to be. There are books full of funny stories about Kobun, and I heard a lot of those kinds of stories from Tim. He was kind of a Zen comedian.

Kobun was also a bit of a mystic. Nishijima Roshi, my ordaining teacher, whom we'll meet in the next chapter, tended to talk in very concrete, down-to-earth terms. The few talks of Kobun's that have been preserved are full of beautiful flights into the more mystical side of Zen philosophy. Tim could be like that too. I'm grateful that I got both sides of Zen from my two main teachers — the very meat-and-potatoes stuff from Nishijima Roshi and Kobun's mystical side through Tim.

But let's get back to the Heart Sutra. As I said, unlike some sutras that are thousands of pages long, the Heart Sutra can be printed on a single sheet of paper, with plenty of room left over to draw band logos and pictures of dinosaurs, which is what I usually did with the handouts I received at college. But I did not do that with my handout of the Heart Sutra.

Because the Heart Sutra blew my tiny little teenage mind. The most famous line in the Heart Sutra is "form is emptiness, emptiness is form." I remember nearly weeping when I heard that line. I had no idea in the world what it meant, but I knew somehow that it was right and that it was exactly what I needed to hear.

Tim also taught us how to do zazen on that first day of class. So I started doing it every morning and every evening.

Maybe this is where I should say a few things about faith. Sometimes the word *faith* means believing in things you can't prove or that you haven't experienced for yourself. For example, I never saw Jesus walk on water. But while I was a student at Kent State I was once told by some guy from the Campus Christian Ministries that I ought to have faith that he did. I was incapable of that kind of faith.

But there's another way of understanding the word *faith*. Sometimes it's a synonym for *trust*. I trusted that Tim McCarthy was not lying to me. He didn't seem crazy either. He'd been doing zazen since he was a little kid. It seemed to have done him some good. Plus, there was a whole tradition of people all over the world who'd also experienced the benefits of zazen for themselves. The things those people said in their books might have been odd, but they didn't seem crazy.

I've now known Tim for well over thirty years. I even lived with him for a while. But I don't know much about him. I think he's from Ohio originally. I know his family is Irish Catholic but that his mom converted to some form of evangelical Protestantism. Tim once told me that his mom had decided he, Tim, wasn't going to hell because he'd been baptized but that he was leading other people — like me, for example — to hell by teaching them about Buddhism. I know he started doing zazen around his middle school years after a chance encounter with a Buddhist teacher whose name he no longer remembers. Later he studied with a teacher who called himself Reverend Thayer. He briefly studied with Joshu Sasaki Roshi, Leonard Cohen's Zen teacher. But Tim's main teacher was Kobun Chino Otogawa Roshi.

A lot of time a Zen student's relationship with his or her teacher takes on a father-son or father-daughter or mother-son or mother-daughter sort of vibe. This is because often your Zen teacher tends to be old enough to be your parent. But Tim was pretty close in age to me. In fact, he was almost exactly ten years older. His birthday is just a few weeks before mine. So it was never a father-son kind of thing with us.

Tim smelled like garlic and made sounds like a duck. The garlic smell came from the cloves of raw garlic he ate daily for health reasons. The duck sounds were inspired by a group of old guys who hung out near one of the monasteries he trained at in California who made quacking sounds when reacting to certain things people said. Sometimes Tim's duck sounds meant something you said was funny. Sometimes they meant you said something stupid. Sometimes they seemed completely random.

Tim was into Frank Zappa, who I also loved. He could quote parts of Zappa's obscene rock opera *200 Motels* from memory, including the spoken-word sections of the song "Penis Dimensions." He was also a musician. But unlike me, Tim was a serious musician. I was just the bass player in a punk rock band. Tim composed orchestral pieces for fun. I never actually heard any of his compositions.

Tim was a big fan of *Star Trek* and *The Prisoner*, a British TV series about a James Bond–type spy who tries to retire and then finds himself imprisoned in a bizarre place called the Village. It was a highly philosophical and weird show. We used to watch it together on his little black-and-white TV set while munching on popcorn.

Tim and I talked about Zen a lot, but Zen wasn't all or probably even most of what we talked about. Every so often I recall snippets of our Zen conversations. But mostly I remember the feeling I got from being around him. He was like an anchor in the stormy sea of early adulthood I was trying to negotiate. He was a mystic, but he never advertised that fact. He seemed to want to keep that part hidden. It only came out when the mood was right.

A lot of stuff happened during my twenties. But most of it doesn't seem to matter much anymore. After Zero Defex broke up I created a fake band called Dimentia 13 and put out five albums on an indie label called Midnight Records. That's how I misspelled the word *dementia*, by the way. The band name came from the title of

Francis Ford Coppola's first movie, which I'd seen on late-night TV once but about which I only remembered the name. I didn't know how to spell *dementia* when I handed over the instructions to my friend Vince Packard, the artist who did the covers for the first two Dimentia 13 records. He asked me if I really wanted to spell *dementia* wrong. I hadn't noticed it was wrong, but it seemed somehow cool to misspell it, so I said yes.

At the time I wanted to make a career out of making Dimentia 13 records. But I never had a touring band, and I never put in the work necessary to start one. A few times I put together versions of Dimentia 13 that could play live. But our shows never attracted many people. Apparently the records sold pretty well in France and Greece, but we never played there. Maybe we would have been stars if we had.

It took me a long, long time to come to terms with the fact that what I really wanted to do most in life was not be a rock star but to study and practice Zen. I think I was raised to be too practical to dedicate myself fully to something as off-the-wall as Zen. Even being a rock and roller for a living seemed more feasible than that. Even though I'd been to Africa, I was raised to think about things like someone from Akron, Ohio, would, in terms of nine-to-five jobs with bosses and paychecks. Running off to a monastery was not on my radar.

And anyway, the only Zen monasteries were in far-flung places like California or upstate New York. One of Tim's friends went off to Minneapolis to study with Dainin Katagiri Roshi, another monk that Shunryu Suzuki had brought over from Japan. Katagiri Roshi's books are some of my favorite books about Zen Buddhism these days. I'll be quoting him a lot in this book.

Sometimes I think about how I could have done that myself. I had the chance to study personally with Katagiri Roshi, a guy I now recognize as one of the greatest Zen teachers ever. Katagiri Roshi first came to America in the 1960s to serve at Zenshu-ji temple in

Little Tokyo in Los Angeles. That's just a little ways from where I live now. He also helped Shunryu Suzuki set up the San Francisco Zen Center and Tassajara Monastery in Northern California.

It wouldn't have been that hard for me to have practiced with Katagiri Roshi when I first started getting into Zen. He was at the Minneapolis Zen Center at the time. I was in Ohio. I could easily have packed up and gone out there with Tim's other student. But I was too stuck on the idea that I needed to do something practical with my life. It's funny the way we think.

So I kept working on getting my bachelor's degree. It took me something like six years, but I finally did it. But after I got my degree I found there were no jobs for someone with a BA in Teaching of History. I got that degree because I figured I could get a job teaching history at a high school. I discovered after a few depressing job interviews that high schools in Ohio did not hire history teachers. They hired football coaches who could double as history teachers to justify their paychecks in the off-season. At every interview I went to I was asked what sport I could coach. When I said I couldn't coach any sport, the interviews were essentially over, though out of politeness they usually kept them going for at least a few more minutes.

So instead of teaching high school, I eked out a meager living doing temp work where I'd be hired for a week here or a couple of days there to replace someone at one of Akron's tire factories who was sick or on vacation. Then I worked for a place that taught adults with intellectual disabilities how to get jobs. Or at least we tried to do that. We generally failed. After a few years of this, my sister told me that a friend of hers had gotten a job in Japan teaching English. The Japanese Ministry of Education, it turned out, hired native English speakers to assist struggling Japanese English teachers. So I applied, and I got the job.

It was in Japan that I met the Zen teacher who would eventually ordain me, a guy named Gudo Wafu Nishijima.

# 4. THE ETHICS OF ACTION

NISHIJIMA ROSHI WAS a very different person from Tim McCarthy. For one thing, he was an elderly Japanese man who had a shaven head and wore Buddhist robes all the time. As far as I know, Tim didn't even own a set of Buddhist robes. At first I didn't like Nishijima Roshi. He seemed arrogant and self-righteous. When he lectured about Zen he had this sort of my-way-or-the-highway kind of attitude that got on my nerves. I mean, he never said "my way or the highway," but he seemed to be saying that he was the only one who truly understood what Zen was all about. Or so I thought.

But let me backtrack a bit and tell you how I came to know Nishijima Roshi. I found him in a free newspaper called *Tokyo Classified*, which was an English-language paper you could find in places where foreigners hung out, like the Tower Records store in Shinjuku or various places in the Roppongi district, where all the embassies are located. There was an ad in there about "Zen Seminars in English" or something like that. They took place on Saturday afternoons in a room on the campus of Tokyo University.

I'd been in Japan for more than a year by then, but I hadn't done much Zen stuff. I'd sat zazen by myself in my apartment most days, just like I had done for ten years already back in Ohio. I didn't go to Japan to study Zen. I went to Japan for a job. During my first year in Japan I'd been an assistant English teacher. I had been hired and brought over to Japan by a program called JET, which stands for

Japan Exchange Teaching. They sent me to a little town called Taka-oka, which even most Japanese people can't locate on a map.

In the year that I worked as a JET teacher, I'd visited three Zen temples. In each case, I or some other foreigner had arranged the visits and we basically went to the temples and sat zazen on our own. Tim had told me that his teacher, Kobun, told him that most Japanese Zen priests had no real interest in teaching Zen to foreigners — or to other Japanese people, for that matter. According to Kobun, they often had no interest in Zen at all. Many of them inherited the job of running the family temple from their fathers. And that's what being a Zen monk was to them, a job. The monks at those three temples I visited were perfect examples. They just ignored us.

After a year in Takaoka, I got a job in Tokyo with a company called Tsuburaya Productions. The company was founded by Eiji Tsuburaya, the special-effects director for all the classic Godzilla movies of the fifties and sixties. Tsuburaya Productions made a TV series called *Ultraman*, which was not a cartoon but a live-action TV series. Each episode was like a miniature Godzilla movie. In every episode a monster — portrayed by a stuntman in an ugly rubber costume — would threaten some Japanese city — portrayed by little buildings made of plywood. Ultraman was a giant superhero from outer space — also portrayed by a stuntman in a rubber costume — who would beat up the monster and save the world week after week. The show was massively popular in Japan and is still going strong more than fifty years after its debut.

My job with the JET program had an automatic cut-off point. You weren't allowed to be a JET teacher for more than three years. So when I was doing that job I wasn't thinking about living in Japan very long. But once I started working for Tsuburaya Productions I realized I might be staying in Japan indefinitely. That's when I started trying to find a Zen teacher over there, which led me to Nishijima Roshi.

Unlike those monks who had ignored us back in Takaoka,

Nishijima Roshi was deeply interested in teaching Zen to non-Japanese people. He'd gotten interested in Zen as a teenager when he was in a used bookstore and came across a copy of Dogen's book *Shobogenzo*. He was fascinated to find a book written in his own language that he could not understand at all. He wanted to know what this strange book was about.

In his twenties, he started attending lectures and retreats run by Kodo Sawaki, the famous "homeless" monk who sought to revive the practice of zazen in Japanese Zen Buddhism. Sawaki Roshi wasn't literally homeless. But they called him homeless because he had no temple of his own, at least not until late in life. His homelessness set him apart from monks who had begrudgingly inherited the business of running a temple, like the monks who'd ignored us in Takaoka.

Sawaki was an orphan who'd been raised by an uncle and aunt who were more interested in drinking and gambling than raising a child. When he was sixteen, Sawaki ran away from home. He walked all the way from the outskirts of Nagoya to Eihei-ji, the temple Dogen had established eight hundred years earlier, and told them he wanted to become a monk. At first they didn't want to accept him, but Sawaki was persistent.

Sawaki studied and practiced Soto-style Zen at Eihei-ji for a time, then practiced Pure Land Buddhism for a bit, and then Yogacara (Vijnanavada or "Consciousness Only") Buddhism for a little while, before returning to Zen and receiving dharma transmission in that lineage. He became convinced that Dogen's style of *shikantaza* — "just sitting" — meditation was what the world needed most and traveled around Japan teaching it to anyone who wanted to learn about it. Lots more details of Sawaki's fascinating life can be found in Arthur Braverman's book *Discovering the True Self: Kodo Sawaki's Art of Zen Meditation*, which also contains a selection of Sawaki's writings on Zen practice.

When he wasn't following Kodo Sawaki around, Kazuo Nishijima, as my teacher was known before he was ordained, got himself a law degree and a job at the Japanese Ministry of Finance. Nishijima told me he had wanted to ordain as a monk with Sawaki Roshi, but there was some sort of miscommunication, and the ordination never happened. After Sawaki's death in 1965, Nishijima continued practicing with Rempo Niwa Roshi, who was the head of the Soto sect and abbot of Eihei-ji. In 1973 Niwa Roshi ordained Nishijima as a monk and gave him the dharma name Gudo, meaning "the Way of Stupidity." He also gave Nishijima dharma transmission, which gave him permission to teach Zen as an independent teacher.

Because Nishijima Roshi wanted to teach Zen to non-Japanese people, he taught himself English by buying a set of instructional tapes and diligently following every lesson. He even considered moving to the United States as several other Japanese Zen teachers had done, although ultimately he decided against it.

Instead, beginning in the 1980s, he taught a class in English about Zen and the philosophy of Eihei Dogen every Saturday afternoon in a room at Tokyo University as part of what the university called its Young Buddhists Association. He also worked on a complete English translation of Dogen's masterwork, *Shobogenzo*, aka *The Treasury of the True Dharma Eye*, with a British student of his named Mike Cross.

*Shobogenzo* is a very long book. Nishijima Roshi had published two volumes of it by the time I started going to his classes in 1994, and the final two volumes came out while I was studying with him. This was only the second time anyone had attempted to translate the entirety of *Shobogenzo* into English, and the previous version was by then long out of print. For a few years, the Nishijima/Cross translation was the only complete version of *Shobogenzo* available in English. There are a few others these days, but Nishijima Roshi's is still the best translation, if you ask me. Then again, I'm biased.

Besides *Shobogenzo*, Nishijima Roshi also published a number of shorter works in English about his take on Dogen's philosophy of Zen. One of these was a twelve-page pamphlet called "The Ethics of

Action." Since this book is about ethics, I'd like to talk about what my teacher wrote on the subject.

He starts off this pamphlet by saying there are two basic categories of ethics: "ethics based on mind, which are founded upon idealistic criteria, and ethics based on the senses, which are founded upon materialistic criteria."

Ethics based on mind, he says, are the ones we are most familiar with. Religious ethics, for example, fall in this category. He defines this style of ethics as being absolute. This idea is best expressed in a slogan you sometimes see on bumper stickers in America: God said it, I believe it, that settles it. To follow these ethics is one of the goals of a religious life.

Ethics based on the senses, Nishijima Roshi says, are materialistic ethics. For a materialist, what is comfortable is good and what is uncomfortable is bad. Often materialistic thinkers have denied the value of ethics and morals. "But," writes Nishijima Roshi, "I believe that even the denial of ethical criteria is itself an ethical criterion; and so I think that there does exist a materialistic ethical criterion."

Buddhist ethics, Nishijima Roshi says, are different. They are based not on ideas or on sense perception but on action. But, he says, we need to define what action is. To do this, he quotes a portion of "Genjo Koan," probably Dogen's most famous piece of writing. The quotation is a little long, but it's important. So I'm going to use it all. It's a little odd, like all of Dogen's writing. But don't worry. I'll explain the weird parts. The quotation Nishijima Roshi uses goes like this:

> When fish swim in water, though they keep swimming, there is no end to the water. When birds fly in the sky, though they keep flying, there is no end to the sky. At the same time, fish and birds have never left the water or the sky. When activity is great, usage is great. When necessity is small, usage is small.
>
> Acting in this state, none fails to realize its limitations at

every moment, and none fails to somersault freely at every place; but if a bird leaves the sky it will die at once, and if a fish leaves the water it will die at once. So we can understand that the water is life and that the sky is life. Birds are life and fish are life. It may be that life is birds and life is fish. And beyond this there may still be further progress. The existence of practice and experience, the existence of a lifetime and a life, are like this.

This being so, a bird or fish that tried to understand the water or the sky completely, before swimming or flying, could never find its way or find its place in the water or in the sky. When we find this place, this action inevitably realizes the Universe. When we find this way, this action is inevitably the state of the realized Universe itself.

This way and this place are neither great nor small; they are neither subjective nor objective; neither have they existed since the past nor do they appear in the present; and so they exist here like this. When a person is practicing and experiencing the Buddha's truth in this state, to get one dharma is to penetrate one dharma, and to meet one act is to perform one act.

This is the state in which the place exists and the way is mastered, and this is why the object of recognition is not clearly defined because the recognition and the perfect realization are experienced together. Do not think that what is attained will inevitably become self-conscious and be recognized by the intellect. The experience of the ultimate state is realized at once. At the same time, the mystery of existence is not always made manifest. Realization is the state of ambiguity itself.

Sorry for the long quotation! But I feel like Dogen wrote "Genjo Koan" so concisely that not a single word is wasted. I didn't want to cut anything out.

In his explanation of this quotation, Nishijima Roshi writes that our life and our surroundings are part of a single continuum. That's what Dogen is talking about when he says that stuff about fish and water and birds and the sky. This is not our usual way of thinking of things. We tend to imagine that we are something separate from our surroundings. But action, Nishijima Roshi writes, always takes place somewhere. The action and the place in which it occurs, he says, are indivisible.

*Surroundings*, by the way, doesn't just mean physical space. It also refers to the times you live in, the attitudes you've absorbed from the people you've interacted with, and much more. It's who and what you are, meshed with where and when you are.

Nishijima Roshi points out that Dogen identifies the scale of our action with the action itself. Dogen says, "None fails to realize its limitations at every moment, and none fails to somersault freely at every place." About this, Nishijima Roshi says, "Our action always fills up the Universe, which is simply the limits of each concrete situation; and we are always free in the state of action."

Our action always fills up the universe. When I first met the old man and he said stuff like that, I just thought he was trying to be poetic. I didn't know yet that he meant it literally. This approximately infinite universe is also very small.

Did I ever really understand Nishijima Roshi? One time he told me that I understood him completely. I think maybe I knew what he meant by that when he said it. Yet, on a personal level, I wonder if I knew him at all the way normal people who say they know each other know each other.

He was a short guy. He barely came up to my shoulder, and I'm just an inch taller than Tom Cruise, who is apparently everyone's go-to guy for "people who are short." As tiny as the old man was, he had a commanding presence. He had utter confidence in himself, which made everything he said compelling. I may not have believed everything he said, but I knew he believed it. And what's more, I knew he meant it!

I didn't know much about Nishijima Roshi's personal history. I still don't. I knew he'd been a track runner in high school. I knew that he served in the Imperial Japanese Army during World War II. Luckily for him, Nishijima Roshi never saw any action during the war. He spent his time guarding a remote outpost where nothing much happened. When he came back home, half his country had been burned to the ground, and millions of his people were dead.

He rarely talked about his wartime experiences. He hardly ever talked about his past at all, really. He wasn't much interested in the past — his or anyone else's. He was focused on understanding and spreading Master Dogen's message. He always called him "Master Dogen," by the way, never just Dogen. To call him just Dogen would have been highly disrespectful. I don't recall him ever admonishing anyone else for calling him just plain Dogen, but he would never do that.

There was a time when I worried that Nishijima Roshi regarded Dogen as infallible. I came to see that wasn't true when I asked him why Dogen had died so young, at age fifty-three. If he was such a wise master, surely Dogen could have figured out a way to live longer. Even in the 1200s fifty-three was a young age to die.

Nishijima Roshi said he suspected the reason he died so young was that Dogen insisted on building a monastery exactly like the one he'd lived at in China. But the area in China where his master had lived was very dry and arid, while all of Japan is extremely rainy and humid, especially the part of Japan where Dogen built Eihei-ji monastery. Japanese buildings are built with humidity in mind. They're purposely made very drafty so that the interiors can dry out. Nishijima Roshi suspected that Eihei-ji, in its original form, must have been damp and prone to growing mold, thereby contributing to bad health among those who lived there.

Of course, no one knows exactly what illness killed Dogen.

Some suspect it was tuberculosis, but there's no way to be sure. In any case, Nishijima Roshi's doubts about Dogen's architectural decisions let me know he didn't think Dogen was incapable of error.

But he did think of Dogen as a genius in his field. No one thinks scientists like Albert Einstein or Stephen Hawking were infallible. But they were geniuses. Most of us aren't qualified to argue with their theories, even if we've studied physics extensively. That's how Nishijima Roshi thought of Dogen. It's not that Dogen's writings were unquestionable. But he knew what he was writing about, and there's very little in his writings that's dubious.

But let's get back to Nishijima's pamphlet about ethics. He wrote, "Master Dogen describes that when we act, we penetrate the dharma, becoming completely one with it; and performing an action with all our being, sincerely, is to meet real action face to face."

Shohaku Okumura Roshi commented about this same section of "Genjo Koan" that Nishijima Roshi wrote about in an essay.* I quoted Okumura Roshi back in the first chapter. Let me introduce you to him properly now, since I'll be quoting him a lot as well.

Okumura Roshi is one of my favorite contemporary Zen teachers. I've never met him, but I've read a lot of his writings, and we've emailed each other a couple of times. He lives in Bloomington, Indiana, of all places. He was ordained by Kosho Uchiyama, Kodo Sawaki's successor, in 1970. He first came to the US in 1981, went back to Japan for a bit, came back to the US, and wrote some really terrific books about Zen. I highly recommend all of them. I also recommend his daughter's short film about Okumura's relationship with his son. It's called *SIT*, and it's on YouTube.

In his comments, Okumura Roshi uses a different translation of "Genjo Koan," so I hope you can follow along: "When we find the path and actually walk on the path, 'as the person realizes one dharma, the person permeates that dharma; as the person encounters

---

* *Dharma Eye* (March 2014).

one practice, the person [fully] practices that practice.' Each and every thing we do in our daily lives becomes our practice and realization. We experience one thing at a time, study it, and understand it. We continue to practice and study who we are, what each thing we encounter and experience is, what our life is, and what this world is like. This is the way we study ourselves and the Buddha way as *genjo-koan*; [which means] actualized reality."

Okumura Roshi also said, "From another perspective, even though we don't perceive what the self is, what the formless life is, and what the world is like, within our activities, the formless life and entirety of the world of interconnectedness are revealed."

I think that captures it beautifully. It can often feel like concepts such as dharma are lofty and far removed from my daily experience. But that's not really how it is. The word *dharma* is a way of indicating our regular, day-to-day existence. We call it dharma to draw attention to the fact that our ordinary lives are something deep and sacred — even when we're just doing something like mowing the lawn or washing the dishes. When we act based on this understanding of the sacredness of all action, we can start to feel the sacred in things we'd otherwise regard as ordinary and unworthy of notice.

Nishijima Roshi always said that the two dominant philosophies in the world were idealism and materialism. And when I say "always," I mean that almost literally. He said it a lot! Sometimes people use the word *idealism* as a synonym for optimism. But that's not the kind of idealism he was talking about. He meant philosophical idealism, the idea that the world of ideas is the true reality. Materialism, on the other hand, is the view that matter is true reality and that all things derive from material interaction.

Religious philosophies are idealistic, while science is materialistic. There are various shades, of course, and not every religion is purely idealistic, and nor is every version of science completely materialistic — especially some of the newer forms of physics. But broadly speaking, that's what he was talking about.

Both ways of looking at things have value, Nishijima Roshi would say. But they are both incomplete. Buddhism, he said, was an alternative philosophy that was neither idealistic nor materialistic. Sometimes people think Buddhism, being usually classified as a religion, is idealistic. Often when Dogen says that everything is the One Mind, that can sound a lot like idealism. But Dogen didn't consider mind to be something apart from matter like most idealists do. Mind and matter are two aspects of the same thing.

Anyway, Nishijima Roshi said that the best way to understand Dogen was to see how he often broke things down into four points of view, which he identified as subjective, objective, action, and reality. One of his students coined the acronym SOAR to help remember this. *Subjective* is a way of indicating idealism, and *objective* is a way of indicating materialism. *Action* combines the mental and physical aspects of reality into one. *Reality* is a synthesis of the other three views.

This is why Dogen contradicts himself all the time. The same thing looked at from the subjective point of view can look like its exact opposite when looked at from the materialistic point of view.

Here's how Nishijima Roshi puts it in that pamphlet about ethics that I've been referencing:

First Master Dogen explains an issue on the basis of abstract thinking, or from the viewpoint of idealistic thoughts…the view from our intellect.

Secondly, he discusses the same issue on the basis of concrete facts, or from the viewpoint of materialistic thoughts. That is, he describes the objective situation, often as perceived by our senses. At times this may appear as a total contradiction to the preceding view.

Thirdly, Master Dogen synthesizes the insistences of the fundamental philosophies above into one philosophy that is based on action. He clearly noticed that actions in our daily life are completely different from our thoughts and from our sense perception. He realized that action itself was real, and thus he made action the basis of his philosophy.

Finally, in what we might describe as "the ultimate phase," he recognized the identity of our action and the Universe, which is just this world in which we live. He said that our life is just our action at the present moment, and so to identify our action with the Universe is to meet and experience reality directly.

He relates this to ethics saying, "The philosophy of action belongs neither to idealism nor to materialism. Action has a number of peculiar factors that establish it as completely different from thoughts and sense perception. When we are acting sincerely at the present moment, it is difficult for us to think or to perceive. We naturally abandon idealism and materialism when we are acting, and so we must conclude that Buddhist ethics are necessarily different from idealistic ethics and materialistic ethics."

Doing something is different from thinking about doing something. Neither our thoughts nor our sense perceptions are particularly reliable. We tend to assume we are accurately sensing the world we live in and that our thoughts proceed from those accurate perceptions. After years of doing zazen, my tendency is to assume the opposite. I assume that all my perceptions are inaccurate and all my thoughts, to quote Led Zeppelin, are misgiven, since they're based on inaccurate perceptions.

Even so, we still need to be able to communicate with each other. And so we use the approximations language allows us. But it's extremely useful to always keep our limitations in mind. I'm never sure that I'm right and someone else is wrong, for example. I might be right from one point of view, while the other person is right from another. Knowing this, and never believing I am entirely in the right, helps me to act more ethically.

Nishijima Roshi says that ultimately "action is the Universe and the Universe is action." He adds that "our usual cultural values, [which are based on] our thoughts and our sense perception, are the complete opposite of real action. In the global civilization of today people usually revere the value of thoughts and sense perception so highly, but in Buddhism we revere our moral behavior in daily life as of the greatest importance."

He goes on: "According to the viewpoint that I have just described, that our life is just our action, we can see that for Buddhism the most valuable thing in this world is just to do right and not to do wrong."

Then he gives us a very interesting definition of the word *Buddha*. He says, "Gautama Buddha... used the word 'buddha' to indicate someone who is able to control themselves." He says, "Getting hold of ourselves, we should make our efforts to follow right teachings and lead meaningful and happy lives. In this state we can regulate our lives with complete freedom."

Nishijima Roshi died in January 2014. At some point when he was in the hospital they decided they needed to intubate him. The doctors began to insert the tube. He stopped them, saying, "I will decide for myself the time of my own death." He died a little while later, at age ninety-four. He always said we should not cling to life or long for death. He lived a long life but chose not to prolong it when his time was clearly up.

Before he died, he asked me to carry on his teaching. To be fair, I wasn't the only one he asked to do that. There are several of us out there trying to keep the thing he started going. Again I ask myself, was he right? Did I really understand him completely? It's hard to say for sure. I've been trying, with various degrees of success, to live according to the teachings he gave me and to pass those teachings on to anyone who wants to listen.

# 5. THE NOBLE EIGHTFOLD PATH

LET'S TALK ABOUT the basic ethical teachings of Buddhism.

There's a story recorded in one of the earliest Buddhist scriptures written in Pali that provides some good insights. Here is my version of that story. On the day that the Buddha was on his deathbed and about to die, a guy named Subbadha, a wandering ascetic, showed up. He was interested in the deeper truths of life, but he wasn't one of Buddha's disciples. Even though the Buddha was seriously sick, he was still answering questions from random people who were interested in his philosophy and way of life.

Subbadha said, "There are a lot of different religious teachers who teach lots of different things. Do all of them know what they're talking about? Or do none of them have a clue? Or is it that some are worth listening to and others aren't?"

The Buddha replied, "Don't worry about whether they have knowledge or not, or where they got their knowledge from. Where the Noble Eightfold Path is not found, there are no enlightened practitioners. Where the Noble Eightfold Path is found, there are enlightened practitioners. If monks would live correctly, there would be enlightened people all over the place."

The Noble Eightfold Path is the fourth of Buddha's famous Four Noble Truths, which were the subject of his very first sermon after his awakening to the truth of the universe. The common understanding of the Four Noble Truths is (1) All life is suffering (or unsatisfactory experience), (2) The cause of suffering is desire, or wanting things to be different from how they actually are, (3) When we stop wanting things to be different from how they actually are, we stop suffering, and (4) The way to stop wanting things to be different from the way they actually are is to follow the Noble Eightfold Path.

The Noble Eightfold Path is basically a path of ethical action. The eight folds are commonly given as (1) right view, (2) right thinking, (3) right speech, (4) right action, (5) right livelihood, (6) right effort, (7) right mindfulness, and (8) right meditation (or right balanced state). There are other ways to translate these. There always are! And we'll get to that. But this version is pretty much the standard way they're given in English.

The Buddha's answer to Subbadha shows how committed he was to ethics. No ethics, no enlightenment! As far as the Buddha was concerned, ethics and enlightenment were one and the same.

Not every spiritual teacher in India saw it this way. A lot of them taught very lofty doctrines about the true nature of reality but said little or nothing about ethics. On the other hand, there were spiritual teachers who were concerned almost solely with morality but who didn't teach much about the nature of reality. The Buddha taught both and tried to show how an understanding of the true nature of reality was intimately tied to ethical behavior.

I think one of the reasons Buddha equated ethics and enlightenment was that he was far more interested in a universal salvation — for want of a better word — than a personal one. To explain why, let's look at the story of Buddha's enlightenment. The story goes that Buddha suffered greatly on his path toward enlightenment. He was born a prince but gave up his throne in order to pursue spiritual awakening. He had a very cushy lifestyle, the kind of life lots of people would envy, but still felt empty and unfulfilled.

He tried being an ascetic, deliberately enduring all sorts of pain in order to free his immaterial spirit from his material body — because most people in India in his day believed we were immaterial spirits trapped inside material bodies. But that didn't work. After six years of trying and failing to free his spirit from his body, he just sat down quietly under a tree and stayed there for a long, long time, avoiding getting caught in thought and trying to experience reality in its purest form, unaffected by his personal views about it. At last he had his big awakening, which — among other things — included the understanding that he was not an immaterial spirit trapped in a material body.

After having this awakening and dwelling in the good feelings of it for a while, he thought to himself that nobody would ever understand it. So he figured he'd just keep it to himself.

The story goes that, at that moment, the god Indra appeared before him. Indra is the chief of the Indian gods, a sort of Zeus-type figure. Indra said to Buddha, "You've got to tell the people about this! They need it!" And so Buddha took Indra's advice and spent the rest of his life trying to teach others about how he had come to this profound awakening.

*That's* what Buddhism is. It's not about a personal enlightenment for one guy. It's about trying to bring about a universal enlightenment of all humankind. One of the reasons Buddha emphasized ethics is that in a world where more people are committed to ethical behavior, more people can do the necessary work to realize the ultimate truth.

People in desperate poverty, or living in war zones, or dealing with constant fear of being attacked or robbed, or dealing with rampant disease, or just living with too many of the kinds of hassles and problems coming from others around them acting unethically aren't going to be able to meditate. They aren't going to be interested in studying the meaning of life. They're too busy dealing with a lot of unnecessary bull crap.

Life is hard enough with the things we all have to struggle against. People being jerks to each other just adds more trouble, and it's completely unnecessary. We owe it to each other not to make things any harder for each other than they already are.

Realization or awakening or whatever you want to call it is difficult even under the best conditions. This is why people climb mountains to get away from everyone else and work on themselves. The Buddha realized that in a world where people could behave decently toward each other, those who wanted to work on themselves wouldn't have to climb mountains. That's the kind of world the Buddha wanted to bring about, one where everyone could reach the level of peace and understanding that he had reached. We all have work to do. That's why it's important for all of us to reconfirm our commitment to ethical behavior all the time.

Not only that, but as a commenter on my YouTube channel put it, "Being an asshole makes it impossible for me to be happy. I'm certain it makes it impossible to find that ultimate realization the Buddha was interested in."

Not only does it cause other people trouble when we act unethically, it causes us trouble as well. Lots of us fail to see that. We think that we can gain something for ourselves by behaving unethically toward others. But that's not true. I can never gain anything by causing pain for someone else. The more I engage in a practice of meditation, the clearer that fact becomes. The best thing for everyone is to act ethically.

So let's look at each of the folds of Buddha's Noble Eightfold Path one by one, shall we?

# 6. RIGHT VIEW

THE FIRST FOLD in the Noble Eightfold Path is right view. Have you ever taken a yoga class in which the instructor asked you to fix your eyes on a "drishti point"? In yoga classes this usually refers to a spot on a wall or some other unmoving object that you can stare at while you hold a balance pose on one leg like tree pose.

*Drishti* is the Sanskrit word for "view" when it comes to the Buddhist concept of "right view." *Samyak-drishti* is how you say "right view" in Sanskrit.

The word *samyak*, which we're translating here as "right," also appears in the Buddhist concept *anutara samyak sambodhi*, or "unsurpassed complete perfect enlightenment." So it also means "complete." In Chinese and Japanese the character that the Japanese pronounce *tadashii* or *shou* is used, and that means "correct." This is why sometimes it's translated as "right (or correct) view" and sometimes as "complete view."

According to Dainin Katagiri, in his book *You Have to Say Something*, this word derives from a term that means "to go together," "to turn together," or "to unite." He says, "Right is a state in which we live together in peace and harmony with all other beings. It is right, beyond our ideas of right or wrong, good or evil."

Just like in English, the word for "view" in Sanskrit can mean to physically look at something with your eyeballs, or it can mean an opinion or a way of understanding things.

In the Dhammapada, a very early collection of the Buddha's

sayings, it says, "And what is right view? Knowledge with regard to suffering, knowledge with regard to the origin of suffering, knowledge with regard to the cessation of suffering, knowledge with regard to the way of practice leading to the cessation of suffering: This is called right view."

In short, to have right view basically means that you understand the Four Noble Truths. But of course, there's more to it than that. As with all things in the Zen form of Buddhism, there's a comparatively easy and straightforward way to understand what right view means and a more difficult and mystical way of understanding it.

The easy way is that right view is just about having the correct philosophical outlook. It means that we understand the basic point of view of Buddhism. Mostly this means knowing that we don't know. It means understanding that our understanding of things is often flawed and one-sided and being open to a wider view of things. It means not having a fixed, rigid outlook.

There's a koan story about this. It goes:

Great Master Hogen once experienced a profound realization and took his community traveling beyond the lake district, where they lived. They had not gone far when they met with a heavy shower of rain. They took shelter at Jizo-in temple. There they met old Master Rakan Keichin.

Master Keichin asked them: Monks, where are you going?

Master Hogen said: We are traveling here and there.

Master Keichin said: What is the purpose of your travel?

Master Hogen said: I don't know.

Master Keichin said: Not knowing is most intimate.

Master Hogen then clearly arrived at the truth.*

The Korean Zen master Seung Sahn liked to use the phrase

---

*   Gudo Nishijima, trans., *Master Dogen's Shinji Shobogenzo: 301 Koan Stories*, Kindle ed. (Tokyo: Windbell, 2003).

"don't know mind" to express this attitude. Shunryu Suzuki Roshi called it "beginner's mind."

Our sense of self is, in many ways, just a collection of things we think we know. I know my shoe size, my address, my mom's maiden name, my favorite Godzilla movie, the names of all six members of the Three Stooges, and so on. I have opinions about various things. I know my own past, at least in broad detail, although there's a lot I've forgotten. All this adds up to something I provisionally call "myself."

But do I really know anything? To know something means to fix it in place. Yet most things won't stay fixed in place. My favorite Godzilla movie has changed over the years, and so has my address. Even my shoe size has changed as I've aged. My attitudes are continually shifting. As for knowing my past, my own past often surprises me. When I made a movie about the punk rock scene that I was part of in my late teens and early twenties I came across a bunch of videos made back then showing me doing things that I had no recollection of.

You'd think that concrete facts like my mother's maiden name and the names of all six members of the Three Stooges never change, and that seems to be true. But often things we take to be facts turn out to be wrong.

And even if I know that one of the Stooges was called Shemp but his legal name was Samuel Howard, although he was born Samuel Horwitz, the real Shemp was far more than his name.

Not knowing is most intimate because the truest thing you can ever say is, "I don't know." But let's get back to the more basic ideas of right view. If there's right view there must be a wrong view too.

Here's what the early Buddhist sutras have to say about wrong views, as opposed to right ones. In the Buddha's *Middle Length Discourses* (one of the oldest records of the historical Buddha's teachings), it says:

> There is the case where an uninstructed, run-of-the-mill person... does not discern what ideas are fit for attention,

or what ideas are unfit for attention. This being so, he does not attend to ideas fit for attention, and attends instead to ideas unfit for attention. ... This is how he attends inappropriately: "Was I in the past? Was I not in the past? What was I in the past? How was I in the past? Having been what, what was I in the past? Shall I be in the future? Shall I not be in the future? What shall I be in the future? How shall I be in the future? Having been what, what shall I be in the future?" Or else he is inwardly perplexed about the immediate present: "Am I? Am I not? What am I? How am I? Where has this being come from? Where is it bound?"*

It goes on:

As he attends inappropriately in this way, one of six [mistaken] views arises in him: The view that I have a self, or the view that I have no self... or the view that it is precisely by means of self that I perceive self... or the view that it is precisely by means of self that I perceive not-self... or the view that it is precisely by means of not-self that I perceive self. Or else he has a view like this: This very self of mine — the knower that is sensitive here and there to the ripening of good and bad actions — is the self of mine that is constant, everlasting, eternal, not subject to change, and will endure as long as eternity.

This is called a thicket of views, a wilderness of views, a contortion of views, a writhing of views, a fetter of views. Bound by a fetter of views, the uninstructed run-of-the-mill person is not freed from birth, aging, and death, from sorrow, lamentation, pain, distress, and despair. He is not freed, I tell you, from suffering and stress.

*    "Right View: Samma Ditthi," *Access to Insight*, 2005, https://accesstoinsight.org/ptf/dhamma/sacca/sacca4/samma-ditthi/index.html.

I know I said this was the easy way of understanding this. Wait till we get to the difficult way!

Basically, all this points to what I said earlier — knowing that you don't know. The first part talks about all the questions that the Buddha deemed unwise. We're never gonna figure out the answers to them, and even if we could, those answers won't help us address the problem of suffering. So we just leave them be and get on with our lives.

The next part, the part about the six mistaken views, is about various theories of the self that circulated in India in Buddha's day. They were based on the notion that there is an eternal, unchanging, nonmaterial self and that this eternal, immaterial, spiritual self lives inside our impermanent, short-lived, gross material body and is our true being. The "self" referred to here is that kind of self.

What gets confusing is that later Buddhists also use words that get translated into English as "self" to mean a bigger kind of self that is the life of the entire universe. Dogen uses the Japanese word *jiko* (usually translated as "self") to refer to that bigger meaning of self.

I'm sorry this stuff is so confusing! But I promise, if you do a regular meditation practice — during which you forget all about even trying to understand any of this — you'll eventually get to a place where this makes a whole lot more sense. Plus, I'll try to explain it more as we go along.

Dogen gets typically obtuse when he talks about right view. In an essay called "108 Gates of Dharma Illumination," he provides very short remarks about each of the folds of the Noble Eightfold Path. He says right view is "a gate of Dharma illumination; for [with it] we attain the noble path on which the superfluous is exhausted." I take this to mean that for Dogen, right view sees things directly, just as they are, with nothing superfluous added.

He also addresses the Noble Eightfold Path in a chapter of *Shobogenzo* called "The Thirty-Seven Elements of Bodhi." *Bodhi* means "enlightenment." What he says in that chapter gets much more complicated.

In his introduction to this chapter, Nishijima Roshi says:

> The thirty-seven methods are usually said to belong to Hinayana Buddhism, because they are discussed in the Abhidharmamahāvibhāṣā-śāstra, which is one of the primary texts of Hinayana Buddhism. In Japan, and especially among Mahayana Buddhist masters, it was very rare for Buddhist monks to discuss these teachings. But Master Dogen has his own views on Mahayana and Hinayana. According to him, there exists only the Buddhism that Gautama Buddha taught. He thought that any distinctions between Mahayana and Hinayana are reflections of the different ages and cultures in which the two schools of Buddhism were taught, and he refused to discriminate between the two Buddhist streams. In this chapter Master Dogen explains the thirty-seven elements of the truth with no division into Hinayana or Mahayana, but based upon the practice of zazen.

Buddhism is usually divided up into two major schools, Hinayana and Mahayana. *Hinayana* is a derogatory term coined by the people from the Mahayana side of the argument. It means "lesser vehicle." The Mahayana folks gave themselves a name that means "greater vehicle."

The so-called Hinayana Buddhist schools were the earliest forms of Buddhism, and most of them have disappeared. The only one remaining is the Theravada school. *Theravada* means "way of the elders." However, it's been suggested that the contemporary Theravada school was actually formed after the other early Buddhist schools went out of business, as a sort of revival of their teachings. So even Theravada might not be, strictly speaking, one of the Hinayana Buddhist sects. But it's the closest we have these days.

In any case, Theravada Buddhism, like those earlier schools of Buddhism, regards only the earliest scriptures of Buddhism as authentic. Mahayana Buddhism, on the other hand, accepts a whole bunch of later sutras and even tends to ignore the early stuff.

So Theravada (and Hinayana) Buddhism is like a crusty old hipster who thinks that only his favorite band's early records are worth listening to, while Mahayana is like a young fan who is into the stuff the band's put out more recently and doesn't really like the old records that much. Dogen is like a young fan who prefers the new stuff but has dug back into the discography to get into the older records and thinks some of those early albums are pretty good.

The Mahayana sutras contain all sorts of sayings attributed to the historical Buddha, as well as dialogues between him and his earliest followers. But none of these sutras appeared until about five hundred years after all those people were dead. The way they used to explain this is to say these later sutras were too deep for the first followers of the Buddha to understand. So they were hidden in a cave guarded by these sort of snake-god things called *nagas* until the world was ready for them.

I'm not sure if anyone ever really believed that story. Maybe some of the rank-and-file folks who attended ceremonies at Buddhist temples mainly out of social obligation or even superstition believed it. But scholar-monks like Dogen always knew the Mahayana sutras were the products of later generations of Buddhists. It wasn't like it was some big revelation one day where everybody went, "Oh my gosh! Those sutras weren't really hidden in a cave and guarded by snake-god thingies? My stars! Hand me the smelling salts!"

Anyway, when talking about right view in the "Thirty-Seven Elements of Bodhi" chapter, Dogen says, "Right view as a branch of the path is the inside of the eyes containing the body. At the same time, even prior to the body we must have the eye that is prior to the body. Though the view has been grandly realized in the past, it is realized now as the real universe and is experienced immediately. In sum, those who do not put the body into the eyes are not Buddhist ancestors."

Weird stuff, right? Let's unpack it.

When Dogen uses the word *eye* metaphorically, he usually means a point of view or a kind of awareness. When he says "inside of the eyes containing the body," he is talking about the awareness of the body. We usually think that awareness is something that occurs inside the body. We think that because the body exists and has senses we can be aware of the outside world as well as the inside of our bodies. That is, we think that awareness is something that happens internally based on things that are external to us. Even knowing what's going on within our own bodies is something we take to be external to the one who knows it. When I have a headache I tend to describe it as if it is something that happens to a "me" to which the head is an external thing.

But Dogen is talking about an awareness that contains the body. He's talking about the understanding that the body exists within awareness rather than awareness being something that occurs inside the body or even inside the mind. Right view is the understanding that the body is inside of me rather than me being inside the body. Which is not our usual way of understanding things. But let's just go with it and see where we end up.

About the part where Dogen says that "even prior to the body we must have the eye that is prior to the body," Nishijima Roshi's footnotes say, "The 'eye that is prior to the body' suggests the ability to regulate our physical actions even before we are conscious of them." That indicates a high level of intuitive ability. We have reflexes that move the body before we are conscious of them. Recent studies suggest that often conscious awareness lags behind even movements that we think of as being done consciously.

Another way to understand what Dogen is saying is that the "eye" is more fundamental than the body. In this reading the word *eye* means "consciousness" or "mind." This is one of the weird aspects of Buddhist philosophy. I grew up learning that because I have a body I am conscious. Consciousness is a phenomenon produced by the body. The Buddhists flip that and say that the body is a manifestation of consciousness or of mind — depending on which term they decide to use that day. We'll get more into this as we go along.

Then Dogen says, "Though the view has been grandly realized in the past, it is realized now as the real universe and is experienced immediately." That's my teacher's translation. Kazuaki Tanahashi's translation of the same line goes, "Because it magnificently sees the self in the past, it actualizes the fundamental point. It is what has been intimately seen in the past."

Here's what I make of that. The "it" that sees the self is right view. So we're talking about right view as if it is a being that can see. Metaphorically, anyway. Right view sees the self of the past through memory, but it experiences the present as reality here and now. This reality is the universe as it is, here and now, of which I am an essential part. And so are you, by the way. We all are.

In the past we were the center of a universe with no center, and we are still the center of a universe with no center.

The way this relates to ethics is that this understanding is the "eye that is prior to the body." As Nishijima Roshi says, this indicates the "ability to regulate our physical actions even before we are conscious of them." In other words, it is an intuitive awareness of what the correct thing to do is, here and now.

Before we are even conscious of the right decision, the right decision has already appeared in our minds. This is something Nishijima Roshi used to say a lot, and it's been backed up lately by studies in human psychology. When I first heard it, I had a hard time believing it was true. Because I often seemed to be at a complete loss as to what the right thing to do was.

Yet the more I worked with zazen practice, the more I began to see that Nishijima Roshi was right. I always know the right thing to do. I'm just very good at shouting over my intuitive sense. That's when I get confused and think that I have no idea what I ought to do. The quieter I get, the easier it is to perceive the quiet intuitive sense and the easier it is to do what really needs to be done. When we maintain right view, the ideas that drive us to do unethical things are undone. We no longer believe ourselves to be separate from others, and therefore we no longer see any valid reason to harm anyone else.

# 7. CAN YOU DO WHAT IS RIGHT WITHOUT BELIEF?

I WANT TO digress a bit here before we go on to the rest of the Eightfold Path. Because one of the ways that right view is often translated into English is as "right belief." And you could make a case that the early Buddhists didn't just want you to *understand* the Four Noble Truths and the Eightfold Path; they wanted you to *believe* in them. Therefore I think I ought to address the matter of belief as it pertains to Buddhism.

The other day, my wife's sister's husband asked me if I could state succinctly what Buddhists believe. He, my wife, her sister, her parents, and I were all sitting around a table, playing Scrabble. Everyone was chatting. The conversations were going this way and that. Topics were shifting. People were talking over each other.

Trying to state what Buddhists believe is difficult even under ideal conditions. Under those conditions it was impossible. The best I could do was to say that it's not really about beliefs. If you believe that Jesus Christ is your lord and savior who died for your sins, I said, you can still be a Buddhist. Your Christian friends might have a problem with that, but most Buddhists would not.

That was the best I could do, and it satisfied him enough that the conversation could continue into other areas. But there's more to it than that.

There are some forms of Buddhism in which having the correct beliefs is important. Stephen Batchelor, who has written a lot of books about Buddhism, wrote a book called *Buddhism Without*

*Beliefs*. Batchelor was distressed because the Tibetan Buddhist organization to which he once belonged insisted that he must believe in certain things. I've forgotten exactly what they said he had to believe in, but it had something to do with a particular deity they were fond of in that sect. And they told him that he had to believe that karma and reincarnation were literally true. Otherwise, they said, he couldn't be a Buddhist. So he left that organization.

Some Buddhists do insist that all Buddhists must hold specific beliefs. But most Zen Buddhists don't. If there's one thing I can say that most Zen Buddhists believe, it's that you don't have to hold specific beliefs in order to be a Buddhist.

This was one of the main reasons I found Zen Buddhism so attractive when I first encountered it. I didn't like being told what to believe. Especially when it came to things that were impossible to verify, like whether Jesus rose from the dead or whether there were dinosaurs on Noah's Ark. When I tried to become a Christian, I found that I was required to believe a lot of stuff that I couldn't believe, which was an insurmountable barrier to my ever becoming a Christian. This was a huge disappointment, because in my late teens I really wanted to be a Christian. When I found out that Zen Buddhism didn't require me to believe anything like that, it was a tremendous relief.

Back then I was a huge fan of the Monkees, the made-for-TV band from the sixties. I'm still a fan today. In the late '80s I even auditioned to be in a TV series called *The New Monkees*. I got as far as having a personal interview with the producers. Most of the thousands who auditioned for the show only made it as far as the "cattle call" auditions with dozens of other hopefuls in the room.

But I failed the audition and didn't get on the show, which turned out to be a good thing. It barely lasted a single season, and their only album didn't sell at all. Sometimes not getting what you want is the best thing possible.

The reason I bring this up, though, is that the Monkees — the original ones, not the "new" ones — made a movie called *Head* in 1968. There's a scene in that film in which an Indian swami gives a little speech to Peter Tork, the Monkees' bass player. One Halloween I decided to go out dressed as a swami. In order to have something to say in character, I memorized the speech the swami gives in that film. I still know it:

> We were speaking of belief. Belief and conditioning. All belief could possibly be said to be the result of some conditioning. Thus the study of history is the study of one system of belief deposing another, and so on, and so on. A psychologically tested belief of our time is that the central nervous system, which feeds its impulses directly to the brain — the conscious and subconscious — is unable to discern between the real and the vividly imagined experience. If there is a difference, and most of us believe there is. Am I being clear? For to examine these concepts requires tremendous energy and discipline. To experience the now, without preconception or beliefs, to allow the unknown to occur and to occur, requires clarity. And where there is clarity, there is no choice. And where there is choice, there is misery. But why should anyone listen to me? Why should I speak, since I know nothing?

It's actually a really brilliant little speech. It was written by Jack Nicholson. Back in the Monkees days, Nicholson was a struggling actor and part-time screenwriter. Apparently he was also a fan of Jiddu Krishnamurti. Krishnamurti was discovered as a child by some folks who were searching for what they called the World Teacher, a charismatic religious leader who they believed would usher in a golden age of peace and enlightenment.

They groomed young Krishnamurti for years to fulfill this role. They established an organization called the Order of the Star, eventually attracting hundreds of thousands of followers eager to do the bidding of the World Teacher. One day they called a huge meeting in which Krishnamurti, now an adult, was supposed to formally announce that he was the World Teacher. Instead, Krishnamurti dissolved the Order of the Star and told them they needed no messiah. "Truth is a pathless land," he said. He spent the rest of his life speaking out against organized religion and saying a lot of other deeply profound stuff. At one point in my life I read every Krishnamurti book I could get my hands on. His philosophy was very influential on the way I understand Buddhism.

Anyway, the swami's speech in the movie *Head* sounds like the kind of thing Krishnamurti might say, even though, as far as I know, it's not based on anything specific he said.

It seems like Jack Nicholson was capable of some pretty profound thoughts. What he wrote for that swami to say about belief is spot-on. All belief is the result of some kind of conditioning. This doesn't apply only to superficial beliefs like the belief I hold that I am an American or the belief I hold that *Monster Zero* (aka *Invasion of Astro Monster*) is the best Godzilla movie and that Curly Howard was the best third Stooge, although Shemp was pretty funny too. It even applies to beliefs that hardly anyone would ever question, like the belief that I am a human being or that I live on planet Earth. Although, as an aside, I also can't imagine why anyone would question that *Monster Zero* is the best Godzilla film or that Curly is the best third Stooge.

Anyway, even beliefs like that I am a human on planet Earth are based on conditioning. We are told again and again that these beliefs are true and undeniable. Eventually we internalize them and think they are our own beliefs, that we reasoned our way to them. But I wonder if that's true.

In the past, religious beliefs have been important tools used by societies to maintain order. For example, if most people in a society believe that murdering someone will anger God, who will then punish them by sending them to hell for eternity, you might have fewer murders.

Whether or not it's true, a lot of people believe that those who have the proper beliefs will behave ethically, while those who do not have the proper beliefs will not. This is why some people get so hot and bothered when they find out that someone doesn't hold what they think are the proper beliefs. That person might be dangerous.

A nonbeliever is thought to be dangerous for two major reasons. First, if, for example, someone doesn't believe he'll be sent to hell for murdering someone, he might murder someone. And second, if someone doesn't hold the right beliefs, he might influence others to stop believing the right things, and if enough people stop believing the right things, the entire social order might break down completely.

At least that's how the thinking goes. A lot of people who think this way don't even realize they think this way. Their belief in belief goes so deep that they don't even recognize it as a belief. The ways people get worked up about what other people believe seem a bit odd to me sometimes. If you tell me, let's say, "Those guys over there believe that all writers of books about Zen should be kicked in the ass," then I can see the sense in my steering clear of those people.

But if you say, "Those guys over there have the wrong beliefs; we'd better go over there and change their beliefs to the right ones," all I can think is, good luck with that! I wish all people believed the right things. But I'm not even sure that I believe the right things. Of course, some beliefs cause more trouble than others. Still, trying to change other people's beliefs is difficult. If that's your plan, you ought to be prepared to put in some serious time and effort.

Can we do what is right without belief? Can we behave ethically even when we don't believe in divine retribution? In the Zen tradition it is generally believed that a person can do what is right and avoid doing what is not right without necessarily holding any specific beliefs around that. Even so, it seems to me that Zen Buddhists kind of hedge their bets when it comes to this belief.

Dogen wrote an essay called "Deep Belief in Cause and Effect."
By "cause and effect" he meant karma, in the sense that if you do
good things, good things will happen to you, and if you do bad
things, bad things will happen to you. This is a common Buddhist
belief, and it's one that Stephen Batchelor finds particularly galling.

Unlike Batchelor, Dogen, who was also a very rational guy, did
not find that idea of karma problematic. The essay I mentioned is
one of two places in *Shobogenzo* in which Dogen writes about an old
koan story from China. It's the story of an ancient Zen master who
is asked by a student if a Zen master is subject to the law of cause
and effect. The Zen master says he isn't subject to the law of cause
and effect. Because of this, he gets reborn as a fox for his next five
hundred lifetimes. In China, foxes were seen as deceptive creatures.

Centuries later the fox/Zen master turns himself into a human
for long enough to ask another Zen master to help free him from
being a fox. He tells this Zen master what happened to him and asks
what he has to say about it. This other Zen master says, "Don't be
unclear about cause and effect." This does the trick and the ancient
Zen master is free from being reborn as a fox.

The point is that everyone is subject to the law of cause and
effect. It doesn't matter how enlightened you are. Dogen wrote this
essay to emphasize to his students that they should have what he
calls "deep belief in cause and effect." He also wrote an essay called
"Karma in the Three Times" (past, present, and future) in which he
makes more or less the same point.

On the other hand, Dogen wrote another essay called "Great
Practice" in which he also comments on the same story of the fox/
Zen master. In this essay, he seems to be saying that an enlightened
person is not subject to the law of cause and effect. Actually, what
Dogen says in that essay is a lot more subtle than I'm making it sound
here. Even so, I think it's fair to say that in the essay "Great Practice," Dogen's opinion about the nature of cause and effect seems

quite different from the opinion he expresses in the essay "Deep Belief in Cause and Effect."

My guess is that Dogen recognized that, for a lot of people, having the proper beliefs was an important factor in their being able to act ethically. Maybe the only reason some people can find to behave properly is that they fear what might happen to them if they don't. Dogen wrote "Great Practice" some years earlier than "Deep Belief in Cause and Effect." Maybe in the years between he realized that some of the people who listened to his talks didn't get his subtler teachings on cause and effect. Maybe he felt that he needed to make things simpler and more blunt.

That's really sad. But I think it's probably true that some people need to believe they'll be punished for doing wrong in order to be motivated to be ethical. Since human law and justice are often unreliable, it might be useful for such people to believe that there's a Great Cosmic Policeman and Judge who sees all and knows all and will make sure justice is done even when human justice fails.

I don't think everyone needs to believe that, though. Plenty of people are clearly capable of being ethical even when they don't believe that God or karma will punish them for doing wrong. And because some people are able to do that, I think it's reasonable to believe that all people have that capacity, even if a lot of them fail to live up to it.

As for me, I've seen karma at work in my own life so often that I can no longer doubt it. I believe in karma, and I believe that my belief in karma is rational. On the other hand, I think it's important to apply ideas about karma *only* to myself and *never* to other people. I don't look at someone who is having a bad time and say, "That guy must have done something wrong in the past. Ha! Ha! He's getting what he deserves!" That kind of talk is really gross and ugly. What's more, it doesn't help. If someone is having a bad time, it doesn't matter if it's because they did wrong in the past. The best thing I can do right now is try to help.

As for the story of the fox/Zen master, in a sense, the fox/Zen master is not subject to cause and effect because he *is* cause and effect. It's not that cause and effect is something that happens to him. He is an example, or even a physical manifestation, of cause and effect in action. We all are.

When it comes to beliefs, I don't believe in them. Not consciously, anyway. But, just like everyone else, I've internalized such a huge catalog of beliefs that it's hard for me to recognize them as beliefs. When I can let go of those beliefs, I feel lighter and happier. I find that holding specific beliefs is not necessary as a motivation for acting ethically. At least not for me. But I believe that not everyone is willing to do that, even if they are capable.

Still, even that is a belief. I might be wrong.

# 8. RIGHT THINKING

USUALLY THE SECOND fold of the Eightfold Path is translated as "right thinking," but sometimes it's translated as "right resolve" or "right intention." And because it's often translated into English as "right intention," you'll sometimes see American Buddhists riffing on how it's about always intending to do good. American new age spirituality gets pretty into this idea of intention, as if the intention to do good things is the same as actually *doing* good things. But as my grandma said, the road to hell is paved with good intentions. Actually, my grandma never said that. But I'm sure somebody's grandma did.

The problem with that interpretation is that it isn't the sort of intention the early Buddhists were talking about. Rather, right intention or right resolve was understood as the specific intention or resolve to leave one's home and family and join the Buddhist monastic order.

On the other hand, in the *Samyutta Nikaya*, or "grouped discourses," one of the early Buddhist scriptures written in Pali, it is defined slightly differently. In that document the Buddha says, "And what is right resolve? Being resolved on renunciation, on freedom from ill will, on harmlessness: This is called right resolve."

In this case it doesn't necessarily mean you have to become a monk or nun but that you should have the mindset of a monk or nun. You should renounce the things of the world, renounce ill will, and resolve to be harmless. Another way of looking at this is that you should have the resolve or intention of following the Noble Eightfold Path and upholding the ethical principles of Buddhism.

If you take this fold of the Eightfold Path to mean right intention in this way, then the ethical implications are easy to see. Renouncing ill will and vowing to be harmless is surely a good way to become a more ethical person. However, there's yet another way to interpret this fold of the Eightfold Path.

The Sanskrit word *sankalpa* can be translated as "will," "volition," "mental resolve," "purpose," "aim," or "intention." Or it can be translated as "thought," "idea," "reflection," or "mind." When the Noble Eightfold Path was translated into Chinese, they chose a word that meant something more like "thought" rather than "aim" or "intention." The word they chose is pronounced *shi-i* in Japanese and is defined as "using wisdom to get to the bottom of things; focusing one's mind; deep contemplation; concentrated thought; deliberating; pondering; reflecting."

In his footnotes to the "Thirty-Seven Elements of Bodhi" — the chapter of *Shobogenzo* in which Dogen writes about the Noble Eightfold Path — Nishijima Roshi remarks that the word *shi-i* is composed of two characters, one that means "to think" and another that means "to ponder, or reflect." He says that the word has a "somewhat general and reflective feeling, whereas the Sanskrit word *sankalpa* seems to carry some sense of definite purpose." Because of the way it was translated, Chinese and Japanese Buddhists in the Mahayana tradition — including Dogen — tended to interpret this fold of the Eightfold Path as being more about right thinking than about right aim or intention. This is why it's often translated into English as "right thinking."

I have to add here that every time I come across the term *right thinking* in Buddhist literature, I immediately recall a *Star Trek* episode from the original (and best) series. It's called "The Cage." In that episode some tiny aliens with giant heads that have big veins all over them capture the first captain of the starship *Enterprise*, Captain

Pike — who was captain before Captain Kirk took over. These aliens can control people's minds and make them see and experience whatever they want them to see and experience. When Captain Pike disobeys the aliens they make him believe horrible things are happening to him. They tell him, "Wrong thinking will be punished. Right thinking will be just as quickly rewarded. You will find it an effective combination."

Just to make the whole deal about what this fold is actually about even more confusing, in "108 Gates of Dharma Illumination," Dogen doesn't even translate *sankalpa* as "shi-i." Instead, he translates it as "funbetsu," which means "discrimination." Of course, the word *discrimination* in this case means the ability to tell one thing from another, not racial or ethnic discrimination.

In "108 Gates of Dharma Illumination" Dogen says, "Right discrimination is a gate of Dharma illumination; for [with it] we eliminate all discrimination and lack of discrimination." Which is another one of those places where Dogen says something that sounds like "I'm not saying it's aliens. But it's aliens."

My take on it is that he is acknowledging that dualistic discrimination is a necessary part of being human, and yet he is also acknowledging that Zen is all about transcending that sort of dualistic thinking. We discriminate in a utilitarian way, because we've got to be able to know the difference between our butts and a hole in the ground and stuff like that. Yet we do our best not to get caught by discrimination.

What Dogen says about right thinking in "Thirty-Seven Elements of Bodhi" is more detailed and complicated:

> Right thinking as a branch of the path: When [we] establish this thinking, the Buddhas of the ten directions all appear. So the manifestation of the ten directions, and the manifestation of the Buddhas, are just the time of the establishment of right thinking. When we establish this right thinking we are beyond self and beyond the external world; at the

same time, in the very moment of the present, when right thinking occurs we go straight to Varanasi [the place where the Buddha first preached the dharma]. The place where the thinking exists is Varanasi. An eternal Buddha says, "I am thinking the concrete state of not thinking." "How can the state of not thinking be thought?" "It is different from thinking." This is right consideration, right thinking. To break a zafu is right thinking.

Weird, huh? Let's take that apart and figure out what it means.

Nishijima Roshi in his footnotes to that chapter of *Shobogenzo* says, "Master Dogen suggests that 'right thinking' is the state in zazen, a state that is different from ordinary thinking, and that this state should be our standard." To which you may slap your forehead and say, "He doesn't say anything about zazen at all!"

Ah, but he does! It's just that, in typical Dogen style, it's a bit obscure. The stuff at the end about "thinking the concrete state of not thinking" comes from the story of a conversation Master Yakusan Igen had with a monk. He told the monk that while doing zazen he should think the thought of not-thinking. When the monk asked what that meant, the master told him, "It's different from thinking."

Lots of people translate this story in other ways. But in the original, the master first tells the monk to do *fushiryo* (not-thinking) and then, upon being asked what that is, the master says *hishiryo* (different from thinking). The word *shiryo* is usually translated as "consideration" rather than "thinking." So it means deliberate thinking rather than the kind of thoughts that just bubble up in your mind on their own.

Both the prefix *fu-* and the prefix *hi-* are negations. But while the prefix *fu-* is a mild negation, the prefix *hi-* indicates total negation. When you use the prefix *hi-* instead of *fu-*, it's like the difference between saying something is "not moral" and saying it's "immoral," or between calling something "not legal" and calling it "illegal."

Dogen's understanding of this fold of the Eightfold Path, then, isn't just about having good intentions. It's about an entirely different way of using your brain.

When Dogen says that breaking a zafu is right thinking, he's saying that you have to do a whole lot of zazen before this becomes your regular way of using your brain. That can sound pretty daunting.

But Dogen also says elsewhere that the mind of a beginner in zazen is no different from the mind of an experienced practitioner. In one of his other essays — called "Bendowa," which means "A Talk on Pursuing the Buddhist Way" — he says, "If a human being, even for a single moment, manifests the Buddha's posture in the three forms of conduct, while [that person] sits up straight in samadhi, the entire world of Dharma assumes the Buddha's posture and the whole of space becomes the state of realization." He even adds that "those who live and talk with them [i.e., people who do zazen], also, are all reciprocally endowed with the limitless Buddha-virtue."

*Samadhi* is usually defined as a rare and special meditative state of intense concentration. In the Hindu tradition it's often identified as a state that occurs to an advanced practitioner of yoga in which she or he achieves union with the divine just before death. Dogen defined *samadhi* very differently.

For Dogen "sitting up straight in samadhi" doesn't mean establishing a special mental state. As far as Dogen was concerned, any time you did zazen, *that* was samadhi. No matter what you thought it was. The "three forms of conduct" just means conduct of body, speech, and mind. When you're doing zazen you are regulating all three, even if it doesn't always feel that way.

In his book *Each Moment Is the Universe*, Dainin Katagiri — that Zen teacher I could have studied with in Minneapolis but didn't — explains zazen like this. "If you try to examine your life analytically, asking yourself who you are, finally you will realize that there is something you cannot reach. You don't know what it is, but you feel the presence of something you want to connect with. This is sometimes called the absolute. Buddha and Dogen Zenji say true self. Christians say God. But even though you are aware that there is something you are seeking, it's pretty difficult to connect with it directly. That's why we practice zazen."*

Doing zazen is a way to connect with this unnamable something directly and immediately. Yet we won't necessarily be aware of this connection. In "Bendowa" Dogen says, "[The state in zazen] is not dimmed by the views of these individuals themselves (i.e., the people doing zazen) because the state in the quietness, without intentional activity, is direct experience."

In the poem "Shinjinmei" ("Inscription of Faith in Mind"), an ancient Buddhist master named Sosan described it like this:

> The empty enlightenment illuminates itself
> There is no need for the slightest mental effort
> It is a realm of nonthinking
> A realm beyond the apprehension of reasoning and emotions.

This kind of right thinking is what goes on constantly as the bedrock of all experience. It's not something you need to try to establish or to bring into being. It's already there. The trick is learning how not to get in the way of it. That is what takes effort.

Someone sent me an email describing some strange sensations and thoughts that ran through his mind every time he did zazen making him feel a little crazy. Here's how I answered:

> Lots of things happen during zazen. It's different for each person. The main thing to do with any sensations or feelings like these is to let them pass.
>
> I myself used to wonder if I was going crazy during zazen sometimes. I think it's what happens when you start loosening control over your thoughts. We all have a lot of filters for our thoughts. We sort of run all of our random

---

* Dainin Katagiri, *Each Moment Is the Universe: Zen and the Way of Being Time* (Boston: Shambhala, 2007), 28.

thoughts through a larger general filter that we believe to be our individual self. This filter censors certain thoughts and allows others to pass. The ones that get censored are not experienced consciously, even though they don't really go away.

Sometimes our filter censors thoughts that are considered "bad," like thoughts of violence or thoughts that are contrary to what it believes "good people" think. Sometimes it censors thoughts that don't reinforce the sense of the existence of a personal self.

When these filters start to become looser, those forbidden thoughts start to be more easily noticed. When that happens, the personal ego can feel threatened. It tries to make sense of these thoughts in a way that will still preserve the idea that it is real and is in control. But this sense of the ego's reality and control was always false.

Anyhow, one of the tricks the ego often tries at this point is to tell you that maybe you're going crazy. It wants you to reestablish those filters.

This part of the practice should be handled carefully. The fact is that none of your thoughts are "you." Those filters are not really necessary if you understand this. If you understand that absolutely none of your thoughts are really your own, then any thought at all can come through your mind and have no effect on your behavior or your emotional state. But the problem is that if you don't understand that none of your thoughts are truly yours, the ego might decide to try to hang on to those forbidden thoughts, and this could cause trouble. That's why the filters exist in the first place — to keep you from acting on some of those thoughts.

But you can also just let those thoughts come into the conscious mind and still not act on them. That's harder for most people to do. It takes practice and discipline. But if you can learn to do it you'll be able to handle a lot of stuff that most people can't handle very well. You'll be less likely to be overwhelmed by strong or difficult emotions, for example.

The most useful lesson zazen ever taught me was that my thoughts are just thoughts. All of them. No matter what they are. They're all just thoughts. No big deal.

Sometimes when my brain stops buzzing with so many thoughts it feels really good. It's like a muscle that's been used so much that it's gotten stiff and sore, but now it's finally getting a little rest. That can feel very nice. I usually just try to enjoy it while it lasts. I think it's good for your brain to get a little rest.

It's ironic how much effort is involved in establishing a state of effortlessness. But we can relate it back to music again. For a skilled musician, playing complex pieces is comparatively effortless. But it's effortless because the musician has put in hours of practice.

The problem in meditation is almost the reverse, though. We don't notice it, but the way most of us view reality is the result of many years of effort and practice. We've been taught to see things a certain way. We've made the effort to learn how to do that, and it wasn't easy. We had to pass a lot of tests in school to demonstrate that we had mastered the proper worldview. We studied hard!

In meditation, we're learning to put all that aside and see things the way we saw them before we mastered the complicated art of seeing things the way our society wanted us to see them. Which is not to say that everything we learned from parents, teachers, and the rest of society was bad. A lot of it is really useful. But it's a specific way of understanding things; it's not the raw experience of seeing things just the way they are.

Right thinking means the ability to step out of the way of what you were taught to think and see things as they really are.

# 9. RIGHT SPEECH

FOLD NUMBER THREE in the Noble Eightfold Path is right speech. In the *Samyutta Nikaya*, the early Buddhist text that we looked at in the previous chapter, *right speech* is defined as "abstaining from lying, from divisive speech, from abusive speech, and from idle chatter."

Those early Buddhists texts say that the criterion for right speech is that what you say must be factual, true, beneficial, and endearing and agreeable to others. But even if what you want to say ticks all these boxes, you still need to wait for the proper time to say it because that's how you demonstrate your sympathy for living beings.

Several of the Ten Grave Precepts in Zen Buddhism, which we will look at after we finish the Eightfold Path, are devoted to right speech, like the vow not to lie, the vow not to speak of the past mistakes of oneself or others, the vow not to praise oneself at the expense of others, and the vow not to slander Buddha, dharma, and sangha. If you wanted to, you could even include the vow not to give way to anger with the precepts about right speech, since anger is often conveyed in words. Almost half the top ten precepts are about right speech.

Speech is a big deal for Buddhists because it's a big deal for human beings in general. No other animal we know of talks at all. But we humans talk all the damn time. Buddhist philosophy is conveyed mainly through talking and through writing, which could be considered a sort of subspecies of talking.

I have a dog named Ziggy Pup. Ziggy has a one-word vocabulary — just the word *woof* at different volumes and frequencies. But he understands a lot of human words. He can be lied to, and lies hurt him. Like if I say, "Let's go for a walk," and then don't actually take him for a walk, he gets really dejected. Not that I do that deliberately. But sometimes I think I can take him outside right away but something comes up and I have to make him wait. When I do that he looks really sad.

So wrong speech can even hurt animals. How much more can it hurt people? It's obvious that using right speech is an important part of being an ethical human being. That's why it's given such priority in Buddhist ethical systems.

Dogen's understanding of right speech is a little different from the way the early Buddhists interpreted it. In "108 Gates of Dharma Illumination" he says, "Right speech is a gate of Dharma illumination; for [with it] concepts, voice, and words all are known as sound." I think Dogen is saying we should understand that, when viewed subjectively, our words have meaning. And yet when viewed objectively, words are just sounds we make with our mouths, the same way Ziggy Pup makes sounds with his mouth. We should understand both ways of looking at speech.

In "Thirty-Seven Elements of Bodhi," Dogen gets more complicated. There he says, "Right speech as a branch of the path is the mute self not being mute. Mutes among [ordinary] people have never been able to express the truth. People in the mute state are not mutes: they do not aspire to be saints, and do not add something spiritual onto themselves. [Right speech] is mastery of the state in which the mouth is hung on the wall; it is mastery of the state in which all mouths are hung on all walls; it is all mouths being hung on all walls."

Strange, as usual, I know. But let's unpack it.

The "mute self" is the silent basis for our being. We are ultimately an expression of great silence, of vast emptiness. And yet we can speak. That right there is a kind of miraculous wonder. When we speak, it is the great silence that speaks. Those who hear us are also manifestations of great silence. When we speak, it is silence talking to silence.

When Dogen says that "mutes among people have never been able to express the truth" he's not talking about people born without the ability to speak. He is saying that, unless we say something, the truth is not expressed. Sometimes we express the truth without actually talking. A good example would be the Buddha's so-called noble silence when he was asked questions that were fundamentally unanswerable. But even this is a kind of speech in that it is a way that humans communicate to each other.

Then Dogen talks about "people in the mute state." Here he means people sitting in zazen. When you sit in zazen you do not aspire to be a saint or to add something spiritual to yourself. Well... you might do both these things. But even if you do, they do not affect your practice of zazen. And those who practice zazen eventually learn to put aside all such aspirations when they come up.

In his footnotes to this essay, Nishijima Roshi says that the phrase "mouths hung on walls" "suggests the situation in the Zazen Hall." He quotes a line from Dogen's *Eihei Koroku*, a book of short talks Dogen gave to his students, in which he describes his zazen practice as, "Sitting on the quiet floor I hang my mouth on the wall. Awareness of sound arrived at this place and took away my vacancy." Hanging your mouth on the wall just means shutting up.

Kobun Chino put this idea in his typically mystical way. He said, "Many times we say 'I' or 'my' or 'mine.' There is something going on which makes it possible to say so. So when I pay attention to this 'I' it is always the true self, in all attempts to express something. Even misspeaking points to the truth. Even very confused talk points to what is to be spoken. It is just the expression which wasn't clear, because the reality of the 'I' was many elements existing in confusion."

Often we don't say the right thing. But someone who is very perceptive can understand us anyway. I experienced this a lot with my two Zen teachers. Even when I said something angry or hurtful, they seemed to hear what was behind the words.

Here's an example. When I lived with Tim, my first Zen teacher, we had another housemate who could be incredibly difficult to deal with. She had some deep-seated psychiatric problems. And although she tried her best to overcome her demons, sometimes she'd lose the battle. Once, after she'd smashed up my answering machine for reasons I never quite understood, I yelled at Tim, "I don't even want to try to help her anymore!"

Later on I apologized for taking that tone with Tim and said that I really did want to help her, but it was just so overwhelming some-times. Tim said, "I knew what you meant." He understood that even misspeaking points to the truth.

I've tried to learn to do that myself, but I'm not as good at it as my teachers were.

If even saying the wrong thing can be considered "right speech" in some way, then maybe you could say that there isn't really any such thing as "wrong speech." We Zen folks say that the truth is beyond words. So in that sense all speech is wrong speech. Yet, in conventional terms, there is right speech and there is speech that is not right.

It is important to understand that neither Kobun nor Dogen were trying to negate the early Buddhist idea of right speech or to say that it's not important to try to say the right things. In a book called *Shobogenzo Zuimonki*, which is thought to have been based on talks Dogen gave between 1236 and 1239 and was compiled by Ejo, Dogen's student and successor, after Dogen died in 1253, Dogen told his monks, "There is a code of conduct that has been carried out by previous Buddhas regarding the manners of body, speech, and mind. Each one of you should follow them. Even in the secular world, it is said that clothes should be in accordance with the law, and speech should be based on the Way. Much more so should Zen monks never follow their own selfish ideas."*

Dogen also said, "In the Scriptures, it is said, 'Though coarse and violent actions may sometimes cause people to wake up, worthless speech obstructs the true Way.' Be it even a word which comes to the lips unintentionally, useless talk hinders the Way. Still more, lewd talk will excite the mind. You must be most careful. Without forcing yourself not to use such language, if you realize it is bad, you will be able to reform gradually."†

Rather than negating the more conventional understanding, Dogen is saying that right speech is very important. The Buddha spoke about right speech because he knew how vital it was. And yet the source of all right speech is the silent ground of our mute self.

---

* Koun Ejo, *Shobogenzo Zuimonki*, trans. Shohaku Okumura and Tom Wright (Tokyo: Soto-Shu Shumucho, 2004), book 1, talk 8.

† Ejo, *Shobogenzo Zuimonki*, book 2, talk 14.

# 10. RIGHT ACTION

THE NEXT FOLD is right action. In one of the earliest Buddhist sutras, right action is explained very simply. "And what is right action? Abstaining from taking life, abstaining from stealing, abstaining from unchastity. This is called right action."

These are also the first three of the Ten Grave Precepts, which we will get to soon, I promise. Most of the other references to right action in the early Buddhist sutras are just expanded versions of that definition of right action.

Even though the sutras only mention killing, stealing, and unchastity, I take those as examples. It seems clear to me that the fuller meaning of right action is ethical action of all kinds.

In "108 Gates of Dharma Illumination" Dogen says, "Right action is a gate of Dharma illumination; for [with it] there is no karma and no retribution." I think he's saying that right action is action done with the knowledge that there is no separation between the doer and the action. Saying that there is no karma or retribution doesn't mean there are no results or consequences for actions. It just means that the idea of results is meaningless when there is no belief in a separate entity that experiences those results.

But what does Dogen say about right action in "Thirty-Seven Elements of Bodhi"? Well, it's funny you should ask. In the last few chapters, I've told you the entirety of what Dogen had to say about the first three folds of the Noble Eightfold Path. That was easy, because what he had to say amounted to just a few sentences.

When it comes to right action, however, Dogen goes on for six and a half pages! You might imagine that if he devoted so much space to right action he's going to tell us in painstaking detail exactly what actions are right and why. Unfortunately, that's not the case.

Instead, he goes on an epic rant about how it's better to be a monk (male or female) than to be a layperson. Here's a small sample:

Notwithstanding scant pursuit of the truth by laypeople, there is no past example of one arriving at the truth. When we arrive at the truth, we inevitably leave family life [i.e., join a monastic order]. How can people who are not able to leave family life succeed to the position of a buddha? Nevertheless, for the last two or three hundred years in the great kingdom of Song [China], people calling themselves priests of the Zen sect have habitually said, "Pursuit of the truth by a layperson and pursuit of the truth by one who has left family life are just the same." They are a tribe of people who have become dogs, for the sole purpose of making the filth and urine of laypeople into their food and drink.

Furthermore, he says, "The monks who speak such words are Devadattas." Devadatta was a monk who allegedly tried to create a schism in the early Buddhist order and may even have plotted to kill the Buddha. Calling people Devadattas is like calling them Judases. He goes on, "In order that they might feed upon tears and spit, they produce childish and demented talk like this. They are deplorable. They are not the kindred of the Seven Buddhas. They are demons and animals."

However, Dogen might be calling himself a Judas here. Because in one of his most famous pieces of writing, "Bendowa," which I quoted earlier, he writes, "Someone asks, 'Should this practice also be undertaken by laymen and laywomen, or is it performed only by people who have left home?' I say: An ancestral master has been heard to say that, with respect to understanding of the Buddha-Dharma, we must not choose between men and women, high or low."

Then right after that we read, "Someone asks, 'People who leave home get free of all involvements at once, so they have no hindrances in practicing zazen and pursuing the truth. How can a busy layperson devotedly do training and be at one with the unintentional state of Buddhist truth?'"

Dogen's answer to this is long and detailed. It begins, "The Buddhist Ancestors, overfilled with compassion, left open a wide and great gate of compassion so that all living beings could experience and enter [the state of truth]; what human being or god could not want to enter? Thus, when we study the past and the present, there are many confirmations of such [experience and entry]." This is followed by several examples of famous laypeople of ancient China who pursued the Buddhist truth and practiced zazen.

Next he says, "In the great kingdom of Song, the present generation of kings and ministers, officials and commoners, men and women, all apply their mind to the Ancestors' truth, without exception. Both the military and literary classes are resolved to practice [za]zen and to learn the truth. Those who resolve it will, in many cases, undoubtedly clarify the mental state. Thus, it can naturally be inferred that worldly affairs do not hinder the Buddha-Dharma."

He concludes that "when Shakyamuni was in the world, [even] people of heavy sins and wrong views were able to get the truth, and in the orders of the ancestral masters, [even] hunters and old woodcutters entered the state of realization, to say nothing of other people. We need only study the teaching and the state of truth of a true teacher."

"Bendowa" was written in 1231. "Thirty-Seven Elements of Bodhi" was written in 1244. According to some scholars, Dogen changed his mind sometime in those thirteen years and decided that what he'd said in "Bendowa" was wrong.

In an article called "Leaving Home," which appeared on the

Dogen Institute website, Shohaku Okumura gives us a somewhat different take. He says, "Dogen had some disappointment after working hard with aristocrats. I think he had some disillusionment about the people in the upper class of society, like emperors. His father was a secretary of the emperor. His grandfather was a prime minister — so he knew that society. When he was young, he was kind of idealistic, he thought that if he presented genuine dharma, people would accept it and support him and create a good dharma-world. But after ten years of his practice in Kyoto he found that was a dream."

Okumura Roshi also says, "For example, from my own experience, one time a Japanese prime minister had a photo of himself in the newspaper sitting zazen — and I really know that was insincere, without any question."

Okumura Roshi continues, saying that later in Dogen's life, after the time "Bendowa" was written:

> He wanted to create a place where sincere people can get together and practice with him. To encourage those people who came to practice with him at this remote place, he wrote this kind of admonition or warning to his disciples.... I'm not sure that he wanted to return to a separation between lay and monastic practice, but he wanted to make a small place where a small number of people could practice. I don't think he rejected lay people, but his idea was for a small number of monks to practice at the monastery in a quiet place, and for lay people to support and join the practice whenever they can. That is similar to the original form of the Buddhist sangha.

I think Okumura Roshi is correct that Dogen isn't so much saying to laypeople that they suck as he is trying to encourage his monks in the hard life that they had chosen in their remote mountain temple. For example, in *Shobogenzo Zuimonki* Dogen says, "Even if we do not have robes, bowls, and so on, we should practice with the resolution that even a layperson can practice the Buddha Way. Anyway, robes, bowls, and other things are simply the ornaments of monkhood. The genuine Buddha Way does not depend on such things."*

Also, Dogen's most famous piece of writing, "Genjo Koan," was written as a letter to a layperson and can be understood as Dogen's advice for lay practice. Although "Genjo Koan" was originally composed in 1233, he revised it several times, the last time being in 1252. I think this supports Okumura Roshi's idea that, as strong as Dogen's language sounds, it probably wasn't intended so much to be anti-layperson as pro-monk.

In fact, the material that seems to put down lay Buddhist practice was probably not meant to ever have been read or heard by laypeople at all. It was a speech intended for the monks who practiced with Dogen. Life must have been hard high in the mountains in that monastery, with no Netflix to watch and no Trader Joe's to shop at, with having to find their own sources of food, water, and heating fuel, and being isolated from the rest of society. Dogen was probably trying to make his monks feel like their hard lifestyle was worth the trouble by telling them how, if they'd remained laypeople, they would have had no chance of experiencing the awakening they were experiencing. He didn't want them to think that pursuit of the truth by laypeople was just the same as what they were doing. That would have been a huge bummer for them!

Dogen does say one really cool thing during this rant, though. One of the ways he admonishes his listeners to remain monks rather than to leave the temple and live as laypeople goes, "Furthermore, this human body, received as a result of the seeds of seeing and hearing the Buddha-Dharma in past ages, is like a tool of the Universe." As such, he says, it should be used in the pursuit of the truth.

The reference to the human body being a "tool of the universe"

---

*     Book 1, talk 6.

echoes what Dogen said in his essay "Inmo": "We ourselves are tools that *it* possesses within this universe in ten directions." "It" in this case is *inmo*, a Chinese word that means something like "something." He's talking about the ineffable and unnamable *something* that is the mind of the universe.

In any case, in spite of this rant, I don't think Dogen believed there was some kind of magic by which going through a Zen monk's ordination made it possible for a person to understand the great truth of the universe, while those who didn't go through it could not. Rather, he was talking about the kind of great dedication required to pursue the Great Matter in earnest. I agree with Dogen's earlier statements, that this can be done with or without a shaved head and a set of Buddhist robes.

I assume most of you reading this book are not Buddhist monastics and probably have no intention or desire to be. What, then, does right action mean for regular folks?

Dogen actually talks about this quite a bit in an essay called "Not Doing Wrongs." I retitled this essay "Don't Be a Jerk" in my book *Don't Be a Jerk*. And that's essentially what it says. Right action is refraining from acting like a jerk. There is no such thing as "evil" that sits around waiting for someone to do it. We bring right action into the world with the things we do or refrain from doing. This is how evil comes into the world too. I'll have more to say about that in a later chapter. For now, suffice it to say that ethical action is what Buddhists call right action.

## 11. RIGHT LIVELIHOOD

THE NEXT FOLD in Buddha's Noble Eightfold Path of ethical behavior is right livelihood. This one is a big topic of discussion and debate, even outside the small circle of nerdy Buddhist scholars who usually debate such things. For example, in an article by Lewis Richmond titled "Buddhism and Wealth: Defining 'Right Livelihood'" it says, "Right livelihood is now a societal, even planetary, responsibility."*

Richmond quotes Bhikku Basnagoda Rahula, who wrote a book called *The Buddha's Teaching on Prosperity* and in turn quotes the Buddha as saying, "The layperson's objective [is to] live a long and dignified life with the wealth obtained through rightful means."

He says this comes from the Buddha's *Numerical Discourses*, which is a legitimate source of the early Buddhist teachings. However, I was unable to find any source that used this precise wording — or, indeed, any recognizably similar wording. In fact, I couldn't find anything in the *Numerical Discourses* that was close enough to this quote that I recognized it as being the same thing. I did, however, find a few vaguely similar statements in the section of the "Adiya Sutta" — which is one of the *Numerical Discourses* — called "Benefits to Be Obtained from Wealth." It basically enumerates several benefits that a follower of the Buddha might obtain from being wealthy. Most of these benefits come down to the ability to help others.

---

* *Huffington Post*, March 16, 2011.

Richmond interprets the quotation, as translated above, to mean, "Clearly, the Buddha saw prosperity and financial security as a good and appropriate activity for laypeople."

I'm less certain than Mr. Richmond about the Buddha's concern for our prosperity and financial security — especially since the Buddha and his monks took a strict vow of poverty and did not own any personal property other than their robes and begging bowls. They seemed to reject the very idea of financial security. But let's leave that aside.

Richmond tells us, "Regardless of our job [or lack of a job] we should be aware of the implications and consequences of what we do. Though *Work as a Spiritual Practice* [Richmond's book], by intention, emphasized the choices and changes an individual could make in his/her workplace, I also feel that conscious livelihood should not be limited to individual awareness and action. Society at large also has a responsibility to be conscious of the consequences of its economic and employment policies. . . . It is not clear whether the Buddha thought of right livelihood in this way, but it behooves us to do so now."

And here's another example of how popular this fold of the Eightfold Path is. The teaser at the top of an article in the Buddhist magazine *Tricycle* called "Why Right Livelihood Isn't Just about Your Day Job" says, "In our messy and entangled world, it is impossible to separate what we do for a living from the larger system that makes living possible."* Author Krishnan Venkatesh says, "Even professions that seem admirable and praiseworthy can be tangled up in negative consequences. A physician today is implicated in a dubious industry that often benefits corporations and shareholders more than patients. My own career as a professor at a private college is mottled with questions about the consequences of the debt these young people take on in order to study."

That's pretty typical of the kind of consternation the concept of

---

*   From the August 13, 2017, issue.

right livelihood inspires in today's Western Buddhists. None of the other folds of the path seem to cause people quite this much concern. On a personal note, this particular fold certainly bugged me a lot too. As I mentioned earlier, I discovered Buddhism when I was just starting out at Kent State University. I probably changed my major more than half a dozen times during my university years. Much of this was because I was deeply concerned that whatever career path I chose had to be right livelihood in the Buddhist sense.

The Buddha defined right livelihood this way: "And what is right livelihood? There is the case where a disciple of the noble ones, having abandoned dishonest livelihood, keeps his life going with right livelihood: This is called right livelihood." Which doesn't tell you much. But he also said, "And what is wrong livelihood? Scheming, persuading, hinting, belittling, and pursuing gain with gain. This is wrong livelihood."

Then he gets a bit more specific, saying, "A lay follower should not engage in five types of business. Which five? Business in weapons, business in [trafficking] human beings, business in meat, business in intoxicants, and business in poison."

In terms of my own struggle with right livelihood, one of my first jobs after graduating from university, as mentioned earlier, was at a place that was then called the Summit County Board of Mental Retardation and Developmental Disabilities. I'm sure they've changed that name by now. It was an organization dedicated to improving the lives of intellectually disabled adults. I was hired as a substitute supervisor for these adults who were ostensibly being trained to get jobs outside the sheltered workshops that the institution provided. Sadly, very few of them ever got those jobs.

In any case, though, my livelihood when I did that job was as right as right could be! No one could argue that I wasn't doing good things for people in need. It was hard work too. And the pay was lousy, which made it seem even more righteous somehow.

I hated it.

It was so not my calling in life. What's more, I was terrible at everything I was assigned to do there.

After two years I quit that job and then spent a year in rural Japan teaching English to Japanese high school kids. That seemed reasonably "right" too. But then after a year of that, I wound up working in Tokyo at Tsuburaya Productions. That's the company I mentioned earlier, founded by Eiji Tsuburaya, the mastermind who directed the visual effects on the early Godzilla films. As you'll recall, the company's most successful production was a superhero TV series called *Ultraman*, in which a Godzilla-size superhero beats the snot out of Godzilla-type monsters week after week, to the delight of millions of Japanese children. Since the show was live action, I regularly got to hang out on the sets as guys in rubber dinosaur costumes destroyed miniaturized re-creations of Tokyo. That was too much fun!

But I felt terribly guilty. I'd given up jobs that were clearly, I thought, right livelihood but that I hated for a job that involved making crazy superhero shows that warped kids' minds. And to make matters worse, I loved that job.

I'd wanted to work for Tsuburaya Productions ever since I was a little child watching dubbed versions of *Ultraman* on Cleveland's channel 43. I really cared about this company. And yet as I continued to work there for a number of years, I began to notice that it was a highly dysfunctional organization. It was a family business and the family could never agree on anything.

I was distraught. It seemed like we — and I really felt like I was part of this big dysfunctional family — were in grave danger of going completely under if we didn't get our stuff together. I couldn't find any way to get us back on track.

So one day I stirred up my courage and asked my teacher, Nishijima Roshi, if I could meet with him to have a talk. I spilled my guts to him about how I wanted to do the right thing for a living. I couldn't keep on working for Tsuburaya Productions, where I was involved in creating violent TV shows for kids. I told him that

I wanted to go to Eihei-ji, the temple that Dogen established in the thirteenth century, get a monk's training, and be a Buddhist monk for a living. I thought he'd be delighted.

He wasn't. He told me in no uncertain terms that he thought it was a terrible idea to be a full-time monk as a profession. He said I should stay with Tsuburaya Productions. He said that while I worked there I could make the things that the company did "a little better."

I was floored.

I'd never thought of it that way. But he was right. It was better to make Tsuburaya Productions "a little better" than to pursue something else because it might have looked like right livelihood to the kinds of people who professionally judge right livelihoods for Buddhist magazines and the *Huffington Post*.

In "108 Gates of Dharma Illumination," Dogen says, "Right livelihood is a gate of Dharma illumination; for [with it] we get rid of all evil ways." This is one of the easiest of his comments on the Noble Eightfold Path to understand. It's pretty general, but it gets the point across.

In "Thirty-Seven Elements of Bodhi," however, Dogen goes on for quite a while about right livelihood. Not as long as he does about right action. But long enough that I've cut it down a bit for you. You're welcome.

In part he says, "Right livelihood as a branch of the path is early-morning gruel and noon rice, is to stay in a temple's grounds and to let the soul play, and is to demonstrate it directly upon the round wooden chair."

The phrase "let the soul play" is one of Dogen's euphemisms for doing zazen. And "demonstrating it directly upon the round wooden chair" refers to the chairs that Buddhist teachers sat on to give lectures. This makes it sound like the only kind of livelihood that Dogen considered right was the one that my teacher advised me not to do — to be a full-time Buddhist monk.

Remember that this comes right after a six-and-a-half-page rant about why it's better to be a monk than a layperson. Dogen wasn't about to follow that up by telling his monks the kinds of jobs they could get outside the temple if they wanted to do right livelihood in the secular world.

But Dogen didn't really think the only thing anyone should do with their lives was be a Buddhist monk. He knew full well how much he and his students depended on folks with regular jobs for financial support. One of Dogen's main financial supporters was a samurai warlord. Talk about being entangled in larger economic systems!

I'm not gonna try and tell you, dear reader, what to do for a living. I'll just say that absolutely anything you choose to do to make your money these days is going to be entangled in something messy if you look at it closely. That's just how it goes. It was probably always that way.

Rather, I'd like to draw your attention to another of Dogen's sayings. This line helped me immensely when I was conflicted about my job at Tsuburaya Productions, which is when I first came across it. In an essay called "Four Elements of a Bodhisattva's Social Relations," Dogen says, "Earning a living and doing productive work are originally nothing other than free giving." Free giving, which is *dana* in Sanskrit, is one of the six Buddhist *paramitas*, which means "transcendent perfections." The others are discipline, patience, diligence, meditative concentration, and wisdom. So it's pretty important stuff.

"We give ourselves to ourselves," Dogen says in that essay, "and give the external world to the external world." He talks about "leaving flowers to the wind and leaving birds to time," meaning, basically, allowing things to be what they are, and he says that these are also examples of free giving. He talks about giving to parents, wives, and children. He talks about the merit in giving up even a single speck of dust. And, most shockingly of all to me, he says that even doing a regular old job to earn a paycheck is also an example of free giving.

"Both receiving the body and giving up the body are free giv-ing," Dogen says. To Dogen, even being alive and dying are exam-ples of free giving. Just the mere fact that you are alive and someday will die are ways that the universe gives itself to the universe.

It's good to give to charity. It's good to work to improve the environment. It's good to leave a bag of coats and blankets next to the homeless encampment in your neighborhood.

All that stuff is great.

Absolutely.

No doubt.

But there are many other ways we can give. Infinite other ways, in fact. When I learned to see my work making movies about rubber monsters as free giving, I started being able to see free giving every-where. And I started to suspect that the entire reason we do jobs for paychecks is that what we *really* want to do is freely give our time and work to our fellow beings. It's just that we need to be able to support ourselves too. And so a complicated system has developed that allows us to do that. But at the bottom of that complicated sys-tem is a desire to give back to others.

When you see free giving everywhere, the mind that believes in self and other begins to fade away. Everything you do can become an example of generosity and an example of right livelihood if you make it one.

Just remember to be careful out there. OK?

# 12. RIGHT EFFORT

NEXT UP IN the folds is right effort. In Japanese, right effort is *shou-shoujin*. The first word, *shou*, means "right" or "correct." As a vegetarian living in Japan, I was very familiar with the next word, *shoujin*, which appears in the term *shoujin ryouri*. *Ryouri* is cuisine. *Shoujin ryouri* is vegetarian cuisine. The word *shoujin* is defined in modern Japanese-English dictionaries as "concentration; diligence; devotion," or as "asceticism; zeal in one's quest for enlightenment," or, finally, as "adherence to a vegetarian diet."

This fold of the Noble Eightfold Path is not nearly as sexy as the previous one. You won't find any *Huffington Post* articles about right effort, and scarcely any in the Buddhist magazines either. Yet the Buddha considered it just as important as any of the other folds. In fact, he considered them all to be of equal importance.

In the early sutras, right effort is basically defined as the effort to follow the other folds of the path. In the Pali scriptures the Buddha says, "One tries to abandon wrong view and to enter into right view: This is one's right effort... One tries to abandon wrong resolve and to enter into right resolve: This is one's right effort... One tries to abandon wrong speech and to enter into right speech: This is one's right effort... One tries to abandon wrong action and to enter into right action: This is one's right effort... One tries to abandon wrong livelihood and to enter into right livelihood: This is one's right effort."

The Buddha also says, "A monk generates desire, endeavors,

activates persistence, upholds and exerts his intent for the sake of the non-arising of evil, unskillful qualities that have not yet arisen; for the sake of the abandonment of evil, unskillful qualities that have arisen; for the sake of the arising of skillful qualities that have not yet arisen; and for the maintenance, non-confusion, increase, plenitude, development, and culmination of skillful qualities that have arisen. This, monks, is called right effort."

Right effort also means the appropriate amount of effort. The Buddha likened it to tuning a stringed instrument. Too much effort is like adding too much tension to the strings until they break. Too little effort leaves them too slack, and everything you play sounds like death metal. But when you put in just the right degree of effort, you're golden.

Another way of looking at right effort is to consider it in terms of the burning question that set Dogen off on his lifelong quest. The Buddhist sutras say that we are enlightened just as we are. "Why, then," young Dogen asked, "do we have to make so much effort? Why all the meditation? Why follow the precepts? Why all the rituals?" None of the teachers he asked had a satisfactory answer.

One good answer to this question is the one often attributed to Shunryu Suzuki. "You're perfect just as you are," he said, "but you could use a little improvement."

In his "108 Gates of Dharma Illumination," Dogen says, "Right effort is a gate of Dharma illumination; for [with it] we arrive at the far shore." Which is nice, but doesn't tell you much.

In "Thirty-Seven Elements of Bodhi," Dogen says some pretty interesting things about right effort. And by "interesting" I mean crazy sounding:

> Right effort as a branch of the path is action that gouges out a whole body, and it is the fashioning of a human face in the gouging out of the whole body. It is to ride upside down around the Buddha hall, doing one lap, two laps, three, four, and five laps, so that nine times nine comes to eighty-two.

It is repeatedly to repay [the benevolence of] others, thousands and tens of thousands of times; it is to turn the head in any direction of the cross, vertically or horizontally; it is to change the face vertically or horizontally, in any direction of the cross; it is to enter the [master's] room and to go to the Dharma hall. It expresses "having met at Boshutei Pavilion, having met on Usekirei Peak, having met in front of the monks' hall," and having met inside the Buddha hall — there being two mirrors and three kinds of reflection.

You're probably wondering what all that could possibly mean. Which is perfectly understandable. Let's go into it weird phrase by weird phrase. In his explanation about "gouging out the whole body and fashioning a human face," Nishijima Roshi says, "Right effort is effort that makes us more truly human in the process of Buddhist training." He says this refers to the words of Dogen's teacher, who said, "Gouging out Bodhidharma's Eye, I make it into a mud ball and work it into a person." This is a poetic way of saying he takes Bodhidharma's understanding of things — Bodhidharma's "eye" — and applies it to himself. Bodhidharma, by the way, was the Indian monk who is credited as being the first to bring the Zen form of Buddhism to China.

Nishijima Roshi says the stuff about people meeting each other in various places expresses the union of subject and object. And he says that the reference to two mirrors "suggests subject and object, their combination resulting in the undivided reality of the present moment. Right effort occurs in balanced consciousness of what is happening both inside and outside, here and now."

Sadly, he says nothing to explain that weird line about riding upside down around the Buddha Hall eighty-two times. Or why Dogen's math is so bad. I wish I had a guess as to what that means, but I don't. If this is an allusion to some old story or koan, I'm sure Nishijima Roshi would have said so. Maybe it meant something to

Dogen's intended audience, something that has been lost to history. Sometimes Dogen is just weird, I guess.

My favorite part is where Dogen says, "It is repeatedly to repay [the benevolence of] others, thousands and tens of thousands of times." That's a simple sentiment but incredibly important. Lots of people have done lots of good things for me, and I can never thank them enough. Even when I eat a bag of corn chips, that bag of corn chips comes from the benevolence and sacrifice of others, like the farmers who grew the corn, the bugs and things that were killed when it was harvested, the truckers who rode all night to get it to the local 7-Eleven, and countless others. And that's just a bag of chips! I don't think I'll ever be able to repay all the benevolence I've received.

Considering Dogen's statement on right effort from "Thirty-Seven Elements of Bodhi" as a whole, I take it to mean that it is the effort one makes to realize one's Buddha nature even when one has learned that no effort is needed. Maybe the "riding upside down" part is an acknowledgment of the seeming absurdity of that needless yet necessary effort.

It's weird that we have to make an effort to realize something that's already there. But every so-called enlightenment moment I've ever had was the profound and unmistakable recognition of something that was already present before I recognized it. I've never heard of anyone who had what sounded to me like an authentic realization who did not say the same thing.

It's like suddenly noticing you have a nose. In fact, Dogen once described his own realization as the recognition that his eyes were horizontal and his nose was vertical. That's what it feels like. Rather than shouting, "Eureka!" you feel like shouting, "Well, duh! How did I ever fail to notice that?"

That's why it's often described with such absurd-sounding phrases as "the face you had before your parents were born." What the people who say these things are trying to describe is something so incredibly basic that it was you before anything you ever thought of as "you" even entered the picture. Something so obvious you cannot help but be aware of it... and yet, somehow you always felt like you had no idea it was there.

Right effort, then, is the effort to recognize what is already so obvious that you can't help but notice it.

# 13. RIGHT MINDFULNESS

THE NEXT FOLD is right mindfulness, another fan favorite! Much as I hate to start off the chapter sounding like a junior high school book report, the *Oxford Online Dictionary* defines mindfulness as "a mental state achieved by focusing one's awareness on the present moment while calmly acknowledging and accepting one's feelings, thoughts, and bodily sensations, used as a therapeutic technique." The fact that you can find that definition online is part of the point I want to make.

And that point is that *everybody's* talking about mindfulness these days! Mindfulness is big business. And whenever there's money to be made, hype must be generated. The website for Headspace, one of the many commercial organizations that offer mindfulness for a fee, says, "You may have heard that mindfulness — the ability to be fully present in the moment — can have numerous benefits, everything from decreased stress and sadness to increased levels of focus and happiness, according to general mindfulness research. Mindfulness meditation practice is one way to truly experience the current moment and integrate that awareness into your everyday life."

If Headspace isn't your jam, you can sign up for another commercial program described this way: "Mindfulness-based stress reduction is an eight-week evidence-based program that offers secular, intensive mindfulness training to assist people with stress, anxiety, depression, and pain."

Most of these organizations like to downplay the fact that the mindfulness they teach is based on ancient Buddhist teachings. They claim that *their version* of mindfulness has been cleansed of all those nasty, yucky religious elements and is purely secular and safe.

But is secular mindfulness really that secular? Here's how the early Buddhist sutras describe right mindfulness: "And what is right mindfulness? There is the case where a monk remains focused on the body in and of itself — ardent, alert, and mindful — putting aside greed and distress with reference to the world. He remains focused on feelings in and of themselves... the mind in and of itself... mental qualities in and of themselves. This is called right mindfulness. ... This is the direct path for the purification of beings, for the overcoming of sorrow and lamentation, for the disappearance of pain and distress, for the attainment of the right method, and for the realization of unbinding." Which sounds suspiciously like the "secular mindfulness" stuff these folks are advertising. Just sayin'!

The early sutras give some techniques for establishing this state of mindfulness. For example:

> There is the case where a monk, having gone to the wilderness, to the shade of a tree, or to an empty building, sits down folding his legs crosswise, holding his body erect, and setting mindfulness to the fore. Always mindful, he breathes in; mindful he breathes out.
>
> Breathing in long, he discerns, "I am breathing in long"; or breathing out long, he discerns, "I am breathing out long." Or breathing in short, he discerns, "I am breathing in short"; or breathing out short, he discerns, "I am breathing out short." He trains himself, "I will breathe in sensitive to the entire body." He trains himself, "I will breathe out sensitive to the entire body." He trains himself, "I will breathe in calming bodily fabrication." He trains himself, "I will breathe out calming bodily fabrication."

The meditation instructions in early Buddhism tend to get extraordinarily detailed — much more detailed even than these examples. There are tons of instructions about what to focus the mind on and how to do that. The above is just the beginning of a very long and involved set of instructions.

Dogen's instructions were far simpler. In "Eihei Koroku Dharma Hall Discourse number 390" he says:

> First you should sit correctly with upright posture. Then regulate your breath and settle your mind. In the lesser vehicle [he means early Buddhism] originally there were two gateways, which were counting breaths and contemplating impurity. In the lesser vehicle, people used counting to regulate their breath. However, the buddha ancestors' engaging of the way always differed from the lesser vehicle. A buddha ancestor said, "Even if you arouse the mind of a leprous wild fox, never practice the self-regulation of the two vehicles."
>
> In the Mahayana there is also a method for regulating breath, which is knowing that one breath is long, another breath is short. The breath reaches the *tanden* [basically the diaphragm] and comes up from the *tanden*. Although exhale and inhale differ, both of them occur depending on the *tanden*. Impermanence is easy to clarify, and regulating the mind is easy to accomplish.
>
> My late teacher said, "Breath enters and reaches the *tanden*, and yet there is no place from which it comes. Therefore it is neither long nor short. Breath emerges from the *tanden*, and yet there is nowhere it goes. Therefore it is neither short nor long." My late teacher said it like that. Suppose someone were to ask Eihei [Dogen is referring to himself in the third person here], "Master, how do you regulate your breath?" I would simply say to him: Although it is not the great vehicle (Mahayana), it differs from the lesser vehicle (Hinayana). Although it is not the lesser vehicle, it differs from the great vehicle. Ultimately ... exhale and inhale are neither short nor long.

Shunryu Suzuki said:

When we inhale, the air comes into the inner world. When
we exhale, the air goes out to the outer world. The inner
world is limitless, and the outer world is also limitless. We
say "inner world" or "outer world," but actually there is
just one whole world. In this limitless world, our throat is
like a swinging door. The air comes in and goes out like
someone passing through a swinging door. If you think, "I
breathe," the "I" is extra. There is no you to say "I." What
we call "I" is just a swinging door which moves when we
inhale and when we exhale. It just moves; that is all. When
your mind is pure and calm enough to follow this movement, there is nothing: no "I," no world, no mind nor body;
just a swinging door.

That's from Suzuki's book *Zen Mind, Beginner's Mind*, which was
the first book about Zen or any other kind of Buddhism I ever read. It
was one of the books Tim McCarthy assigned us in that class I took
at Kent State. That paragraph stuck with me for a very long time. I
probably could have quoted it by heart back when I first started sitting.
It's an almost perfect miniature statement of the Zen worldview. A lot
is packed into that little paragraph! So let's look at it a little closer.

We talk about an "inner world" and an "outer world," and most
of us think there is an absolute division between the two. We imagine
that the outer world is eternally separate from our inner world. We
imagine that the outer world can exist without the inner world. We
imagine that the outer world existed before we were born and will
continue on long after we're gone. We imagine that the inner world
came into existence around the day we were born and will probably
disappear when we die.

The Zen view is entirely different. The outer world is the same
as the inner world. They are born together and pass away together.
Our assumption that they are eternally divided is a mistake.

Suzuki Roshi also said that both the inner world and the outer world are limitless. That's not at all how I understood things before I got into Zen. I believed that the outer world was probably limitless, although there was some dispute about that. Nobody knew if outer space went on forever, but it sure was big. As for the inner world, though, it was totally limited and small. Tiny! To hear someone say confidently that the inner world was limitless was a huge surprise to me. I couldn't imagine what that might mean. Nowadays, after a few decades of Zen practice, I think I'm beginning to understand.

Think of it this way. We're used to the idea that space is limitlessly big. If distances can be limitlessly large, they can be limitlessly small too. And limitless smallness is just as limitless as limitless bigness. Perhaps the very concept of space itself is an illusion. But let's leave that for later.

Suzuki Roshi says that when we say "I breathe in," the "I" is extra. If the idea of the inner world being limitless was surprising to me, the idea of "I" being "extra" was baffling. I couldn't make any sense of that one! Of course I breathe! How could "I" be "extra"? And yet something about that statement felt right. It was one of the many ideas I came across in Zen literature early in my study that I couldn't understand intellectually but that hit me in the gut as being right.

When he said that when we become pure and calm enough "there is no 'I,' no world, no mind nor body; just a swinging door," I had no clue what he meant, and yet I was certain that's what I wanted in my life.

I've strayed a bit away from the topic of mindfulness. So let's go back to that. Here's what Dogen says about mindfulness in "108 Gates of Dharma Illumination." "Right mindfulness is a gate of Dharma illumination; for [with it] we do not consider all dharmas intellectually."

This is an important point regarding mindfulness. All too often these days, mindfulness becomes a kind of intellectual exercise. It's all about *me* being mindful of *my* breath, or *me* being mindful of each step *I* take, and so on. The notion of the separation of subject and object is strongly reinforced. Mindfulness in Buddhist practice is meant to overcome this false idea.

In "Thirty-Seven Elements of Bodhi," Dogen addresses this:

> Right mindfulness as a branch of the path is the eighty or ninety percent realization of the state of being duped by ourselves. To learn that wisdom occurs following from mindfulness is "leaving the father and running away." To learn that wisdom occurs within mindfulness itself is to be fettered in the extreme. To say that being without mindfulness is right mindfulness is non-Buddhism. Neither should we see the animating soul of earth, water, fire, and wind as mindfulness. Upset states of mind, will, and consciousness are not called mindfulness. "You having got my skin, flesh, bones, and marrow" is just right mindfulness as a branch of the path.

Whenever Dogen refers to realization as being 80 or 90 percent, he means actual realization rather than an idealized image of realization. He also sometimes refers to "half realization." Actual realization never feels complete.

What we realize is that we are duped by ourselves. We have fooled ourselves into believing that we are the subject and the rest of the universe is made of objects that we, the subject, perceive.

Dogen says that the idea of wisdom following mindfulness is like "leaving the father and running away." This is a reference to a story in the Lotus Sutra that goes like this: "A wealthy man had a son, but the son went away from his father and lived as a poor wanderer for a long time. His father moved to another country, looking for his son, who had disappeared. Not knowing that the wealthy man was his real father, the poor man by chance came to the place where his father resided. Terrified by the wealthy man's dignity he soon ran away."

But the story has a happy ending. Later on the father convinced his son to work for him, and at the end of his life he revealed to everyone that the man was really his son and left all his property to him. Dogen is saying that the idea that wisdom follows mindfulness is a mistake, just as the son's running away was a mistake.

He explains this by saying that the idea of wisdom occurring within mindfulness is "fettered in the extreme." Rather than wisdom occurring within mindfulness or following — that is, being produced by — mindfulness, mindfulness occurs within wisdom. Mindfulness *is* wisdom. Here the word *wisdom* is another way of saying Mind, as in the Big Mind that is the universe and is ourselves. We exist within mind rather than mind existing within us.

Next Dogen says, "To say that being without mindfulness is right mindfulness is non-Buddhism." This refers to the idea that having a completely blank mind is mindfulness, which Dogen does not agree with.

Kodo Sawaki said that the only time your mind is a complete blank is when you're dead. Sawaki Roshi's student Kosho Uchiyama Roshi said, "Having no thought is not necessarily good zazen. Thoughts are important as secretions from our brain. Secretion oozes out of life. . . . In the same way that saliva in the mouth or gastric juice in the stomach is secreted, thoughts oozing out of our brain are an important function of life. But too much secretion of gastric juice causes an ulcer, or even cancer. Excessive secretion of thought is also dangerous to our life. Saliva, gastric juice, and thoughts should ooze in an appropriate amount for a natural condition."

Kosho Uchiyama Roshi is the guy who took over Kodo Sawaki's temple Antai-ji after Sawaki Roshi died in 1965. "Homeless Kodo" had a home the last few years of his life, it turns out. In addition to being a Zen Buddhist monk and priest, Uchiyama Roshi was a poet and a master of origami. He wrote a number of really good books on Zen, the most popular of which is *Opening the Hand of Thought*, which is where that quotation I just gave you comes from. The title is from another one of his ways of describing zazen. Most of the time, when we have a thought, we — metaphorically — grab it and hold on tight. Rather than doing this, Uchiyama Roshi recommended that we "open the hand of thought."

We are not working toward a state of emptiness in which emptiness is the opposite of fullness. The mindfulness we're talking about cannot be described in words and so in that sense could be described as "emptiness" — in that it is empty of anything we can describe. Yet it is not empty in the sense of containing nothing rather than something. It is the ground of all being and nonbeing. Emptiness is the source of you and me and everyone and everything else.

Then Dogen says we should not see the animating soul of earth, water, fire, and wind as mindfulness. Kazuaki Tanahashi translates that line as, "Do not regard spirits of earth, water, fire, and air as mindfulness." In Japanese there are no true plurals. So the line is ambiguous as to whether it refers to a single soul/spirit of earth, water, fire, and air or to multiple souls/spirits. In either reading, mindfulness is not something external to ourselves that makes the universe work. Rather, we are not separate from that *something* that makes the universe live and move.

Finally, Dogen says, "'You having got my skin, flesh, bones, and marrow' is just right mindfulness as a branch of the path." This is a reference to Bodhidharma's words to his four disciples. Bodhidharma, as you may remember, was the Indian monk who is thought to be the first to bring Zen Buddhism to China. Even though he had only four students, his influence was profound. He was the founder of the famous Shaolin Temple, as seen in dozens of kung-fu movies. The martial arts are said to have originated in this temple, but that was long after Bodhidharma's time.

Near the end of his life, Bodhidharma asked his monks to express their understanding of his teaching. The monk Dao Fu said, "We shouldn't be attached to words of teaching, nor should we ignore words of teaching, but we should just let the dharma flow freely."

Bodhidharma said to Dao Fu, "You have got my skin."

The nun Zong Chi said, "My view is like the joy of seeing the land of the Buddhas. Once seen, it is never seen again."

To the nun Zong Chi, Bodhidharma said, "You have got my flesh."

The monk Dao Yu said, "The four elements and the five aggregates don't exist. Therefore there is nothing to be attained." "The four elements" just means matter. The ancient Chinese believed there were four types of matter: earth, water, air, and fire. As for "the five aggregates," in Buddhism a human being is said not to have a soul but to be a combination of five aggregates, which are form, feeling, perceptions, impulses, and consciousness. I'll explain those later on.

To Dao Yu, Bodhidharma said, "You have got my bones."

The monk Huike said nothing at all in response to his teacher's question but just bowed deeply. To Huike, Bodhidharma said, "You have got my marrow." Huike received Bodhidharma's robe and bowl and officially became his successor.

This is usually understood as meaning that Huike had the deepest understanding and was therefore superior to the other three. Dogen rejected that idea. He said that each of Bodhidharma's disciples had a complete understanding. Dao Fu completely got his skin, Zong Chi completely got his flesh, and Dao Yu completely got his bones.

The idea here in "Thirty-Seven Elements of Bodhi" is that the understanding transmitted from teacher to student is right mindfulness. It's not exactly that a teacher transmits anything to the student. Rather, teacher and student establish the same understanding, and the teacher formally recognizes that understanding.

Phew! That was a workout!

I hope this makes some kind of sense. Mindfulness is a damned difficult subject.

One of the biggest problems in contemporary commercial

mindfulness programs is that its teachers often don't understand just how deep and difficult mindfulness really is. When it's sold to the public as a way to relieve stress, anxiety, depression, and pain, problems can arise.

Since mindfulness is so deep and difficult, some people who practice it can sometimes find themselves suffering more stress, anxiety, depression, and pain rather than less. This is because when we open our minds, we can begin to consciously be aware of things that had been buried deep, hidden from the conscious mind. An eight-week course is not nearly long enough to understand the true depth of mindfulness. Try a lifetime instead.

Anyone with enough experience in Buddhist meditation practice to be given permission to teach it has gone through these less pleasant parts of the journey and is, therefore, able to guide new practitioners through the rough stuff. This usually involves the teacher saying, "Don't worry about it. That's just one of the things this practice brings up." Hearing that from my teachers was all I ever really needed. But I don't want to trivialize that. It was all I ever really needed, but I *really needed* it! It meant a lot to hear that from a teacher I trusted and who I knew was not lying to me.

Those who haven't actually experienced that kind of difficult stuff for themselves are unable to be convincing even if they too say, "Don't worry about it. That's just one of the things this practice brings up." The student can tell if the teacher isn't being truthful.

It's not that I am against mindfulness as a method for psychologists and others to use in helping their patients and clients. It's just that I think "secular mindfulness" is a very new thing, whereas Buddhist mindfulness has 2,500 years of research and development behind it. A lot of what is regarded as merely "religious" stuff and is therefore discarded by the enlightened scientific folks of today is part of that research and development. The philosophical outlook of Buddhism can help a student make sense of the difficult stuff they encounter while meditating. The rituals and ceremonies help support and reinforce the sense of calm that comes with meditation.

Because much of that research and development stuff looks "religious" to Western people, the folks who are trying to establish purely secular mindfulness practices figure they can just toss it out. I understand why they think that way. But I don't think that's entirely correct.

The Buddhists have been working with meditators for a very long time. They've seen a lot. All sorts of levels of experience are represented in Buddhism. New meditators look to experienced meditators for advice and guidance. Buddhism has traveled through many countries. Westerners tend to think of Asia as a single entity. It's not. It's a lot of very different cultures. Many of the techniques that Buddhists have developed to handle the inherent difficulties of meditation have proven themselves in multiple cultural settings that are often very different from each other.

Many of these techniques involve ritual. Sometimes there's chanting and bowing involved. Sometimes there are stories in which mythological beings speak and interact. These are useful in helping students understand some of the more surprising aspects of ourselves and the world we live in that the practice of mindfulness can bring up.

One way to approach the literature and mythology of Buddhism is to look on it not as religious dogma but as a set of memoirs and accounts of the meditative journeys of individuals and communities. This is one of the reasons I'm drawn to Dogen's writings. He writes in a very contemporary way sometimes. Some of his writings feel like a bridge between the ancient way of expressing this stuff and a more modern approach. He references the older Buddhist literature, but he personalizes it. He makes it come alive in ways that the old literature doesn't — at least for me.

Reading this kind of literature can help people who meditate put their experiences into a framework and thereby make sense of some of the stranger aspects of the practice. For me, it provided a way to think about things. Ideas like Shunryu Suzuki's description of the personal self as a swinging door between the inner and outer world, the idea of the inner and outer world being essentially the same thing, even such weird things as when the Heart Sutra says that form is emptiness and emptiness is form, these helped me navigate the changes that meditation practice brought up.

It's a set of strategies and techniques that have been honed over a long time and have proven themselves valuable. Modern secular mindfulness hasn't had time to develop equivalent variations. Perhaps one day it will.

# 14. THE WORLD OF DEMONS

THIS BRINGS UP another thing we ought to talk about, which is a phenomenon that the Buddhists call the world of demons. Every few months somebody comes out with an article telling people that it's dangerous to meditate. As I was working on this book, *Harper's* magazine came out with an article called "Lost in Thought: The Psychological Risks of Meditation," by David Kortava.* I found it online, where it was illustrated with an animated GIF of a meditating person with undulating lightning bolts coming out of her or his head. Oy vey.

Most of the article is taken up by a long, heartbreaking story of someone the author calls Megan who has a psychotic break at a meditation retreat and — spoiler alert — ends up committing suicide sometime later.

During her retreat Megan reported that she felt "zoned out into space." She said, "I can't remember where I am. ... Is it the end of the world? Am I dying? Why can't I function or move? I can hear the Buddha now. He is telling me to meditate. I can't, I'm so confused. Is this a test? Am I supposed to yell out 'I accept Jesus as my Lord and Savior?' What am I supposed to do? I am so confused."

The article points out that Ariana Huffington, of *Huffington Post* fame, wrote a self-help book called *Thrive*. In the book Huffington

---

* April 2021 issue, https://harpers.org/archive/2021/04/lost-in -thought-psychological-risks-of-meditation.

says, "The list of all the conditions that these [meditative] practices impact for the better — depression, anxiety, heart disease, memory, aging, creativity — sounds like a label on snake oil from the 19th century. Except this cure-all is real and there are no toxic side effects."

"Unfortunately Huffington was wrong," says the author of the article. "Although there is data supporting the positive effects of meditation, the scientific literature is murkier than some champions of the practice would like to believe, and the possibility of negative outcomes cannot be so easily dismissed. As early as 1976, Arnold Lazarus, one of the forefathers of cognitive behavioral therapy, raised concerns about transcendental meditation, the mantra-based practice then in vogue. 'When used indiscriminately,' he warned, 'the procedure can precipitate serious psychiatric problems such as depression, agitation, and even schizophrenic decompensation.' Lazarus had by then treated a number of 'agitated, restive' patients whose symptoms seemed to worsen after meditating."

As early as 1976, eh? Wow! So early. I'm impressed ... *not*! This sort of stuff has been recognized by Buddhists for thousands of years. Entire books were written about the subject before Sigmund Freud "discovered" the existence of the subconscious mind — which the Buddhists had also written about for centuries.

Anyway, back to the article. The article quotes Vinod Srihari of the Yale School of Medicine as saying, "for people already at risk for a psychiatric disorder, to have a first break on an extended meditation retreat makes sense logically." After a while the article brings up the work of Willoughby Britton, who runs an organization called Cheetah House. This organization works with meditators who are having troubles like this. Britton herself was a meditator. She says that "every meditation center we went to had at least a dozen horror stories" like the one about Megan. One meditator told her that the practice of letting go of concepts was "sabotaging my mind's ability to lay down new memories and reinforce old memories of simple things, like what words mean, what colors mean." Another one said, "I had two young children. I couldn't feel anything about them. I went through all the routines, you know: the bedtime routine, getting them ready and kissing them and all that stuff, but there was no emotional connection. It was like I was dead." Britton herself says, "It took me three years of trauma training to realize, oh, that's dissociation. And I hadn't realized it." She says that "if you can sit for long periods of time and not feel any pain and not have any thoughts, most meditation teachers are going to say that you're doing great."

They would? I sure wouldn't!

After going on and on like this for a while, the article finally gets to what I think is the real issue at hand. It talks about how these practices of meditation have been removed from their roots. It says, "Gone was the cosmology of hell realms and hungry ghosts and karma and rebirth.... Gone, too, was the open acknowledgment of the sundry mental and physical tribulations that might surface in the course of a serious meditation practice."

One of the problems with the way meditation has been commercialized these days is that if you're trying to make money on selling people meditation practices, then telling them that there are probably going to be some rough patches if you do a meditation practice long enough is not good for business.

Often the horror stories about people freaking out during meditation are centered on people who jump into very intensive practices without any prior experience. They'll go to a ten-day silent retreat, for example, where you're not allowed to speak or read or even make eye contact with anyone else — and they have never meditated before in their lives. Often these retreats are centered on very secularized versions of Buddhist meditation in which all the cosmology and mythology surrounding Buddhism has been removed. Even the word *Buddhism* is not mentioned. It's presented as a kind of psychological exercise.

But ten days, ten hours a day, meditating in total silence is a lot to put somebody through who has never practiced before. It took me more than ten years of daily zazen before I felt like I was ready to go on my first three-day zazen retreat. And that three-day retreat included maybe five or six hours of meditation a day, not ten or more.

Another problem with these secularized retreats is that far too often the people leading them have very little experience with meditation. In the Zen tradition, no one would be allowed to lead a retreat unless they had done zazen for decades. Before being allowed to teach, any certified Zen teacher would have already gone through their own version of what Britton rightly calls the "dark night of the soul."

All my teachers have had those kinds of difficult experiences in zazen. Nearly everybody I know who's practiced long enough has had times where they've gone through a really dark patch in their meditation. Having come through that, you know how you dealt with it. And you presumably had a teacher you could consult about it. So you have a sense of how to talk another person through it because you've experienced that from the side of the person freaking out.

And as I said, there are traditional ways of understanding these kinds of experiences — all that cosmology and all those heaven and hell realms and that sort of stuff. These days lots of people pooh-pooh that stuff because it sounds like superstition. And we don't want superstition anymore! We want science!

But that stuff about cosmology and so forth is a mythological way of expressing the kinds of things a person encounters in a meditation practice. You don't have to actually believe that out there somewhere in the cosmos is a hell realm. Even if you don't take it literally, you can still use the mythology of hell realms as a way to understand what you might be going through when you hit one of these rough patches in meditation practice. When you've got some sort of framework for understanding this kind of experience it doesn't feel as scary or as potentially permanent. On the other hand, if you think that the only explanation for what you're experiencing is that you're going insane, that can be a lot scarier than the idea that you're temporarily entering into a so-called hell realm that lots of other people — including your teacher — have experienced and have come through just fine.

Before I ever experienced any of this sort of thing myself I had heard and read a lot of teachings that I could reflect on when it did come up for me. I could go, "Okay, Tim warned me that this might happen. Nishijima Roshi has lectured on this. I've read about it in books." I understood that this sort of thing was common.

Just so I don't scare the bejesus out of you and make you never want to meditate again, I have to point out that most people don't get into this stuff right away. It generally takes a long time to develop.

Magazines like *Harper's* or the *Atlantic Monthly*, which published a similar article about the dangers of meditation a few years ago, love the story of the person who, the very first time they meditate, has a complete crack-up and ends up going psychotic. But that's not a very common story. The more common story is the one where meditation is just so boring and uneventful that the person gives up on it.

If you get through the boring part and still keep doing it, it's pretty likely that you'll also have been steeped in the mythological traditions surrounding meditation. That stuff is not there to try to make you believe in ghosts and supernatural beings. It's there as a part of the 2,500 years of research and development of this practice. People have been experiencing this kind of thing and working out how they and others can deal with it for a very long time. It's a shame to ignore all their efforts just because it doesn't sound like "science."

Willoughby Britton says, "The science of meditation is pretty much exclusively focused on the positive effects of meditation. But if we want to understand the entire trajectory of the contemplative path and everything that it entails, we need to be more even handed and more balanced in our investigations, and begin to investigate the full range of experiences, including the ones that would be considered negative, difficult, challenging, or maybe even problematic."

I totally agree. But the "science" she is referring to is contemporary Western psychology and psychiatry, much of it driven by commercial interests. Western psychology and psychiatry are useful in a lot of areas. But Westerners in general haven't had much experience with meditation the way that the cultures from which traditions like Buddhism derive have. To write off all that cultural learning as mere unscientific superstition is a big mistake.

People often ask me about the benefits of meditation. They want me to sell them on the benefits of meditation. I hate doing that because I think it's usually better not to talk too much about the benefits at the outset. Just do it for a while. See the benefits for yourself. Don't come in with expectations, especially grandiose ones that you might be inclined to push yourself hard to fulfill. When people asked him about the benefits of zazen, Kodo Sawaki said, "Zazen is good for nothing!"

I know that's a hard sell. But the people who are selling folks on the benefits of meditation are probably not doing them any favors by downplaying or even denying that there can be serious challenges.

One way of understanding these challenges is the concept of *makyo*. It's a Japanese word that means something like "world of demons." I got introduced to this idea very early on in my Buddhist practice. I probably first encountered it in the book *The Three Pillars of Zen* by Philip Kapleau. My first teacher also talked about it.

This idea of a world of demons doesn't have to be taken literally, like there are literally demons in a world somewhere out in space, or underground, or wherever demons dwell. It's a way to express the sort of phenomena that sometimes arise through Zen and other meditation practices. But maybe the best way to get into it is for me to tell you a little bit about my worst *makyo* experience. I wrote about it in *Hardcore Zen*, but it's worth talking about it again.

Leading up to my major *makyo* experience were a number of

other strange events. Things were getting weird for me. I was living in Japan by then and doing a lot more zazen, but I didn't have a good strong connection with Nishijima Roshi yet and my first teacher was far away in America. This was before the internet made communicating with people overseas easy and cheap.

Anyway, things were getting strange for me psychologically. It was probably a combination of a lot of things besides just zazen. I was living in a foreign country. I could barely speak the language. I didn't have a lot of friends. In fact, I didn't have anyone in my life at the time who was both a friend and a native speaker of English. So even among the friends I did have, there was always a communication barrier.

As a result of all this my worldview was starting to fall apart. The understanding that I had up until then of who I was, and what the world I lived in was, was starting to crumble. This is not an uncommon thing for Zen practitioners. But I want to emphasize again that this is not something that usually happens at the beginning of zazen practice. As I said before, in the beginning it's mainly just tedious. My circumstances were unusual, and that led to an acceleration of the process I was going through.

I remember being on a commuter train in Tokyo, probably the Odakyu Express going to work at Tsubaraya Productions, and just feeling like this wasn't reality anymore. At least, it wasn't reality the way I'd always understood it. I felt like my life was sort of a dream and that reality was something entirely different.

Fast-forwarding a bit, I attended one of Nishijima Roshi's summer retreats at Tokei-in temple in Shizuoka, where Mount Fuji is. This wasn't my first retreat, or my second. I'm not sure which one it was. But I'd been going to these retreats for a few years. I was probably having a rough time in zazen that day, although I don't particularly remember. It's just that I remember a lot of rough times in zazen at Tokei-in temple. It was hard to get through. Stuff was always coming up in my mind that I didn't like.

But it really hit that night. I don't know if it was the first or second night of the retreat. We all slept in one fairly large room with tatami mats on the floor. The women would sleep in one room, and the men would sleep in another. So I was in the room where the men slept, and I woke up in the middle of the night from a horrifying nightmare. I don't remember exactly what the nightmare was about, but I remember my stomach was doing flip-flops. I could feel it right in my gut.

I woke up in total terror. It was as if every fear that I'd ever had in my life had come all at once. I've never felt terror like that before or since. People who've read this same story in *Hardcore Zen* have said I had a panic attack. I've never had a panic attack — at least not anything any psychiatric professional has diagnosed and labeled as such — but this felt like something more than the phrase *panic attack* can encompass. Then again, maybe panic attacks are more than the words *panic attack* can encompass. But this was a sense of heavy, saturated, total fear.

I was rational enough that when I looked around the room and everybody was asleep I realized there was nothing for me to be scared of. Yet even so, I was in total, absolute, utter terror.

I didn't know any of the people at the retreat very well. They weren't complete strangers, mind you. I knew their names and had been on retreats with some of them before, but I didn't know them well enough to wake any of them up in the middle of the night saying, "I'm scared! Read me a bedtime story!" Especially when we all had to get up at four the next morning.

One thing I'd started doing when I went on these retreats was to bring some magazine or book or something with me that had nothing to do with Zen. I did this because I'd already had a couple of little minor freak-outs before. It seemed like it helped in those situations to distract myself with something that wasn't the least bit "spiritual."

So I went and got my backpack in which I had a copy of *Fortean Times* magazine. It's a magazine that looks at unusual phenomena like UFOs and werewolves and whatever in a rational and scientific way but doesn't necessarily try to debunk them. It's pretty fun.

Anyway, I had this copy of *Fortean Times*, and I went to the *hondo*, which is the Buddha Hall, the main area in the temple where the Buddha statue is, because they kept the lights on there all night. So I went in there and I was just looking at my magazine. Actually, I was not even really reading the magazine but just kind of using it as something to distract me and calm me down. I don't know how long I sat out there with that magazine, but eventually I got settled enough that I wasn't feeling a big adrenaline rush and total fear. I went back to the room where everyone was sleeping and somehow managed to go to sleep.

At four the next morning I got up with everyone else and did my zazen. There was this interesting moment, though, during one of Nishijima Roshi's lectures that day. Somebody asked him a question, which I don't remember. But Nishijima Roshi answered the question by saying, "Just don't drink alcohol."

And when he said "Just don't drink alcohol," he was making eye contact directly with me. At that moment I understood my problem completely. It wasn't that I had a drinking problem. I don't drink alcohol at all. It wasn't about alcohol. It was about the kind of delusions that I was putting into my head around that time.

I've never spoken to anybody about the specific nature of what was scaring me or what the nightmare was about — not even to a close friend or significant other. And I never will because it doesn't matter.

The deal with *makyo* is that it's very personal. Whatever the particular thing is that you think is the worst thing in the world, the thing that you're protesting about, or writing tweets about, or saying how terrible it is that anybody would do this thing, whatever that thing is, it is part of you. And you crave that terrible thing just as much as any of the people you point fingers at for bringing that thing into the world. That's what I discovered that night. It was heavy and it was difficult.

But there's an upside to this. Having gone through that, there's not much anybody else can say or do that could be worse than what I now know to be part of myself. That doesn't make me completely immune to ever freaking out again. But it takes a lot more to fluster me now than it did before.

I did initially make the mistake of thinking I was absolutely beyond the point of being rattled by anything. That seems to be a common mistake. But I think if you're honest with yourself, you'll see that there are still things that can set you off. Even so, it's nice to get past some of the stuff that used to really wind me up and be able to keep making progress so that fewer things are able to get to me.

Getting back to that *Harper's* magazine story about Megan and how she committed suicide after a meditation retreat, I would guess that what she encountered was something like what I did — the unmistakable understanding that whatever she hated the most about humanity was part of her. Without the proper training to know that whatever that was, it was not she herself, because she had no "self" to begin with, such an encounter could be psychologically devastating. I can see why someone would want to commit suicide after having the sort of experience I had. If I had thought that stuff in my head was me, then I might have decided I'd better kill myself for the good of the world.

I'll say it again. Under most circumstances this kind of *makyo* experience is not going to happen to you on the first day, or the first month, or the first year, or probably even the first decade of your practice — as long as you take it slow and don't get ambitious about achieving something through meditation.

If you somehow get involved with a teacher or organization that encourages you to have altered states of consciousness or reach some kind of "higher level of awareness" or whatever, my advice would be to say sayonara and look for somebody else. You can find a teacher who's more sensible than that if you look around. Those ambitious meditation practices that get you to have these big experiences really fast are the only ones that are truly dangerous.

On the other hand, if you acclimate yourself slowly to the understanding that your practice helps you develop, you'll be okay. The reason things go wrong sometimes is that we've lived our whole lives with one way of understanding life, the universe, and everything, and we've gotten comfortable with that. But what the Buddhist teachers will tell you is that the thing most of us think of as normal life is a kind of deep mass hallucination that almost everyone in the world is partaking in. Getting into a better, more realistic understanding of how things really are is like being talked out of a bad acid trip. You have to take it slow, or you'll just end up making things worse.

# 15. RIGHT BALANCED STATE

THE FINAL FOLD in the Noble Eightfold Path is what Nishijima Roshi called "right balanced state." He's probably the only one who translates it that way. The much more common translation is "right concentration," although I've also seen it translated as "right meditation," "right meditative absorption," "right union," and "right single-mindedness."

The actual word the early Buddhists used was *samadhi*. We ran across this term before when I told you how Dogen defined it. Let's go a little deeper this time. *Samadhi* comes from a root word that means "collect" or "bring together." It's often understood as bringing the mind together to concentrate on a single object. As I said earlier, generally people tend to think of it as a rare and special meditative state.

In early Buddhism samadhi was described as follows:

> There is the case where a monk — quite withdrawn from sensuality, withdrawn from unskillful [mental] qualities — enters and remains in the first *jhana*: rapture and pleasure born from withdrawal, accompanied by directed thought and evaluation....
>
> With the stilling of directed thoughts and evaluations, he enters and remains in the second *jhana*: rapture and pleasure born of composure, unification of awareness free from directed thought and evaluation — internal assurance....

With the fading of rapture, he remains equanimous, mindful, and alert, and senses pleasure with the body. He enters and remains in the third *jhana*, of which the Noble Ones declare, "Equanimous and mindful, he has a pleasant abiding." ...

With the abandoning of pleasure and stress — as with the earlier disappearance of elation and distress — he enters and remains in the fourth *jhana*: purity of equanimity and mindfulness, neither-pleasure-nor-pain. [This is called right concentration or samadhi.]*

*Jhana* is the Pali pronunciation of the Sanskrit word *dhyana*, which is usually translated as "meditation." This same word was pronounced *chan* in Chinese, and *ʒen* is how you pronounce it in Japanese. So Zen Buddhism could be called Jhana Buddhism, and we could talk about first zen, second zen, and so on. Since that's the case, you might expect Zen folks to be all about the *jhana* states as described above.

In fact, though, in the Zen tradition we rarely talk about *jhanas*. At least not in the sense of there being distinct levels. As you can figure out from context, in older forms of Buddhism the various *jhanas* were different states or levels of meditation. In this example, they seem to lead from one to the other, getting better and better, until at last you end up in the fourth *jhana*, which is the best-est *jhana* of them all.

The problem with this system for me is that it involves comparing things that cannot be compared. How do you judge which number *jhana* you're in? I suppose you could compare it to the descriptions you've heard or read of that *jhana*. For example, you could ask yourself if you're feeling "rapture and pleasure born from withdrawal." If the answer was yes, then you'd know you were in *jhana* number one.

---

*    "Jhana," *Access to Insight*, 2005, https://www.accesstoinsight.org/ptf /dhamma/sacca/sacca4/samma-samadhi/jhana.html.

But what does "rapture and pleasure born from withdrawal" feel like? I certainly don't know. Maybe I could guess based on what sort of feelings and images words like *rapture*, *pleasure*, and *withdrawal* evoke. But then I'm really just comparing my actual state at this moment with my imagination.

Or maybe if I've accomplished *jhanas* number one and two — leaving aside for the moment how I'd know I did that — I could compare my memories of those states with whatever I'm feeling at this moment. If I'm not feeling what I remember feeling in those states, and if instead I feel "equanimous and mindful" and have "a pleasant abiding," I might declare that I'm in *jhana* number three.

What's a "pleasant abiding," you ask? I'll be darned if I know! I'm not even sure what being "equanimous" feels like. I guess it feels kinda equal all over? Or something. You tell me.

I suppose I could make a vague guess as to what feeling neither pleasure nor pain would be like. But if I had to guess at that one, I'd say that it just feels kind of normal. Like maybe the feeling I get on a day that's not too hot or cold while sitting on a couch that's not very nice but also not too bad and watching a TV show that I neither enjoy very much nor hate.

But how would I be certain if I'd accomplished *jhanas* one and two and hadn't made a mistake? I guess I could ask my teacher. Which would mean I could describe to her my memories of how I felt at a particular time in the past. This would invoke in her images and feelings associated with the words I used, and she could compare those images and feelings to memories of her own past states of *jhana* and use that comparison to guess if I'd reached those states too. Then she could either confirm my meditative accomplishments or deny them.

I hope I'm conveying what my problem with this sort of stuff is. People in the world of nerdy meditators toss around descriptions like these ideas of the states of *jhana* as if they mean something. But to me they're just gibberish. I can't make heads nor tails of them.

I know that by questioning this stuff I could be accused of questioning the wisdom of the Buddha. But that shouldn't be a big problem because the Buddha himself told his students to question his words and find out for themselves if they were true. Besides which, I have some serious doubts about how much of the early Buddhist scriptures — written hundreds of years after the Buddha died — contain the actual words of the Buddha.

In the Zen tradition, on the other hand, the word *samadhi* is used very differently, especially by Dogen, as I noted earlier. The most famous example of Dogen's way of defining *samadhi* is the section of his essay "Bendowa" called *Jijuyu Zanmai* (the Samadhi of Receiving and Using the Self).

This is a bit long, so forgive me, but I think it's really important. Here's how *Jijuyu Zanmai* goes:

When you practice zazen with the whole body, speech, and mind, even for a short time, the entire universe immediately becomes the posture of Buddha. The whole sky immediately becomes enlightenment. It enables all beings everywhere, in Heaven, on Earth, or in Hell, to increase their dharma joy of their original nature. It enables all beings to be Buddhas. It renews their awakening.

Together, all beings in every direction and in every realm become clear in body and mind. They realize great liberation. Their original face appears.

Thus, the supreme, complete, and perfect awakening of all things returns to you when you sit zazen. You and this awakening assist each other intimately in ways that cannot be perceived. You drop off body and mind absolutely and without fail.

At this time grass, trees, walls, tiles, and fences carry out Buddha work. Everyone and everything receives the benefits of the movement of wind and water caused by this practice of zazen. The influence of Buddha helps them realize the enlightenment that they already possess. Although they do not perceive this, it is true.

All of you who receive this wind and fire spread the Buddha influence of original enlightenment. All who live and talk with you also share this virtue. They too spread and circulate this truth throughout the universe. This truth is limitless. It never ceases. It cannot be understood. It cannot be measured.

However, when you are sitting zazen you do not notice this. Your perceptions do not interfere with it. This is because this stillness is not something you have created. You directly experience the stillness that already exists. Within this stillness, you are enlightenment itself.

Many believe that practice and enlightenment are two different things. They think that practice and enlightenment can be perceived separately. This is not the case. Enlightenment is not associated with perception. Our human thoughts and our human feelings are deluded. They cannot reach the standard of enlightenment.

Mind and object appear and disappear within stillness. This takes place in the realm of the samadhi of receiving and using the self. Not even a speck of dust is moved. Nothing is destroyed. And yet buddha work and buddha influence occur.

Grasses, trees, and walls praise and proclaim this truth for the sake of all beings. It does not matter whether these living beings are ordinary or saintly. In turn, all beings praise and proclaim the truth for the sake of grasses, trees, and walls. It does not matter whether these grasses, trees, and walls are ordinary or saintly.

Awareness of self lacks nothing. Awareness of the external world lacks nothing. Both are concrete, real experience. Both are always happening. Realization occurs at every moment. Realization is practiced endlessly.

If only one person sits zazen even for a short time, zazen is one with all existence and completely fills all of time. It is mystical cooperation. It guides all beings and all things in the past, present, and future.

Each moment you sit zazen is complete practice and complete realization. If all of the Buddhas came together and combined all of their wisdom to try to calculate the goodness of one person sitting zazen for one moment they could never come close.

So for Dogen, zazen was samadhi. It doesn't matter if it feels like samadhi to the individual doing zazen. This samadhi is not limited to a single individual. The entire universe partakes of it. Nor could it be limited by any notion of rank or number. For Dogen there was no sense in ranking states of samadhi because every instance of it is complete in and of itself. Remember what he said about skin, flesh, bones, and marrow?

In "108 Gates of Dharma Illumination," Dogen said, "Right balanced state is a gate of Dharma illumination; for [with it] we attain undistracted samadhi." Here again he's just talking about plain old zazen. We may judge our own experience of zazen as good or bad, or compare it to other times we've done zazen, or compare it to stories we've read or heard about other people's experiences in zazen. But that's irrelevant. This instance of zazen is exactly what it is, no more and no less.

In "Thirty-Seven Elements of Bodhi," Dogen says, "Right balance as a branch of the path is to get free of Buddhist ancestors and to get free of right balance. It is others being well able to discuss. It is to make nose holes by cutting out the top of the head. It is the twirling of an udumbara flower inside the right Dharma-eye treasury. It is the presence inside the udumbara flower of a hundred thousand faces of Mahakashyapa breaking into a smile. Having used [this] state of vigorous activity for a long time, a wooden dipper is broken. Thus, [right balance] is six years of floundering in the wilderness and a night in which a flower opens. It is [when] 'the Great Fire at the end of a kalpa is blazing and the great-thousand world is being totally destroyed, just to follow circumstances.'"

I know. That's weird. Let me try to explain it.

He says that right balance is getting free of Buddhist ancestors and getting free of right balance. This means we no longer have to worry about comparing ourselves with practitioners of the past or present or about comparing ourselves with whatever we think of as "right balance."

The stuff about making nose holes by cutting off the top of the head is especially bizarre. But it's really not as crazy as it might sound. Nostrils are a symbol of liveliness. In his footnotes about this, Nishijima Roshi says, "Right balance is a lively state realized by ceasing the more sophisticated mental activities (cutting off the top of the head) that take us away from the here and now." So Dogen is saying that in zazen we stop worrying about making intellectual judgments — we metaphorically cut off the top of the head — and we get into the real experience of living just as it is. We make nose holes.

About the stuff concerning udumbara flowers, an udumbara flower is a symbol of something that doesn't exist. The flower of the actual udumbara plant doesn't look like a flower, so for many years people assumed the plant did not produce flowers at all. "Twirling a flower" is a reference to the time when the Buddha indicated that his student Mahakasyapa was his successor by picking up a flower and twirling it in his hand, at which point Mahakasyapa smiled in recognition of the moment.

In the original version of the story about Mahakasyapa the flower Buddha twirled is not specified as an udumbara flower. The reason it's an udumbara flower — that is, a flower that was thought at the time not to exist — in this retelling and not just an ordinary flower, as in the original story, is that Dogen wants to emphasize that we do not need to be aware of our own enlightenment. It's there whether or not we notice it.

When he says that a "wooden dipper is broken," he means that a Buddhist practitioner has become completely free from conditions that restricted her/his ability to understand and appreciate this real moment.

"Six years of floundering in the wilderness" alludes to the Buddha's six years of ascetic practice in pursuit of the truth before he came up with the middle way and found his enlightenment. The line about a flower opening one night refers to the Buddha's experience of balance on the night of his enlightenment when he just sat in the lotus posture without any specific goal or intention.

The Buddha's six years of ascetic practice are often seen as a mistake or a waste of time. But they were not. In an essay called "Sesshin Sessho" ("Expounding the Mind and Expounding Nature"), Dogen says:

> From the time we establish the bodhi-mind [when we decide we really want to know the meaning of life, the universe, and everything] and direct ourselves toward training in the Way of Buddha, we sincerely practice difficult practices; and at that time, though we keep practicing, in a hundred efforts we never hit the target once. Nevertheless... one hit of the target now is by virtue of hundreds of misses in the past.... We can never attain the Buddha Way by abandoning the Buddha Way.... The Buddha Way, at the time of the first establishment of the will, is the Buddha Way; and at the time of realization of the right state of truth, it is the Buddha Way.... t is like someone walking one thousand miles: the first step is one in a thousand miles and the thousandth step is one in a thousand miles.

Just because you might feel like your practice right now is going nowhere, it is by virtue of your misses that you finally become able to hit the target.

The stuff at the end about the Great Fire refers to a koan that goes like this: "A monk asks Master Daizui Hoshin, "[They say that] when the Great Fire at the end of a kalpa is blazing, the great-thousandfold world [i.e., the whole universe] will be totally destroyed. I wonder whether or not this place will be destroyed."

The master says, "It will be destroyed."

The monk says, "If that is so, should we just follow circumstances?"

The master says, "We just follow circumstances."

When the monk asks whether "this place will be destroyed," he doesn't just mean whatever place he and his master happen to be at that moment. He means himself, he means the great Self of all things.

This story doesn't necessarily imply that there will come a time when everything will be destroyed. Rather, it means that in every situation we "follow circumstances." In other words, we need to accept what is and do what is appropriate for the real situation.

I know that was a lot. But the bottom line, for Dogen, is that right balanced state simply means doing zazen. No matter how it feels or what sort of judgments you or anyone else passes about your zazen experience. Right balanced state doesn't mean that you have to achieve some kind of special state while doing zazen. Just doing zazen is enough, as far as Dogen was concerned.

This is a very tricky point. Lots of people give up on zazen practice because they feel they're not getting anywhere. They expect progress. They expect achievements. And often it's hard to feel like you've progressed or achieved anything at all. As I said when talking about *makyo*, most of the time zazen is just boring, boring, boring.

But what is achievement? What is progress? Isn't all progress and all achievement based on comparing how things are right now to how you remember them being in the past, or to how you wish they were, or to how you think they could be in the future, or about comparing yourself to someone else?

If meditation practice is about being in the here and now, are the concepts of achievement and progress relevant at all? Is any sort of comparison relevant at all?

In actual practice, though, it's really hard to give up the idea of achievement and progress, and it's hard not to compare. I know this very well. Even after all the zazen I've done and all the times my teachers have told me that it's not about achieving anything, I still find myself frustrated sometimes at how dull and ordinary my zazen experience often is. I still find myself comparing my real experience in zazen to what I think it ought to be like.

But when I feel that way I try to remember how Dogen said that even what I might define as "bad zazen" is still the supreme state. It's still samadhi. The fact that I fail to recognize it as samadhi is unimportant.

And when I fail to remember even that, I just try to sit still until the little timer on my phone goes off. I always feel at least a little better for having done some zazen. And that's something.

# 16. THE HEART SUTRA

I MENTIONED THE five aggregates a few chapters ago and said I'd explain that to you, so that means I need to talk about the Heart Sutra. I first encountered the Heart Sutra when I was a student at Kent State University. On the first day of my Zen Buddhism class I heard the Heart Sutra for the first time. The translation that Tim presented to the class was the one done by his teacher, Kobun Chino Otogawa Roshi. It goes like this:

Avaloketeshvara Bodhisattva, when practicing deeply the prajna paramita, perceived that all five skandhas are empty and was saved from all suffering and distress.

Shariputra, form does not differ from emptiness. Emptiness does not differ from form. That which is form is emptiness, that which is emptiness form. The same is true of feelings, perceptions, impulses, consciousness.

Shariputra, all Dharmas are marked with emptiness. They do not appear or disappear, are not tainted or pure, do not increase or decrease. Therefore in emptiness, no form, no feelings, perceptions, impulses, consciousness.

No eyes, no ears, no nose, no tongue, no body, no mind. No color, no sound, no smell, no taste, no touch, no object of mind. No realm of the eyes and so forth until no realm of mind consciousness.

No ignorance and also no extinction of it and so forth, until no old age and death and also no extinction of them. No suffering, no origination, no stopping, no path. No cognition, also no attainment. With nothing to attain a bodhisattva depends on Prajna Paramita and the mind is no hindrance. Without any hindrance, no fears exist. Far apart from every inverted view, he dwells in Nirvana. In the three worlds, all Buddhas depend on Prajna Paramita and obtain anutara samyak sambodhi.

Therefore, know the Prajna Paramita is the great transcendent mantra, is the great bright mantra, is the utmost mantra, is the supreme mantra, which is able to relieve all suffering and is true, not false. So proclaim the Prajna Paramita mantra, proclaim the mantra that says gaté, gaté, paragaté, parasamgaté, bodhi svaha.

And that's it. That's the entire Heart Sutra. Short as it is, it's probably the most important sutra in the Zen form of Buddhism. There are so many ways to get into it, but I'll tell you what it means to me.

This little sutra is the distillation of several much longer sutras about Prajna Paramita, which means "great transcendent wisdom." Let me take you through it slowly and try to explain the stranger parts.

Avaloketeshvara Bodhisattva is the Bodhisattva of Compassion. This bodhisattva is also called Kanjizai Bosatsu or Kanon in Japanese, and Guanyin in Chinese. Initially, Avaloketeshvara was pictured as a male, but in order to show that he represented compassion, artists often gave him very feminine-looking features. After a while it became more common to depict the bodhisattva as female.

Bodhisattvas are beings who supposedly put off their own complete and total enlightenment and entry into nirvana in order to save all the other beings first. So they won't go across to the other shore of enlightenment until everybody else is over there already.

*Prajna* is a compound of two words. The first is *pra*, which is related to the prefix *pre-* as in *prefix* in English, meaning "before." The second is *jnana*, which is "knowledge."

So the wisdom that the word *prajna* refers to comes before knowledge. It's more basic than mere knowledge. *Paramita* means something like "the best" or "the greatest."

The storyline of the sutra, such as it is, is that while in this state of highest wisdom the bodhisattva of compassion perceived that all five skandhas are empty. Skandhas are the constituents of a person. Sometimes the word *skandha* is translated as "aggregate." It literally means "heap."

Even though my family was not religious, I grew up around Christianity more than any other religion, and I was aware that Christians believed that we are all immaterial souls living inside material bodies. I wasn't sure I believed that myself. But I figured all religions had a similar idea that the real person was a nonmaterial entity that lived inside a material body.

Back when I was hanging around the Hare Krishnas on campus, I learned that they very strongly insist that the true essence of a person is a thing called atman, which is basically the soul, and is eternally separate and completely different from the material body. Unlike the Christians, who believe that after you die God judges you and sends you to either heaven or hell for eternity, the Hare Krishnas believe that when you die, your soul leaves your current body and goes into another body.

The Buddha was also aware of that idea because he was Indian, and the concept was pretty common. Through a long process of examining the idea of an immaterial soul that inhabited a material body, he came to the conclusion that there was no such thing as a soul. He instead proposed this idea of five skandhas, which in this version of the Heart Sutra are given as form, feelings, perceptions, impulses, and consciousness.

So form is the physical body and the material world. Nishijima

Roshi would say that matter was ultimately just sensation. For example, you have a particular set of sensations when you hold this book in your hands. It has weight and texture, and the words have meanings that create mental sensations. Based on those sensations you form an image that there is a material substance "out there" made of paper and glue and ink and ideas.

The next skandha is feeling, which is the standard translation of a Chinese character that also means something like "reception" or "acceptance." So you can think of it as a combination of those things. It's physical as well as emotional feelings.

The next skandha is perceptions. Katagiri Roshi explains the difference between feeling and perception by saying, "With perception, you can receive something through the consciousness. Feeling is more basic; before you can get something through consciousness, you can receive it."

The next one is impulses, but that one takes a bit of explaining so I'll leave it to last.

The final skandha is consciousness. In Buddhist terms, consciousness is what happens when you add up the first three skandhas. The form, feeling, and perception of something gets formed into a conscious impression of the thing. Buddhists often talk about six consciousnesses, one for each of the five senses — visual consciousness, auditory consciousness, and so on — and a sixth for mind consciousness.

But let's get back to impulses. The original Sanskrit term is *samskara*. D. T. Suzuki translates it as "confection." So it's like candy, I guess. Poet and translator Red Pine gives it as "memory." Some people translate it as "concepts." In the standard English translation of the Heart Sutra used by lots of Soto Zen temples in the US, it's translated as "formations." Kobun Chino chose "impulses." There are probably other translations I'm not aware of too.

According to the *Shambhala Dictionary of Buddhism and Zen*, *samskara* means "impression or consequence, generally translated as formations, mental formational forces, or impulses. Samskara refers both to the activity of forming and the passive state of being formed.... Since actions can be either physical, verbal, or mental, impulses that are physical, verbal, and mental are distinguished." And so on and so forth. It's a really long definition!

Katagiri Roshi says that impulses are "sort of the basic nature of consciousness" or the "original nature of action." He points out that action is impermanence. Action is change. Even mental activities are changes in the state of our brain moment by moment.

Don't worry. There's not going to be a quiz on that. I just wanted to give you an idea of what all the translators are dealing with. *Samskara* can mean a lot of things! The same is true of all the other skandhas. I went through them pretty quickly, but you can find people who get into endless discussions about the precise meaning of each one.

To me, it's kind of useless to study in detail what each of the five skandhas are. The real point of the teaching is that we are not just one indivisible thing. Rather, we are a collection of things that come together for a while and then come apart. That's all you really need to know. Precisely what those things are is beside the point.

This idea that we are a collection of things rather than one indivisible something makes sense if you look at science and evolution. The first creatures that lived on Earth that we know about from the fossil record were single-celled organisms. There were two types of these single-celled organisms — prokaryotes and eukaryotes. And the theory is that one of these single-celled organisms swallowed another one of these single-celled organisms. But instead of the second one being digested, it became incorporated into the first. And that new organism became the basis for us, for all life on Earth, because it was a more efficient sort of cell.

Nobody really knows if that's the way it happened, but the theory seems to be well supported by the fossil evidence. Somehow these different single-celled organisms began to live in colonies.

And then the colonies became specialized. Then these specialized colonies came together to form super colonies that functioned as if they were a single unit. Our highly evolved physical bodies, then, are actually colonies of specialized colonies of individual cells that are all cooperating together.

So the idea that we are just one thing, even in the physical sense, is mistaken. Even so, we do appear to be one single thing, at least to ourselves and to each other. We talk about ourselves and each other as if we were each just one individual thing. Yet we shouldn't take that idea too seriously.

The next funny word that comes up in the Heart Sutra is the name Shariputra. Shariputra was one of Buddha's main disciples. He was said to be very wise and analytical and is known as the smartest of the smarty-pantses among Buddha's original followers. Because the sutra is addressing Mr. Smarty Pants, we can assume it's trying to address that side of things, the intellectual side.

The most well-known lines in the sutra come right after Shariputra gets introduced. "Form does not differ from emptiness. Emptiness does not differ from form. That which is form is emptiness. That which is emptiness form."

The word *emptiness* is pretty complicated. Let me see if I can uncomplicate it. This word is often misunderstood. There was a tendency among early scholars of Buddhism in the West to think that Buddhism was a kind of nihilism because they saw this word *emptiness* all the time.

It's a subtler concept than that. Emptiness can be thought of in a lot of ways. I tend to think of it as silence or as that which is unnamable. It's that *something* that we can't really understand but that underlies everything. If you think about it, silence is everywhere.

Even if you go to the noisiest place in the world, there's this undercurrent of silence beneath the noise. Noise just kind of sits on top of silence. That's the way I think of emptiness. We are something that has grown out of emptiness. We are the manifestation of essential emptiness. So emptiness doesn't mean nothingness as opposed to somethingness. My first teacher, Tim, would often use the phrase "the ground of all being and nonbeing" to describe it.

Form is emptiness. Also feelings are emptiness, perceptions are emptiness, impulses are emptiness, and consciousness is emptiness. All these things are emptiness.

The sutra goes on, saying, "All Dharmas are marked with emptiness. They do not appear or disappear, are not tainted or pure, do not increase or decrease."

So emptiness is something that doesn't appear or disappear. And if what we are is really emptiness, then we don't appear or disappear either.

Then the sutra says, "Therefore in emptiness, no form, no feelings, perceptions, impulses, consciousness. No eyes, no ears, no nose, no tongue, no body, no mind. No color, no sound, no smell, no taste, no touch, no object of mind. No realm of the eyes and so forth until no realm of mind consciousness."

Where it says "and so forth" it means no realm of the eyes, no realm of the ears, no realm of the nose, and so on. What you see is the "realm of the eyes," what you hear is the "realm of the ears," and so forth. Indian philosophy divides things up like that. They liked to come up with categories and lists for everything. Ancient Indian philosophers even had a categorization system for different types of sneezes.

Then the sutra says, "No ignorance and no extinction of it and so forth until no old age and death and also no extension of old age and death." That's the Twelvefold Chain of Codependent Coorigination. Although it only mentions the first link and the twelfth link.

Just FYI, the twelve folds are (1) ignorance, which is the cause of (2) action (actually the Sanskrit word is our old friend *samskara* again), which is the cause of (3) consciousness, which is the cause of (4) name and form, which is the cause of (5) the six senses, which are the cause of (6) contact, which is the cause of (7) feeling, which is the cause of (8) love (also sometimes translated as "craving" or "desire"), which is the cause of (9) taking, which is the cause of (10) coming into existence, which is the cause of (11) birth (also sometimes translated as "becoming"), which is the cause of (12) old age and death.

The Twelvefold Chain of Codependent Coorigination is fascinating stuff. You can find discussions of it in lots of places, including in my book *Sit Down and Shut Up*. But the bottom line as far as we're concerned here is that, again, we are not just a single independent unit. We are part of a chain of causes that somehow has come to imagine itself to be a single independent unit.

Then the sutra says, "No suffering, no origination, no stopping, no path." Those are from the Buddha's first sermon, "The Four Noble Truths," which I mentioned earlier. The common way of translating the Four Noble Truths is, "All life is suffering. There is an origination to suffering. There is a way to stop suffering. And there is a path that you can follow to stop suffering." And that path is what we were just looking at in the last few chapters, the Noble Eightfold Path.

So in a way, the Heart Sutra is denying all the foundational aspects of Buddhist philosophy. It's like finding a secret passage in the Bible that says "no savior, no resurrection, no heaven, no eternal life" or something like that. It's taking all the things that everybody thinks they know about Buddhism and saying, "No, it's not any of that. Sorry!"

But it's not trying to refute those ideas so much as to help us understand that all these concepts, even though we agree that they're good concepts, are in the end just concepts. Even the best concepts are not the same as reality. They're just ways of describing reality. They're just names.

Names do have utilitarian value. People call me Brad, and I respond to it. But "Brad" doesn't encapsulate everything about me. It doesn't really get to the true core of what I am. It's just kind of a place marker. Still, it's a useful place marker. It's the same with these Buddhist ideas about suffering and so forth.

Then the sutra says, "No cognition, also no attainment. With nothing to attain, a bodhisattva relies on Prajna Paramita and the mind is no hindrance."

I talked about achievement and progress in an earlier chapter. Attainment is another way of saying the same thing. No attainment is really key to what we're practicing when we do zazen. We are trying to just sit with nothing to attain. We're not trying to have a special experience or a special state of mind or anything like that. We're trying to leave all that behind and just be exactly what we are. There is a certain irony in trying to attain "nothing to attain."

But the irony is more a linguistic trick than anything that you really need to worry about. People will say, "If the goal is no goal, then you still have a goal." I asked my Zen teacher Tim about that once, and he said that semantically that's true. But in actual practice, the goal of having no goal is very different from any other goal you can have. So it's just a language trick. In practice it doesn't mean you actually have a goal when the goal is to leave all goals behind. Try it sometime and see.

The next weird term in the sutra is *anutara samyak sambodhi*. Kobun Chino Roshi left that untranslated, but it means unsuppressed, complete, perfect enlightenment. It's what you attain when you don't attain anything.

Then there's the little mantra at the end. Translated it means "gone, gone, gone all the way, gone to the other shore, Hooray!" Tim told me that somebody once asked Kobun what that meant and why it was tacked on to the end of the sutra. Kobun's response was, "I don't know, that's just Indian stuff."

It was a convention in ancient India to end a sutra with a mantra. Personally, I don't worry too much about the mantra at the end. Other people comment on it extensively, and if you like that sort of thing you can read what they have to say. To me, it doesn't really mean much. It's just how the Heart Sutra ends.

There's a lot more I could say about the Heart Sutra, and I'm sure I'll end up talking about it more as this book goes on. But for now, those are the basics. So let's get back into the Buddhist ethical system, shall we?

# 17. THE ZEN BUDDHIST PRECEPTS

BUDDHIST OFTEN TALK about the Three Poisons, which are greed, hatred, and delusion. We all know these are bad things. But where do greed, hate, and delusion come from? People have been working on that question for centuries, so I don't think I'll be the one to give the definitive answer. But I have a guess.

If you want to look for the origin of greed, hate, and delusion, you've got to talk about the small self, the ego-based sense of being an individual entity separate from everyone and everything else in the universe, a subject as opposed to the objects that the subject encounters.

It might be that greed, hate, and delusion are inseparable from this "small self." There is a word in Sanskrit, *avidya*, which is often translated as "ignorance." *Avidya* means "the lack of *vidya*." And *vidya* means "knowledge" or "understanding."

*Avidya* is the root of the illusion of small self. It's the first link in the Twelvefold Chain of Codependent Coorigination that I introduced in the previous chapter. Buddhists, as well as followers of other Indian philosophical systems, see *avidya* as the root of most basic delusion about who and what we are. It is also the root of greed, hate, and all other smaller delusions.

When we see ourselves as the Big Self — the self that includes everyone and everything — then greed and hatred don't make sense. There's nothing to be greedy for and no one to hate. But when we see ourselves as individuals in competition with other individuals, greed and hate seem to make sense — even though they don't.

When we choose to do the wrong thing, to act out of greed and hate, we're choosing to serve the small self. Only the deluded small self could see any sense in acting out of greed or hatred. We think there is something to be gained for the small self by doing that sort of thing — whatever it happens to be. But we are wrong.

The thing the small self thinks will enhance it will not. By acting out of greed it can move some object from one part of the Big Self to another part of the Big Self. By acting out of hatred it can transfer some sensation from one part of the Big Self to another part of the Big Self.

But this is temporary. Big Self always wants to be in equilibrium. So any such action will be corrected and the balance restored. In the mind of the individual small self, this will often be perceived as pain and suffering, for example when the thing it thinks it has gained by stealing from another is taken away. But from the point of view of Big Self, equilibrium has been restored and everything is fine; the imbalance has been corrected.

For me, studying the Buddhist precepts has been a useful way to come to understand this. At first the precepts just looked like a bunch of rules that restricted me and kept me from having fun. But after working with them for a while, I could see the practicality of them. The precepts aren't meant to be restrictive or moralistic. They're meant to help you have a better life, to help you not disturb the balance of things by demanding stuff that won't really help you even if you were to get it.

The regular practice of zazen has made me see the benefits of doing good, or at least doing better if I can't always do good. It's a sort of inverted form of selfishness. I've seen that doing good is better for my self — both small self and Big Self. I feel better when I do what's right, and I feel worse when I do what's wrong.

This doesn't mean I never make mistakes. I do. But each mistake seems to be a learning experience. So I try to learn from my mistakes and not repeat them.

The Buddhist precepts are the Buddhist code of morality or ethics. All religions have these codes. Before I get into explaining what the precepts are and what they mean to me, I want to get something out of the way. In the past, I've used the words *morals* and *ethics* somewhat interchangeably. Some readers have objected, saying that Buddhism is concerned only with ethics and not with morals. If you look the words up in the dictionary, their definitions overlap so much they might as well be the same. But in common contemporary usage, I get the sense that the word *morals* has more of a feeling of a dogmatic set of rules, whereas the word *ethics* has a lighter sense of simply knowing what's right and wrong.

If that's the case, then you could indeed say that Buddhism is more concerned with ethics than with morals. But there are precepts in Buddhism. And although the Buddhist precepts are not dogmatic rules enforced by a judgmental God, they are taken very seriously. They're not rules, but it would be wrong to think of them as merely suggestions. They're a lot more important than that. In that sense, then, Buddhism does have something like morals as well as ethics.

Either way, the words overlap so much that I'll continue to use them more or less interchangeably, if that's OK with you.

In her book *Circle of the Way: A Concise History of Zen from the Buddha to the Modern World*, Barbara O'Brien explains the reason that Buddhism addresses ethics/morals like this:

> Morality is important not because a god has commanded us to behave but because our misbehaviors stem from belief in a self. We lie, cheat, scam, assault, and do various other damaging things to other people ultimately because we are trying to protect or gratify the self. Through living honestly and harmoniously with others, we learn that "I" am not the center of the universe, after all.
>
> The cultivation of such selfless virtues as compassion,

loving-kindness, empathy, and equanimity (remaining upright in distress, not being sucked into "taking sides") is an essential antidote to the ego's demands. Somewhat paradoxically, the practice of these virtues is both prerequisite for realizing enlightenment and the living manifestation of enlightenment. Likewise, the moral precepts of Buddhism describe the natural activity of enlightened wisdom in the phenomenal world, but they are spelled out and codified in order to function as training wheels for those who are still deluded.

This is a wonderful definition, I think. But let's dig into why religions in general all seem to have codes of ethics.

Evolutionary biologists have suggested that ethics are adaptive. Societies that have codes of ethics will last longer than those that don't. In fact, there probably isn't any such thing as a society that lacks a code of ethics. Even in prisons, where notions of right and wrong are questionable at best, codes of ethics develop and are often harshly enforced.

Probably when humans made the transition from wandering hunter-gatherer societies to settled farming societies, people quickly understood the need for establishing more stringent rules of conduct than they had needed during their years of wandering. This was also the time when the seminal forms of the world's major religions began to appear.

The idea of an all-powerful God who made rules and enforced them must have been very appealing to early human societies. As I said earlier, the more people in a society who believed that God was watching them and would punish them for breaking his rules, the better. That kept things stable in early human societies and made it possible to do the kind of repetitive work that farming necessitates. You need a predictable society if you're going to base it on an activity that follows the cycles of the weather and depends on people being able to know what to do and when to do it.

But religious people tend to want more rules than most folks. They voluntarily forgo activities that other people find pleasurable and acceptable. For example, some will practice sexual abstinence. Or they won't partake of alcohol and drugs even when the rest of society considers it OK to do so. Some will be far more careful with the words they use than the rest of society. Things like that.

The Buddhist precepts first appeared when the Buddha decided to share his teachings with a group of like-minded people who agreed to live together to try to put his teachings into practice. Pretty much as soon as they got together, conflicts sprang up.

Interestingly enough, the very first Buddhist rule was about sex. The Buddhist monks decided that having sex was a barrier to practice. Probably one of the main reasons for this was that in those days, reliable contraception was not available. A male monk who had sex risked getting someone pregnant, and female monastics risked getting pregnant themselves. Trying to have a functioning community dedicated to meditation was not going to work out if there were lots of babies around. Sex is also a very exciting activity centered on bodily pleasure and as such was one of the greatest distractions to a life of meditation.

The very first Buddhist monastic rule we know of came about when the mother of a monk named Sudinna talked Sudinna into having sex with the wife he had left behind when he'd joined the monastic order. His mother wanted a grandchild to carry on the family. Sudinna figured there was no harm in that, as long as he returned to the order after doing the deed. So he agreed and got his former wife pregnant, then returned to the fold.

When word got back to the Buddha, he wasn't too happy about what had happened. So he made a rule that sexual activity was forbidden for monks, no matter the circumstances.

From then on, whenever there was a problem with someone not acting right, the monks would ask Buddha for his opinion, and he'd let them know what he thought was right. All the Buddha's decisions were committed to memory by the collective and came to form the first set of monastic rules. But after a while it became clear that there were way too many of these rules and that some of them covered very specific instances that weren't applicable to people who weren't directly involved in the controversies that had inspired them. For example, one of those early Buddhist precepts said it was OK to run up a tree if an elephant was chasing you. Which is nice advice, but do we really need a religious precept to cover that situation?

Eventually, centuries later, the folks in the Zen tradition whittled the whole cumbersome lot of rules down to just sixteen far more general precepts that were thought to contain all the important elements of the original big long list. The first three are called the Three Devotions. They go like this:

1. I devote myself to the Buddha.
2. I devote myself to the dharma (Buddhist teachings).
3. I devote myself to the sangha (Buddhist community).

Next up are the Universal Precepts, and they are:

1. I vow to observe the rules of society.
2. I vow to observe the moral rule of the universe.
3. I vow to work for the salvation of all living beings.

The next are called the Ten Grave Precepts, and they are:

1. I vow not to kill.
2. I vow not to steal.
3. I vow not to hold excessive desires.
4. I vow not to lie.
5. I vow to refrain from intoxicants.
6. I vow not to dwell on past mistakes.
7. I vow not to praise self and berate others.
8. I vow not to be covetous.
9. I vow not to give way to anger.
10. I vow not to disparage the Buddha, dharma, and sangha.

I should note here that these are the versions of the precepts that I use. Not everyone agrees on how these sixteen precepts ought to be worded. Within the Zen school, the versions I use are fairly standard. What I call the Universal Precepts, however, are often called the Pure Precepts, and they usually go something along the lines of (1) Avoid all evil, (2) Do only good, and (3) Purify the mind.

Within the Grave Precepts, number three is most often expressed as something like "I vow not to misuse sexuality." I received the more generalized version I use — I vow not to hold excessive desires — from my teacher Gudo Nishijima Roshi, although he didn't just make that up himself. A lot of Zen teachers prefer to make this one a more inclusive vow about having excess desires rather than a specific vow about sex. Even so, it was originally more of a blanket prohibition against having any sex at all. I wrote a whole book about this precept. But don't worry. If you don't want to go out and get that book, I'll talk about this precept some more later on in this book.

Also, Grave Precept number six is usually a vow not to speak of the faults of Buddhist monks or laypeople. The version I use comes from Kobun Chino Roshi, my first teacher's teacher. I like it because it's about not dwelling on the past mistakes of *anyone*, including yourself, and, of course, including people who don't consider themselves Buddhists. The standard version of precept number six has sometimes been used as an excuse to hide the wrongdoings of Buddhist teachers. Which is unfortunate. That's another reason I decided to go with Kobun's version. And by the way, Kobun didn't make that up himself. It's one of several variations you can find out there. We'll be looking at some of them later.

The others on this list are pretty much the same, no matter what Zen temple you choose to take the precepts from.

Here's how Nishijima Roshi explained the reasoning behind having Buddhist precepts in a pamphlet called *The Buddhist Precepts*:

> Master Dogen said that following the precepts is only the custom of Buddhists; it is not their aim. He felt that the precepts were only standards by which to judge our behavior. As such they are very useful to us, but we should be careful not to make them the aim of our life.

The precepts have been described as a fence which sur-
rounds a wide, beautiful meadow. We are the cows in that
meadow. As long as we stay within the fence our life is safe
and serene...; but when we step outside the fence we find
ourselves on shaky ground — we have entered a dangerous
situation and we should return to the pasture. When we do,
our life becomes safe and manageable again.*

Nishijima Roshi also says that "as Buddhists we realize that in
our long life there will be many situations in which we will be unable
to keep the precepts. This should not prevent us from receiving the
precepts. We receive the precepts sincerely, recognizing their value
and purpose in our life.... We are living here and now so we must
find rules which can be used here and now. We must find our precepts at every moment. Reality is changeable so our rules must also
be changeable. True rules must work in the real world. True precepts
are changeable and at the same time unchangeable."

I think that's a great way to put it. The Ten Commandments
are commands from God. If you disobey them, it is said, you will be
punished by God. As far as the precepts go, though, the only thing
that happens when you disobey them is that you put yourself on
shaky ground. If you stumble and fall, that's on you. You're the one
that chose to leave the safety of the meadow.

But Nishijima Roshi acknowledges that it's not always possible
to keep the precepts. And sometimes, even when it is possible to follow them, we break them anyway. So we have to find our precepts at
every moment. If we want to follow them to the best of our ability,
we have to understand the fundamental reasons for the precepts.

On the other hand, one of the most important functions of the
precepts is to get us through times when we don't know what to do.
If you're in doubt about a situation, remember what the precepts say
to do, and do that. This is usually the best option.

---

*   *The Buddhist Precepts* (Tokyo: Windbell, 1992), http://www.zen.ie
    /downloads/Precepts.pdf.

Kobun Chino related the precepts to the practice of zazen, saying:

> You don't use the precepts for accomplishing your own personality, or fulfilling your dream of your highest image. The precepts are the reflected light world of one precept, which is Buddha's mind itself, which is the presence of Buddha. Zazen is the first formulation of the accomplishment of Buddha existing.
>
> The more you sense the rareness and value of your own life, the more you realize that how you use it, how you manifest it, is all your responsibility. We face such a big task that naturally such a person sits down for a while. It's not an intended action, it's a natural action.

There's an interesting conversation in the book *I Am That* by Sri Nisargadatta Maharaj that I think might help explain why ethics are so greatly emphasized in Buddhism, even with its ideas on nonduality. But before I get into the conversation, I'd better explain who Nisargadatta Maharaj was.

For starters, he was not a Buddhist. He was a teacher of the Advaita Vedanta form of Hinduism. Even to call Advaita Vedanta a form of Hinduism is stretching the definition of *Hinduism* almost to the breaking point. It comes out of the Hindu tradition and sometimes makes reference to Hindu concepts. But its relation to Hinduism is a lot like Zen's relation to Buddhism, or the relationship between Christian mysticism and the rest of Christianity, or the relationship between Sufism and Islam. All these traditions take their parent religions in directions that many mainstream followers of those religions sometimes find baffling.

Nisargadatta was an interesting fellow. He ran a little cigarette shop in Mumbai, India, when it was still called Bombay. In his thirties he met a guru who told him that he was not what he thought himself to be and said that he should attend to the feeling of "I am" as a way of discovering his true nature.

This he did for about three years, at which point he had a profound experience of awakening. Afterward, he returned to working at his cigarette shop. But now he also met with spiritual seekers from around the world who came to sit in his tiny apartment above the shop and talk things over. These talks were translated into English and published as the book *I Am That*. Later a number of other books of these dialogues with seekers were compiled. I discovered Nisargadatta Mararaj's work only a few months ago. I think it's pretty great.

In any case, even though the Maharaj wasn't a Buddhist, his teachings are often very similar to the ideas you find in Zen Buddhism. In *I Am That* a student asks the Maharaj about sin and virtue. He wants to know if there can be any such thing as absolute sin and absolute virtue that have nothing to do with social norms and conventions. This is one of the questions that comes up a lot for Buddhists too.

The Maharaj says, "Sin and virtue refer to the person only. Without a sinful or virtuous person what is sin or virtue? At the level of the absolute there are no persons; the ocean of pure awareness is neither virtuous nor sinful. Sin and virtue are invariably relative."

The student then asks, "Can I do away with such unnecessary notions?"

The Maharaj answers, "Not as long as you think yourself to be a person."

That's a great answer. It reminds me a lot of a dialogue between my teacher Gudo Nishijima Roshi and a student, as recorded in his pamphlet about the Buddhist precepts.

Nishijima Roshi says, "A Chinese priest once said, 'No rule is our rule.' This statement expresses the Buddhist attitude precisely. The precepts are valuable to us. They can help us before and after we act, but in the moment of the present we cannot rely on any rule. We must make our decisions directly: at the moment of the present to be without precepts is our precept. No rule is our rule."

Nishijima Roshi's student asks, "So is it important to keep the precepts or not?"

To which Nishijima Roshi replies, "It is important to keep the precepts."

Because we are confused about who and what we are, and confused about our role in the scheme of things, we need some sort of guidance. The precepts can provide that guidance.

Furthermore, it's important not to get overconfident. It's important not to make the mistake of thinking we know better than the folks who came up with the precepts when maybe we really don't. As long as I think myself to be a person, I need to be a decent person. This is important to everyone.

But there is another way to think of things that doesn't involve thinking of myself as a person. In an article in *Dharma Eye*, Shohaku Okumura said:

> The basis of the Bodhisattva precepts is the reality of all beings to which the Buddha awakened. In other words, impermanence, egolessness, and the interdependent origination of all things. When we awaken to the reality that we ourselves and all other things are impermanent and egoless, we see that we cannot cling to anything. We are then released from attachment to ourselves, our possessions, and all other objects. When we awaken to the fact that each thing is interconnected to every other thing… we see that we are supported by everything and live together with everything. We can exist only within relationship with others. That reality is the source of the precepts. When we see the interconnectedness of all beings, we can only try to be helpful to them and avoid being harmful to them.*

We begin to see that acting in unethical ways to others is about the same as punching ourselves in the face.

So that's why we have the precepts. Let's look at them one by one.

-------

* In the February 2004 issue, https://www.sotozen.com/eng/dharma/pdf/13e.pdf.

# 18. THE BUDDHIST CONFESSION BOOTH

I'M GOING TO go through the Buddhist precepts in the order they appear in a ceremony called jukai. *Jukai* means "receiving the precepts." It's a ceremony in which you make a formal and public vow to follow the Buddhist ethical precepts. The ceremony can get pretty fancy, depending on where you do it. Though it doesn't need to be that fancy, and some Zen places do simpler versions. The most important part is the vows, and those don't change very much from place to place. So that's what I'm going to focus on rather than the ceremonies surrounding them.

Making a public vow to do something is powerful. That's why we have weddings, for example. It's why we used to pledge allegiance to the flag in school. Vowing to do something publicly is often a good way to make a person more serious about whatever they've vowed to do or not do. It doesn't always work, of course, but it seems to work for a lot of people.

The jukai ceremony starts with a confession, hence the title of this chapter. Buddhists don't actually use confession booths like the Catholics do. But repentance and confession have been an important part of Buddhism right from the beginning.

This often surprises people who expect that a rational practice like Zen would have done away with anything as primitive and superstitious as confession or repentance. They're sometimes shocked to hear groups of American or European Zen monks chanting in unison, "All my ancient twisted karma; from beginningless greed, hatred, and delusion; born of body, speech, and mind; I now fully avow," followed by a seemingly endless series of bows, and topped off with a group recitation of the Buddhist precepts in call-and-response fashion. But not only is this a time-honored Zen Buddhist tradition, it's one of the very oldest traditions within all Buddhism. As I said earlier, when the first Buddhists gathered to practice as a group, they quickly realized that they needed to set up some rules. Meditating with a group is not like meditating alone. In a way, it's sort of like how sleeping with someone else — and I mean actually *sleeping* — is different from sleeping by yourself. You have to adjust your usual sleeping habits so that both of you can actually get some shut-eye. Things you could do without any problems while sleeping on your own — rolling around, snoring, farting, and suchlike — are often unacceptable when sharing a bed with someone else.

Practicing meditation in a group requires a similar approach. Everybody has to agree on how, when, and where to meditate, or else nobody is gonna be able to get any meditating done. Compromises may have to be made as far as individual lifestyles. A lone meditator might not be as concerned with personal hygiene as he'd have to be when meditating with a group, for instance. People who want to chant and people who want to meditate silently will either have to form separate meditation communities, or they'll need to compromise. A lot of stuff like that has to be worked out.

Because these rules were so important for the maintenance of the group, the early Buddhists developed a ceremony in which they recited the rules together as a group twice a month on the occasion of the full and new moon. This is related to jukai, in that it's basically the same ceremony except practiced by the entire group rather than by an individual with her or his teacher.

Part of the ancient full-moon ceremony involved ritual confessions by monks and nuns who had violated the rules during the two weeks between ceremonies. If they'd violated one of the really important rules, like killing, stealing, lying, or having sex, they might be kicked out of the group altogether. If the violation was less serious, they had to confess in front of at least twenty fellow monastics and might be suspended from attending group activities until the next ceremony, two weeks later. For smaller offenses, they'd have to confess before five other monastics, and the penalty would be lighter. Violations of rules that were considered very minor, such as those dealing with food, often required confession to only one person. And some violations required no confession at all.

The criteria for which rules required which sort of confessions and what sort of penalties varied from group to group and changed over time. In some of the stricter Buddhist communities practices like this are still in place. But you generally won't find European or American Zen groups doing things this way.

None of the Zen groups I've been to in America or Europe required their members to publicly confess to specific violations of the precepts. Although I did hear about an incident at one Zen monastery in California involving a couple of male monks who had been taking sexual advantage of women who came to the monastery during the summer season when it was open to paying guests. After they were caught, these guys were asked to publicly confess what they'd done in front of the other monastics before they were allowed to continue staying at the monastery. But as far as I know, this only happened once.

What happens instead of a public confession of specific violations is that everybody chants a general confession together, the one that goes, "All my ancient twisted karma; from beginningless greed, hatred, and delusion; born of body, speech, and mind; I now fully avow."

As I mentioned earlier, this is usually followed by a lot of bowing, which accompanies a call-and-response recitation of the Buddhist precepts. It's all very stylish and beautiful when it's done right. The person who leads the call-and-response chanting does so in a funny singsong voice with an elongated pause in the middle of certain words. The first time I heard it, I thought the guy chanting either had run out of breath or had forgotten what he was supposed to say next. It's a cute ceremony.

"Confession is good for the soul," they say. In Psalms, King David says, "I acknowledged my sin to you, and my iniquity I have not hidden. I said, 'I will confess my transgressions to the Lord,' and you forgave the iniquity of my sin." In the Gospel of John it says, "If we confess our sins, God is faithful and just to forgive us our sins and to cleanse us from all unrighteousness."

If you believe in a God who can hear your confession and forgive you, this makes perfect sense. But what if you're a Buddhist who doesn't believe in God at all? Or at least not in the kind of God who listens to confessions?

When you're part of a monastic Zen community, the point of confession is to confess to the community. So there's no need to invoke any supernatural deity who also hears your confession. As I said, these days the confession most Buddhists do is ritualized and nonspecific. Still, making a public admission to having done wrong can be meaningful.

According to the *Encyclopedia of Buddhism*, after a while a "form of repentance and confession arose as a way to cope with bad karma (action) and had a very different goal from maintaining monastic purity. These confessions referred to unexpiated guilt resulting from unknown or unremembered past wrongs, and were a plea for forgiveness to alleviate suffering and harm in the present life. The goal was not merely to escape the social penalties of rule breaking, but to avoid the larger karmic consequence of wrongful actions, thoughts, and attitudes."

I don't want to get into the arguments for and against rebirth and reincarnation. But that's part of how this tradition came to be. So let's just take it as a given that most Buddhists in the early days took it for granted that rebirth/reincarnation was a real thing.

If you believe that you have lived many, many lives before this one, then it follows that you've probably done all sorts of bad things in those past lives and that you don't remember that stuff. In fact, many Buddhists believe that the very fact of being born at all is evidence that you've done bad things in other lifetimes and that you need to atone for them in this one. You've also done good things in those past lives, by the way. Maybe lots more good things than bad, in fact. But we don't usually confess those good things.

The idea of repenting for wrongs done in previous lifetimes first appeared in a text called the *Sutra of Golden Light* a few hundred years after the Buddha and his original followers died. Supposedly the writer of this sutra experienced a vision of a shining drum and heard voices saying that this drum had the power to relieve troubles and afflictions. One was supposed to confess these wrongs to a celestial Buddha named Golden Light. Even the act of saying this Buddha's name, the sutra said, had spiritual powers. In case you want to try it out for yourself, his name in Sanskrit is Suvarnaprabhasa. Heck, I said it a few times as I was writing this chapter. What could it hurt?

This was the first time that the purpose of confessing wrongdoings was shifted from the social function it served in the early sangha to something more like a plea for supernatural protection and forgiveness. And not just forgiveness from the folks one might have harmed or offended with one's bad conduct, but from a celestial figure. The chanting of the name Suvarnaprabhasa was supposed to destroy evil actions and their consequences. Repentance became a devotional matter, not just a communal one.

This led to other developments along the same lines. After a while you were supposed to visualize a bodhisattva named Samantabhadra to help you deal with wrongdoings from previous lives in the distant past. You were supposed to consider the functions of your sense organs, which often lead you to do bad things, then you were to recite a vow of repentance.

Attachment to phenomena perceived by the senses was said to be the cause of wrongdoing. Which makes sense. When you try to gain something at the expense of another person, it's because it makes you feel good in some way. Furthermore, attachment to the senses is what supposedly caused you to manifest in this world as a living organism. Meditation, on the other hand, was thought to give you a better understanding of the fundamental emptiness of the senses and their functions and was said to relieve you from attachment to them.

These confessional models eventually came to be streamlined into that chant I told you about, "All my ancient twisted karma," etc. Enlightenment was seen as a way to correct all past, present, and future wrongdoing.

Later on, in Zen Buddhism, it was said that one should recognize the emptiness of doer, deeds, and karma, thereby transcending them all. This led to something they call "formless repentance." Since we are all really emptiness itself, no one gets merit for good deeds or demerits for bad ones. Of course, that's just one side of things. On the other side, here you are living with the consequences of all the bad things you've done in the past. And so you confess and try to do better. You also empathize with the pain of all beings whom your bad actions have affected and do your best to help them out in any way you can.

Just as we are affected by the bad actions of others, our own bad actions affect other people. So we have to be really careful about what we do. And we hope that our own carefulness influences others to be careful as well.

In the book *Embracing Mind*, Kobun Chino talked about the Japanese word *sange*, which is often translated as "repentance" or "confession." In defining the word *sange*, he said that it's "recognition and acknowledgment of one's own personal, individual faults, mistakes, or dissatisfactions. If this occurs in reality, it is a universal occasion because it is revealed in the universal scene. This reverse recognition appears in each individual's life. So this word, 'repentance' is personal, and it is also universal."

We tend to think of repentance or confession as only an individual matter. I did something wrong, and so I repent for it. Why should I repent for someone else's wrongdoing?

But Kobun sees something that most of us miss. Recognition and acknowledgment of our own faults "is revealed in the universal scene," he says. When he says "this reverse recognition" in the next sentence, he means that the universe "out there" recognizes repentance "in here" as the understanding that the individual's ethical actions are a reflection of a universal ethics, which does not belong to the individual and is not the creation of human ideas and thoughts.

In the Zen tradition, when we do the repentance chant, we acknowledge our ancient twisted karma. About this part of the chant Kobun says that it refers to "the mind which is very huge and covers the world. It sees present life from beginningless ancient time, in which we know that we were there because we are here. It knows there are no gaps in life, which burns as a candle. Even if one burns out, the next one goes. In that way, in our life lineage, everyone is carried."

One way to think of what Kobun is saying here is in terms of the common understanding of reincarnation. But reincarnation in Buddhism is a bit different from what a lot of people imagine it to be. Since Buddhists don't believe we have souls, the image of a candle lighting another candle is often used to explain how rebirth happens. If you use one candle to light another, and then you blow out the first candle, is the flame on the second candle the same flame or a new one? It's hard to say.

But Kobun isn't really talking about rebirth. He's talking about the "mind which is very huge and covers the whole world." This is much greater than any concept of individual self — even one that has been reincarnated millions of times. In a sense, because we are not truly separate from anyone or anything in the entire universe, then every wrong ever committed by anyone is a wrong we have committed ourselves.

Now, that's pretty heavy! But I don't think it's necessary for each of us as individuals to take on the guilt and shame of every bad thing anyone, anywhere, at any time has committed. We couldn't handle that, even if we tried.

But we acknowledge that we are connected to all of it. And so, on behalf of all who have ever done wrong, we repent. Many of those who have done wrong would never even consider repenting, so we do it for them. And it counts because we are all intimately connected.

Kobun also said, "The relation between the Precepts and the words of avowal is like a person who is always thankful, and is always able to say, 'I'm sorry.' It is the bright side of things and the shadowy side of things."

It's hard to always be thankful. Often it looks like we don't have much to be thankful for. And yet when we lead our lives with a sense of gratitude toward everything, it feels so much better than resenting what life presents us with. The ability to say "I'm sorry" seems rare sometimes, but we all possess it. When we can repent our wrong-doings, the weight they carry becomes so much less. Thankfulness and repentance are the bright side of things that balances out the shadowy side of things.

In an essay included in *Shobogenzo* called "River Voices and Mountain Forms," Dogen suggests that we should recite the following: "Although our past evil karma has greatly accumulated, indeed being the cause and condition of obstacles in practicing the way, may all buddhas and ancestors who have attained the buddha way be compassionate to us and free us from karmic effects, allowing us to practice the way without hindrance."

For people who got into Zen because they thought it was completely free of anything that sounded the least bit supernatural or anything that was in any way reminiscent of prayer, this probably sounds really wrong. Yet praying for Buddha to relieve us of our past wrongdoings is exactly what Dogen is asking us to do. Weird.

Before this, Dogen tells us that "if the mind or the flesh grow lazy or disbelieving, we should whole-heartedly confess before the Buddha. When we do this, the power and virtue of confessing before the Buddha saves us and makes us pure."

This might seem really out of character since Dogen is often depicted as a person who advocated only self-reliance. Dogen's contemporary, Shinran, who founded the Pure Land School of Buddhism, on the other hand, is known for advocating "other-power" rather than "self-power." He said that people should pray to a Buddha named Amida to be reborn in the Pure Land, where they could find the enlightenment they were unable to achieve in this lifetime. In contrast, Dogen said that ordinary human beings could get enlightened in this very life. Yet here is Dogen advocating that we pray for forgiveness from a supernatural being.

Dogen adds, "In the past, Buddhist ancestors were [the same as] us, and in the future we may become Buddhist ancestors. When we look up at Buddhist ancestors, they are one Buddhist ancestor, and when we reflect upon the establishment of the mind, it is one establishment of the mind." Now, that sounds more like Dogen.

But then Dogen sums it all up by saying, "Quietly, we should master this reasoning. This is direct experience of realizing the state of buddha. When we confess like this, the mystical help of the Buddhist ancestors is invariably present. Disclosing the thoughts in our mind and the form of our body, we should confess to the Buddha. The power of confession causes the roots of wrongdoing to dissolve. This is unadulterated right training; it is right belief in the mind and right belief in the body."

Again we're back to the idea that confessing things to the Buddha, who was long dead even in Dogen's time, will bring us mystical help from the Buddhist ancestors. It sounds very religious and not terribly rational.

But is it irrational to ask for help from the Buddhist ancestors?

Well, I've chanted that chant myself, and I feel like the Buddhist ancestors have helped me a lot. They've helped me by leaving me words that have been important to my life and my practice. They've helped me by teaching their students, who taught their students, and so on until the living teaching reached me.

Dogen says that "in the past, Buddhist ancestors were [the same as] us, and in the future we may become Buddhist ancestors." The Buddhist ancestors were not supernatural beings with amazing powers. They were people like us who did difficult work to learn the deep truth about themselves and the world they lived in. We and the Buddhist ancestors are part of a tradition of human beings who asked impossible questions and made efforts to find inexpressible answers.

Also note that "the same as" is added in brackets to the text. What the original version actually says is that they *are* us. Did Dogen mean to suggest that the ancient worthies were — somehow — us?

Maybe he did. The universe is one thing. Everything on Earth just recycles endlessly. The atoms and molecules that make up your body now were parts of other bodies in the past. Buddhists would also say that the consciousness that you think of as your own is part of a larger consciousness that has been around forever. In this sense, the Buddhist ancestors weren't just the same as us, they were us — they *are* us.

Ultimately we are repenting to ourselves and asking ourselves for help.

# 19. THE THREE DEVOTIONS

IN THE JUKAI ceremony, after you repent, you vow to pay respectful devotion to Buddha, dharma, and sangha. Sometimes, instead of respectful devotion, it's phrased as "I take refuge in Buddha, dharma, and sangha." My teacher called these the Three Devotions, but sometimes they're called the Three Refuges.

In Nishijima Roshi's lineage we say, "I take refuge in Buddha, honored among bipeds. I take refuge in dharma, honored as beyond desire. I take refuge in sangha, honored among communities."

I like that it says "honored among bipeds." It makes it sound like we're trying to take bipedal aliens into account. In fact, it is a legitimate way of translating the original vow as it appears in Chinese. I wonder what those ancient Chinese folks were thinking...

Aliens aside, I have often pondered this idea of "taking refuge." It conjures up the image of someone fleeing for his life from some wild animal or angry band of ruffians intent on his destruction, or maybe hiding from a storm or other natural disaster.

For today's Buddhist monks and nuns in the West, the idea of taking refuge is usually symbolic. That wasn't always the case for monks and nuns in the past. Back in the old days, a lot of people literally took up life at a Buddhist temple to take refuge.

Societies weren't as law-abiding in the past as they are today. Life could be much more dangerous. In many societies in Asia, monks and nuns were considered a special class. They weren't bound by a lot of the duties and obligations that others were. In medieval

Japanese society, for example, monks and nuns were not required to abide by the strict caste system that existed in Japan at that time. A monk was a person of no status in ancient Japan, which was often far better than being a person of low status. This is why pretending to be a monk or nun when you really weren't was very dangerous in medieval Japan. There were laws that said if a monk was caught breaking his vows he could be severely punished, or even executed.

Lots of people I talk to have trouble with the idea of making a vow to take refuge in Buddha, dharma, and sangha. For one thing, those are three foreign words. Most of the folks I talk to don't have a clear understanding of what they're taking refuge in. So let me try to tell you what taking refuge in Buddha, dharma, and sangha means to me.

What I really am is not this body that is typing these words or this mind that is thinking about what word to type next. By doing loads of zazen, I have learned this very clearly. Yet the habit of believing that I am this body and this mind is deep. I slip back into it all the time. It's a way of understanding things that is reinforced by nearly everyone I meet; it's the basis of nearly every book I read, every TV show or movie I watch, every newspaper article, every YouTube video ... the list goes on and on.

I live most of my life surrounded mainly by people who never question whether they are their body and their mind. To them it's an undeniable fact. It doesn't even occur to them that it could be otherwise. If they encounter someone who tells them they are not their body or their mind, they generally think that person is crazy.

Even though I've been doing Zen practice for literally most of my life, and even though I've had some experiences around this practice that have confirmed for me that its philosophy is true, it's difficult — perhaps even impossible — to avoid falling back into old habits of thought and behavior. When that happens, my old programming reasserts itself and I fall into depression and despair, or I pursue shallow amusements that may relieve my depression for a little while but only end up reinforcing it in the long run.

I've found three things that always help me work on this problem. They don't necessarily solve it once and for all. But they help a lot. The first is that somehow I had the great good fortune of meeting someone I could trust who showed me there was a different way of understanding things and that a different way of living was possible. And then I met another one of these rare people! And they both showed me a practice that could help me understand this other way of living.

Just being around Tim McCarthy or Nishijima Roshi felt different from being around anyone else. Of course, everyone's different. But there was something extraordinary about those two that I never felt in anyone else. Any conversation I ever had with Tim or with Nishijima Roshi was useful, even if it was a conversation about nothing of any importance.

The second thing that has helped me is reading and listening to good teachings. It doesn't matter what tradition they come from, but having established myself in a particular tradition — Soto-style Zen Buddhism — I find it useful to make that my main source. It's not my only source, mind you. But it's the one I always come back to. I don't always understand the things I read, but reading them seems to help reorient my mind in a different direction. I may not *be* the mind, but reorienting the mind can be useful.

Along with this, I've also found that it helps my practice to be as ethical as possible, which is a huge part of what I get from these books that I've read and the teachers that I've spoken with. I try to be kind and honest and helpful whenever I can. It doesn't always have to be any grand gesture or huge sacrifice. As Dogen says, even one added speck of good makes a mountain of goodness that much bigger.

The third thing that has helped me is to associate with people who see things from a truer perspective. I recognized that my teachers did this. Being near them was extraordinarily helpful, but I couldn't just hang around them all the time. Luckily, I found a few other people who, like me, questioned the prevailing understanding of things that most people believe in.

Associating with others who question the common view of life, the universe, and everything has always been useful to me. They don't have to be Fully Awakened Masters. They can just be ordinary people who are engaged in a practice of trying to fully embrace the truth.

I wouldn't call all these people "friends." Not exactly. Often they're people I see only in the context of Zen practice, at a retreat or temple or something. In a way, they're more like coworkers than friends. We're friendly with each other, and we understand that we are working together. We don't necessarily have to hang out at each other's houses or go to Cedar Point amusement park together.

I originally wrote the material you just read as part of something completely different, having nothing to do with the subject of this chapter. It was going to be part of a blog, I think. But after writing it, I realized that another way of saying what I said above is that I revere Buddha, dharma, and sangha.

That's how you'd say it in the traditional Buddhist way. Buddha does not have to mean the historical Buddha as represented in the canonized scriptures. The Buddha can be any person who helps you realize the truth. The dharma also doesn't need to be the approved scriptures of Buddhism. It can be any teaching that points in the direction of reality. And the sangha doesn't always have to be a group that is organized around Buddhism and has the word *sangha* in their official name. It can just be friends or acquaintances who recognize that there is a truth beyond the conventional understanding of how things are. In other words, they are people who have renounced greed, hatred, and delusion. Or at least they're trying to. Even if they sometimes regress a little and lapse into bad behavior, as long as they are headed in the right direction and are able to recognize when they haven't acted correctly, they can be good friends or acquaintances to associate with. They can be a sangha.

So Buddha, dharma, and sangha don't have to fit some narrow definition of those terms. Anyone can be a teacher, the teachings come in a wide variety, and the people who follow those teachings are whoever they happen to be. When I vow to pay respectful devotion to Buddha, dharma, and sangha, I'm just vowing to respect those people and teachings that help me get clear about who and what I really am.

As for "taking refuge," I take that to mean that these are the things I turn to to stay on track. I don't regard them as infallible or absolute. They are just the things I depend on. It's good to have a community, a set of teachings, and a teacher.

People often ask me how to find a Zen teacher and a group to practice with. I never quite know how to answer because I found my two main Zen teachers almost by accident. As I already said, I was not looking for a Zen teacher when I found my first teacher, Tim, when I signed up for his class at Kent State. I found my second Zen teacher, Gudo Nishijima, in a newspaper ad.

It often seems that many of the people who ask me how to find a teacher and a group fall into two broad categories: those who haven't really looked very hard, and those who've looked too hard. If you're serious about finding a teacher, you might have to do some work looking for one. A combination of dumb luck and possibly karma worked for me and made it easy. Your luck/karma might be different.

My teachers happened to be very conveniently located. Yours might not. You may have to actually go somewhere. I've found that some of the people I've exchanged emails with have very unrealistic expectations in this regard. More than once I've had someone moan to me that the nearest teacher to them is an hour's drive away. One guy even said the nearest teacher took forty whole minutes to get to.

It's hard for me to muster a whole lot of sympathy for those people. Because, while Tim lived about a minute and half's walk from me, those weekly meetings in Tokyo with Nishijima Roshi took about an hour and a half to get to (on a good day!) and required a long walk, plus two changes of train lines. An hour or so to get to see a Zen teacher sounds totally sweet.

Maybe the age of the internet has made some people demand

absolute convenience. I don't really know. But Amazon does not deliver everything right to your doorstep. There's value in working for things that are important.

Even if your nearest teacher is two hours away or four hours or six, that might just be how it goes. Those ancient teachers and students you read about in stories — some of them met maybe once or twice in their entire lives. That's how it was before there were trains, planes, and automobiles. They didn't always all live together in one house like the Monkees. So if it turns out you can meet your teacher only once a month or twice a year or whatever, that's no reason to give up. Maybe that's just how it's gotta be.

As for the people who look too hard, what I mean is that some of the folks who ask me how to find a teacher seem like maybe they're being a little too picky. They tell me stories about how they've gone to a dozen meditation centers and none of them seemed quite right.

Now, maybe some of these centers really are pretty dodgy. Ever since meditation became the "it" thing to do among the rich and privileged, a lot of centers have sprung up that, frankly, don't really have much to offer. Some are cults. Some are just clueless. Some are set up by entrepreneurs who see a market and assume that teaching meditation must be pretty easy. If you find yourself in one of those kinds of places, just stop going.

On the other hand, looking for the perfect match is a losing strategy. You'll never find it. I never have. As I've said, I disliked Nishijima Roshi pretty strongly when I first started going to his talks. I mainly went because the time was convenient. The only places in Tokyo that I'd found before I found his place had their meditation meetings at, like, six in the morning on Wednesdays and things like that. I kept going to Nishijima's classes, thinking that eventually I'd manage to find something better. It took me maybe two or three years to finally recognize that he had been my real teacher all along.

## 20. THE UNIVERSAL PRECEPTS

AFTER YOU TAKE the Three Devotions in the precepts-receiving ceremony, you take the three Universal Precepts, sometimes referred to as the Pure Precepts. As I said, the Universal Precepts, in my teacher's tradition, are:

1. I vow to observe the rules of society.
2. I vow to observe the moral rule of the universe.
3. I vow to work for the salvation of all living beings.

In his pamphlet about the Buddhist precepts, Nishijima Roshi explained the Universal Precepts as follows:

> The first is the observance of rules. Every society has its rules. If we fail to follow the rules of our society our life will be disturbed, so as Buddhists we should observe the rules of society.
>
> The second universal precept is called observance of the moral rule of the Universe. To observe the rule of the Universe is to act appropriately in all situations. It is to act correctly — to act right. Thus observance of the rule of the Universe can be called the observance of morality. There are many social rules, but we need to follow a morality which transcends the social situation. We need to follow a morality based on the order of the Universe itself.
>
> The salvation of all living beings is the third universal

precept. Buddhism teaches us that we are part of the Universe. We are not isolated entities, but elements of a system — a grand system which is reflected in every small part: in every being. So all beings in the Universe share a quality or essence which cannot be named or described; it is an ineffable something — it is the basis of life itself. So if we are to express our true nature as human beings, it is natural for us to care for that which we have in common with all living beings. It is natural for us to want to save other living beings.

Nishijima Roshi's version is a bit different from some other versions of the Universal Precepts, which are often expressed as something more like: (1) Refrain from all evil, (2) Practice only good, and (3) Actualize good for others.

The one that really bugs certain people whenever I talk about Nishijima Roshi's version of the Universal Precepts is the first one, "I vow to observe the rules of society."

That sounds pretty different from "I vow to refrain from all evil," I'll grant you. But It's not far off from some of the variations out there. For example, the San Francisco Zen Center's version of that one is "I vow to embrace and sustain right conduct," and an older version they used to use went, "I vow to embrace and sustain forms and ceremonies."

Nishijima Roshi's version derives from the way he translated the Chinese characters into English. If you look at the Chinese characters used to express this precept, it means something like "I vow to follow the rules." It originally meant that you vowed to follow the monastic regulations. This is still what it means if you take the precepts as a prelude to entering a monastery. Nishijima Roshi was trying to take a precept that originally meant following monastic regulations and make it applicable to people who were not going to join a monastery. Thus his version became "observe the rules of society."

The reason it's often given as "refrain from all evil" probably also follows from the idea of making a precept about obeying monastic rules more universally applicable. Many Zen groups in the West choose a variation on "refrain from all evil" as their translation because the precept is thought to derive from an old saying by Gautama Buddha that went, "Avoid all evil, practice all good, this is the teaching of all Buddhas."

Other translations of the first Universal Precept include, "I vow not to commit evil" (Great Vow Zen Center), "I vow to refrain from all action that creates attachments" (Dainin Katagiri), "I vow to refrain from all action that is rooted in ignorance" (Sojun Mel Weitsman), "The precept of restraint and religious observances" (Cheri Huber), and "Abstain from unwholesomeness" (Tozen Akiyama).

I think the reason Nishijima Roshi's choice of "follow the rules of society" bothers some people is that they interpret it as meaning something like "follow every law and custom of the nation you live in, no matter what it is." Then they jump to examples of societies where things have gone very wrong ethically — Nazi Germany mostly, but sometimes Imperial Japan — and imagine that the precept is saying that if everyone else is a Nazi you should be a Nazi too. But that is not at all what the precept is saying. I would have thought that would be obvious, but I've had enough unpleasant discussions around this precept to know otherwise.

I read the Nishijima Roshi version as something more along the lines of "observe the rules of polite society" or maybe "obey social norms." In other words, be a decent, law-abiding person. Don't be a jerk. Or, if you want, refrain from all evil.

"Follow the rules of society" does not necessarily mean you have to observe every law and custom of the place you live in even if those laws and customs are clearly in violation of the version of the precept that says "refrain from all evil." But I think that, in most cases, you ought to obey the law.

The second Universal Precept is often phrased as "embrace and sustain every good." The reference to the "moral rule of the universe" is Nishijima Roshi's preferred wording. He often talked about the moral rule of the universe.

The idea that ethical behavior is the moral rule of the universe might be difficult to accept. It seems as though lots of people behave unethically and get away with it. They often even profit from it. It's impossible to prove this is not the case, so I won't even try. But I will say that I don't believe anyone ever really profits from unethical behavior.

I say this because when I observe my own life, I can see very clearly that I have never benefited from unethical behavior. Not even once. Whatever benefit I might seem to have derived from acting unethically was always offset by other effects of that behavior, such as feelings of shame and guilt or the fear of being caught. It seems that somehow the universe always finds a way to restore balance. If this is the way it always works for me, it's hard for me to believe it doesn't work the same way for everyone else.

Some alternate translations of the second Universal Precept include, "The precept of obedience to all good laws" (Cheri Huber), "I vow to cultivate goodness" (Great Vow Zen Monastery), "I vow to make every effort to live awake and in the truth" (Dainin Katagiri), and "Do what is wholesome" (Tozen Akiyama).

Let's move on to the last of the Universal Precepts. At least Nishijima Roshi's version of the third one — I vow to work for the salvation of all living beings — is pretty standard. The idea that we should work for the salvation of all living beings is part of what's called the Bodhisattva Vow, which goes, "Beings are numberless, I vow to save them."

Of course, the whole idea of saving all living beings sounds pretty daunting. My friend Rob rephrased it in a way I really like — and that I've used in other books — which is, "I vow to save all beings... from myself."

This brings the vow into line with the other two Universal Precepts. You may not be able to be like Superman and save everyone, but you can at least not cause them any more trouble than is absolutely necessary. Another good rewording of this one comes from Kosho Uchiyama Roshi, who put it, "Beings are numberless, I vow to be of benefit to all of them."

Some alternate translations of the third Universal Precept include, "Actualizing good for others" (John Daido Loori), "I vow to help others" (Great Vow Zen Monastery), "I vow to live to benefit all beings" (Dainin Katagiri), and "With purity of heart, I vow to live and be lived for the benefit of all beings" (Shunryu Suzuki).

The Universal Precepts derive from a verse in the Dhammapada, which is one of the oldest compilations of the sayings of Gautama Buddha. In verse 158 the Buddha says, "Avoid all evil, practice all good, this is the teaching of all Buddhas." In the chant that Zen Buddhists recite before eating meals during retreats, there's another variation of the Universal Precepts. At one point in the meal ritual everybody holds up their bowls and chants, "The first portion is to end all evil, the second portion is to cultivate all good, the third portion is to free all beings. May we all realize the Buddha Way."

About the Universal Precepts, Kobun Chino Roshi said, "These three [precepts] are a precise description of the contents of awakening that was contained in Buddha's mind." So it's not that the precepts are advice on how to act in order to become enlightened. They are the content of enlightenment and the expression of enlightenment.

Nishijima Roshi often said that following the precepts was a way of doing what we really want to do. I used to think he was crazy for saying that. Eventually I realized he was right. What I most truly want to do is what is most beneficial to everyone. It took me a few years to understand that, though.

The next ten precepts are the ones that people like to discuss at length. So I'll go through them one by one.

## 21. I VOW NOT TO KILL

NOW WE COME to what are often called the Ten Grave Precepts. These precepts are also known as the Prohibitory Precepts because they're a list of things you shouldn't do. The first one is "I vow not to kill."

Bodhidharma supposedly had his own version of the Ten Grave Precepts. As you'll recall from an earlier chapter, Bodhidharma is the semilegendary guy who brought Zen to China from India in the fifth or sixth century CE. He supposedly rephrased the first Grave Precept this way: "Self-nature is mysteriously profound. In the midst of eternal dharma, not to give rise to the view of stopping and extinction is called the 'No Killing Life Precept.'"

Kobun Chino Roshi was fond of the Bodhidharma's version of the precepts. I heard these precepts from Tim McCarthy during that class at Kent State. They made a big impression on me. They're not the most widely taught version of the precepts, but I think they're really interesting.

The reason I said that Bodhidharma "supposedly" had his own version of the precepts is that, although attributed to Bodhidharma, the so-called Bodhidharma One-Mind Precepts were probably not composed by Bodhidharma. The earliest versions we have come from the fifteenth century, and although written in Chinese, they may very well have originated in Japan. It's quite possible that they were part of the Japanese Tendai sect of Buddhism's attempt to establish their own version of the Buddhist precepts. The Tendai sect is really into esoteric, mystical-sounding stuff. Lots of Zen folks also make use of the Bodhidharma One-Mind Precepts, although Dogen never mentioned them in his writings.

So what does the precept about not killing mean? And what does the other version of it as interpreted by someone who probably wasn't Bodhidharma mean? I'm glad you asked!

On the one hand, this precept in its original form sounds like the biblical commandment "Thou shalt not kill." Most Christians understand that as meaning "Thou shalt not kill other people." I once heard a guy from the Hare Krishna movement say the biblical commandment can't possibly mean just not to kill people. He said that God knows there is a specific word for killing people, and that word is *murder*. According to the Hare Krishna guy, if God had meant the commandment to be limited to human beings, it would have been "Thou shalt not murder." Therefore, according to the Hare Krishna guy, the commandment meant that good Christians and Jews ought to be vegetarians.

There is a problem with the idea that "Thou shalt not kill" means you shouldn't kill anything at all ever and that being a vegetarian or a vegan is the way to accomplish this. Even the strictest vegetarian or vegan in the world ends up engaging in some form of killing in order to stay alive. All sorts of little creatures are plowed under whenever crops are harvested, blood is often used in fertilizer, plants are killed when we eat them, and so on.

All life forms that I know of depend on the death of other life forms in order to survive. Even plants that are nourished by sunlight are also nourished by minerals and other elements in the ground that come from the decaying corpses of other plants, as well as insects and animals. And certainly no human being can survive very long without taking the life of something.

In the strictest sense you can't uphold this precept unless you kill yourself, which is still killing, so even that's not an option. In a way, all of the Grave Precepts are asking you to vow to do something you can't possibly do. That's where Bodhidharma's One-Mind Precepts come in. But before we get into those in detail, I'd like to show you a few different ways various English-speaking Zen groups have translated the original version of this first precept.

Some of these translations are really elaborate. The Appleton Zen Center's version goes, "I respect all sentient and insentient beings and always act with compassion towards them. In order to live, it is necessary for me to take life. I do so with reverence for the life taken. In gratitude, I do not take my own life for granted." Diane Eshin Rizzetto of the Bay Zen Center in Oakland, California, has a version that goes, "I take up the way of supporting life. I resolve to look squarely and with an open heart at the rage, fear, and sense of separateness that feed my impulses to harm others. Remembering that my life on earth must cause the death or suffering of many fellow creatures, I resolve with gratitude to abstain from cruelty and relieve the suffering that I can."

Other versions are briefer. Here are a few: "Affirm life, do not kill" (John Daido Loori), "Abstinence from willful killing" (Akiyama Roshi), "I vow not to kill but to cherish all life" (Great Vow Zen Center), and "A disciple of the Buddha abstains from willful taking of lives" (Shunryu Suzuki).

The original precept in Chinese is just four characters that, if translated literally, would come out something like "Not kill life vow."

One of the earliest documents to spell out what this precept means was the Brahmajala Sutra, composed in China in the fifth century. That sutra defines the first precept this way: "A disciple of the Buddha shall not himself kill, encourage others to kill, kill by expedient means, praise killing, rejoice at witnessing killing, or kill through incantation or deviant mantras. He must not create the causes, conditions, methods, or karma of killing, and shall not intentionally kill any living creature. As a Buddha's disciple, he ought to nurture a mind of compassion and filial piety, always devising expedient means to rescue and protect all beings. If instead, he fails to restrain himself and kills sentient beings without mercy, he commits a major offense."

Another even earlier document, the Abhisanda Sutta, explains the vow of not killing as a kind of gift to the world. It says, "There is the case where a disciple of the noble ones, abandoning the taking of life, abstains from taking life. In doing so, he gives freedom from danger, animosity, and oppression to limitless numbers of beings. In giving freedom from danger, animosity, and oppression to limitless numbers of beings, he gains a share in limitless freedom from danger, freedom from animosity, and freedom from oppression. This is the first gift."

Nishijima Roshi explained this precept, saying, "We all have our life, the Universe is life itself. We should not destroy that of which we are a part. We should not destroy life in vain."

In his "Commentary on the Precepts," Dogen says, "Life is non-killing. The seed of the Buddha grows continuously. Maintain the wisdom-life of the Buddha and do not kill life."

As we shall see with the rest of the precepts, it's up to the person who receives them to decide what they mean. The more elaborate translations of this and the other precepts we'll be looking at seem to be imposing the teacher's understanding of the precepts on those who receive them. Which is not necessarily a terrible thing. That's part of their traditions. But I tend to prefer the shorter, more open-ended versions.

Having said that, I pretty much agree with most of the longer, more elaborate versions of this precept. I think the precept means that we have to respect life and avoid killing whenever possible. I'm one of those people who tries to let flies out of the house and leaves spiders alone when I see them in the bathroom. On the other hand, I have had places I've lived in fumigated for roaches. And I light mosquito coils when we're all getting bitten. I feel bad for doing this, but sometimes such actions are necessary.

I've been a vegetarian since I was about eighteen years old. But

I'm not a vegan. So there's that too. I got into vegetarianism before I got into Buddhism, by the way. I had a friend in junior high school who was a vegetarian, long before it was hip to be one. He explained to me why he didn't eat animals, and I thought it was a great idea. I couldn't really get my mom into cooking me vegetarian food as well as the usual dinner for everyone else, and I was too lazy to cook for myself. But as soon as I started living on my own I became a vegetarian.

I'm not trying to impress you or justify anything. I'm just letting you know how I deal with the precept on a personal level. Buddhists are all over the map with this precept. Tibetan Buddhists eat meat, for example. The climate in Tibet makes it hard to grow vegetables, so that was a compromise they made. In Japan, some Buddhists eat meat and some don't.

In the earliest days, Indian Buddhists had been mostly vegetarians, as was the established custom in the Hindu religion. But the Buddhist monks lived by begging for food. The early monks asked the Buddha what to do if someone put meat in their begging bowls. He told them that as long as they had no reason to believe the animal had been killed specifically for them, they should accept the offering with gratitude and eat it. As I said, you can't live a life that's perfectly free of killing. But you can take some steps to try to minimize the amount of lives you take. And I think that's worth doing.

But let's put aside the arguments about diet and look into that other version of the precept I told you about right at the beginning of this chapter, the one attributed to Bodhidharma. To refresh your memory, it goes, "Self-nature is mysteriously profound. In the midst of eternal dharma, not to give rise to the view of stopping and extinction is called the 'No Killing Life Precept.'"

Each of the Bodhidharma One-Mind Precepts begins with the statement "Self-nature is mysteriously profound." Whoever wrote these precepts wanted to emphasize this point. To me this means that we don't really understand exactly what we are, and we probably never can. So we do our best within what we are able to understand while accepting that we are never going to comprehend the final answer. Plus, remember that when Buddhists say "self" they mean everybody and everything, not just the individual self.

"In the midst of eternal dharma" is what it says next. The author is pointing out the eternal nature of the universe. Everything we encounter and everything that we are has been around literally forever and will stick around forever. The elements of our bodies were present at the moment of the big bang. And if there was a time before the big bang, they were present then too. This is true even if they were nothingness, as some people now suggest. Nothingness became all this, and now here it is. No matter what happens to all this stuff in the far, far future, it's still going to be around in some form, forever and ever.

Buddhists would say that what we call our "consciousness" or "mind" was also part of everything from the beginning of time too. You can choose to accept that or not.

Eternity is also now. The present moment is eternal. It is always now, no matter when it is. It was now when the last tyrannosaurus keeled over, it's now right now, and a bazillion years from now it will still be now.

In the midst of this eternal dharma, the precept says, we uphold the precept of "not killing life" by not giving rise to the view of stopping or extinction.

This could be taken a lot of ways. For example, you could read it as saying that there is no such thing as death, so you might as well not worry about following the precept of not killing things. But that's clearly not what it means. You have to consider the context. The Bodhidharma One-Mind Precepts come out of a tradition that already had under its belt a thousand years of observing the standard version of the precept. In no way is this version intended to overturn or replace the original one. It's intended to expand the meaning of it.

In *Each Moment Is the Universe*, Dainin Katagiri explains his understanding of the first precept in a way that seems influenced by the Bodhidharma One-Mind Precepts. He uses the example of an inanimate object, in this case, a table:

> The Buddhist precept that tells you not to kill doesn't just mean not to physically kill people or animals. If you deeply understand the meaning of the precept of not killing life, you know that not killing the life of the table means not handling the table according to an egoistic view that separates you from the table. Not killing life means to see the table as it really is and handle the table as a manifestation of eternal time, where there is no gap between subject and object. This is to animate the life of the table as Buddha.
>
> How can you do this? As much as possible, try to handle the table as something more than an object in the realm of twelve hours. Handle the table wholeheartedly, with compassion and kindness. At that time practice comes up very naturally, just like water from an underground spring, and this practice deepens and develops your life.

Commenting on this precept, Kobun Chino Roshi takes things even further. He says:

> One hundred thousand million lives came into our life, which is each of these dynamic lives, and we are fulfilling their wish of who they wanted to be. That is the way to live the Precepts. We listen to all existences, how every being wanted to be, not only what we ate, what we took, but all existences.
>
> Continuous existence is in each moment of our life. Whether you are being aware of your deeds or not it is happening in that way. It is like eating a meal, our body is big and the food is little, so we say, "I took this life." But when you compare the amount of food you took and the amount of energy of your life, they are actually the same.

This is a very interesting way to keep one moment of the universe. All beings offer their life for it and return to nothing. All beings return to nothing, offering their lives and making one moment possible. This is how we humans live, how vegetables live and die.... The question of how you are going to live is answered by expressing, not just understanding, what life is all about.

The Bodhidharma One-Mind Precepts ask us "not to give rise to the view of stopping and extinction." This is what Kobun is doing here. He acknowledges that things live and die, and yet he sees how life itself is continuously moving from place to place. Since we are fated to have to take the lives of other beings in order to continue our own existence, we must make an effort to be worthy of their sacrifices. Even if it is just the sacrifice of the life of a head of lettuce, that's still important.

We should continually ask ourselves if we are doing all we can to be worthy recipients of the lives that are sacrificed so that we can continue to live. That's how we uphold the impossible-to-uphold precept that says "I vow not to kill."

# 22. I VOW NOT TO STEAL

THE SECOND GRAVE Precept is usually given as "I vow not to steal."
The Bodhidharma One-Mind Precepts version of this precept goes,
"Self-nature is mysteriously profound. In the dharma in which nothing can be attained, not to give rise to the mind of attaining is called
the Precept of 'No stealing or robbing.'"

Like the vow not to kill, this precept also matches one of the
Ten Commandments, "Thou shalt not steal." It's pretty much a
no-brainer that stealing is bad.

As I said, the original version of the Buddhist precepts came
about when the first group of followers of the Buddha began living
together. People being what they are, I'm sure there were incidents
of monks taking stuff from each other. And so a rule about stealing
had to be made.

For the early monks, stealing was one of four major offenses that
could get you kicked out of the group. As you know, the others were
sexual intercourse, murder, and making false claims with regard to
one's spiritual attainment. Later on other Buddhist groups decided
that there were ten major offenses. These were killing, stealing,
engaging in sexual conduct, lying, buying and selling intoxicants,
finding fault with Buddhist laypeople or monks/nuns, praising oneself while putting down someone else, being greedy, getting angry
and refusing an apology from another, and slandering the Three
Treasures. These were refined to become the Ten Grave Precepts
that we're looking at in this section of the book.

The Brahmajala Sutra defines the precept against stealing as follows:

> A disciple of the Buddha must not himself steal or encourage others to steal, steal by expedient means, or steal by means of incantation or deviant mantras. He should not create the causes, conditions, methods, or karma of stealing. No valuables or possessions, even those belonging to ghosts and spirits or thieves and robbers, be they as small as a needle or blade of grass, may be stolen. As a Buddha's disciple, one ought to have a mind of mercy, compassion, and filial piety — always helping people earn merits and achieve happiness. If instead, one steals the possessions of others, one commits a major offense.

Some contemporary English-language versions of the second Grave Precept include, "I resolve not to steal, but to honor the gift not yet given" (Mel Weitsman, Oakland Zen Center); "I take up the way of taking only what is freely given and giving freely of all that I can. At times when I feel I am entitled to what others want, need, or own, I resolve to hold this hard ball of entitlement, of separation, to feel its texture, and to wait until its nature is clear" (Diane Eshin Rizzetto); and "Act Generously — I act with generosity and open-handedness. I receive only things that are freely given to me. I remember that clinging and attachment are the root of suffering" (Appleton Zen Center). Many contemporary versions of the precept define stealing as "taking what is not given."

Gudo Nishijima Roshi explained this precept by saying, "We have our own place in the world; our own position and property. We should not invade another's position. We should not steal."

But perhaps there's more to this precept than simply not taking stuff from other people. In his "Commentary on the Precepts," Dogen says, "The mind and the externals are just as thus. The gate of liberation has opened."

Commenting on Dogen's definition, in *Embracing Mind* Kobun Chino says, "To understand the broader meaning of this Precept, think about your existence before you existed, and after you will finish existing. In between, we have this issue of 'no stealing.' The subject opens up, in a very big way, the question of whether our practice and behavior is encouraging life as one identity. In other words, do we 'possess'?"

Kobun also says, "The basic recognition of this Precept contains the dilemma of possessing everything and anything, and possessing nothing. This is the human contradiction. The more wealth you have, the more effort you need to take care of it. On the other hand, the fewer possessions you have, the more you are free."

We never really own anything. Not even ourselves. What we take ourselves to be is actually the possession of the universe. Anything we could steal is something we already own.

Kobun says:

The ordinary meaning of stealing is to take something from others, make another's thing your own. Together with this meaning, we can observe what the whole thing is about. Something happened, and we appeared on this earth as a very small drop of life, which grew up as matter. A little circle of energy appeared in your mother's circle of energy, and when the time came, it started to separate. It looks like two, but, as you know, mother and child cannot be separated. Even if the mother passes away, that mother is the mother of this child, always. Yet we think this human being is an individual existence. Because this human shape is dynamic, and moves among many things, we do not question that it has a separate existence.

And yet that sense of separation is ultimately an illusion. We are no more an independent being now than we were when we were in the womb. It just seems that way.

In the legal sense, of course, stealing is forbidden. You can't just walk into my apartment, grab my bass, and say, "Everything belongs to the universe! See ya later!"

Buddhists don't deny this. Even in training temples, where pretty much everything is owned communally, individual monks are allowed to have a small number of personal items that other monks aren't allowed to take from them. And if you were to walk into a Zen temple in Japan and try to make off with the Buddha statues, they'd call the cops. When we discuss the wider meaning of whether one can be said to own or possess anything, we acknowledge the conventional sense of ownership as a given. Even so, we ought to look closely at the deeper meaning of this precept.

"Self-nature is mysteriously profound," said whoever claimed to be Bodhidharma when composing the One-Mind Precepts. "Unattainable dharma. Not to raise the mind of attainability is called 'No stealing or robbing.'"

If you look at it that way, then the subject of this precept isn't stealing. It's unattainability. In the Heart Sutra it says, "With nothing to attain the mind is no hindrance. Without hindrance there are no fears. Far beyond all inverted views one realizes Nirvana."

We go through our whole lives trying to attain things. We strive for money, for status, for true love, for exciting experiences, and for all sorts of other things, viewing them as objects that we can acquire and then possess. This creates fear. On the most basic level, we fear that we might not get the essential things we need to survive, like food, water, or shelter. But even when the basics are taken care of, we're still scared. Maybe my investments won't work out. Maybe I won't get that promotion. Maybe she'll say no.

But perhaps the Heart Sutra is right. Maybe if we were able to completely give up even the idea of being able to attain anything, we would have nothing to fear. That, of course, is easier said than done.

Our usual understanding of who and what we are makes it seem like we can attain things. We are used to the idea that we can enhance ourselves by attaining material things like cars, or money, or a signed copy of the first Ramones album or by attaining immaterial things like status, or knowledge, or power, or even spiritual things like mindfulness, or unsurpassed complete perfect enlightenment.

This is based on the idea that there is a fundamentally unchanging "me" who at one time lacks the thing in question and then later gains that thing. Our whole lives we've been told that this is how it works. The structure of our thinking has been ordered by language to picture things in these terms. It may, in fact, be impossible not to think in terms of attainment.

The Bodhidharma One-Mind Precepts version of this precept asks us not to see the precept just as an admonition not to run off with our neighbor's power drill. It asks us to look into the very nature of the concept of attainment. It asks us to look into who and what we really are and question whether it is even possible to attain anything — including enlightenment.

When I have seriously looked into this question, I've seen that it is never possible to attain anything at all. This is why I do the practice of *shikantaza*, which is sitting still for the sake of sitting still, with nothing to attain. When we do nothing but practice sitting still for a certain amount of time each day, it becomes clear that past and future are an illusion. There is no past. There is no future. There is only this moment. This one tiny moment. That's all there is.

And in this moment what can you attain? You have what you have right now. Maybe in the future you'll get something. But that's not now.

Attainment always happens in the future or in the past. It's always a matter of comparing the state at one moment to the state at another moment. But it makes no sense to compare one moment to any other moment. Every moment is complete unto itself. It contains what it contains and lacks what it lacks. Or perhaps it lacks nothing because each moment is the entire universe.

Given that, why would anyone even think about stealing or even attaining anything?

## 23. I VOW NOT TO HOLD EXCESSIVE DESIRES

THERE'S A PASSAGE from Nisargadatta Maharaj's book *I Am That* that I found to be extremely helpful when it comes to the matter of desires:

> Merely assuaging fears and satisfying desires will not remove this sense of emptiness you are trying to escape from; only self-knowledge can help you. By "self-knowledge" I mean full knowledge of what you are not. Such knowledge [of what you are not] is attainable and final, but to discover what you are there can be no end. The more you discover, the more there remains to discover.... Your desire just happens to you, along with its fulfillment or nonfulfillment. You can change neither. You may believe that you exert yourself, strive, and struggle. Again, it all merely happens, including the fruits of the work. Nothing is by you or for you. All is in the picture exposed on the cinema screen; nothing is in the light, including what you take yourself to be, the person. You are the light only.

The part about a picture on a cinema screen is a metaphor that Nisargadatta used a lot. He said that the activities of our lives are like a movie on a screen. We think that we are the characters in the movie. But actually we are more like the light of the projector. Or perhaps not even that.

None of our desires is really our own possession or even our own creation.

The Bodhidharma One-Mind Precepts version of the precept about not holding excessive desires is, "Self-nature is mysteriously profound. In the truth in which there is nothing to grasp, not to give birth to attaching to loving is called the Precept of 'no desiring,' 'no wrong, no scattered desiring.'"

The translation of the precept I'm using — "I vow not to hold excessive desires" — is the one my teacher Gudo Nishijima Roshi settled on, although for a time he gave this precept as "I vow not to lust." Kobun Chino gave this precept as "No attaching to fulfillment."

The more common version of this precept is "I vow not to misuse sex." A variation of this precept was, apparently, the very first Buddhist precept, and it was originally a vow of strict celibacy. Earlier I mentioned the story behind the original version of this precept, the one about the monk whose wife, whom he'd left to join the sangha of celibate monks, begged him to give her a child, so he did it with her one last time. As Buddhism spread beyond monks and nuns to regular people, the precept was modified from one of celibacy to one of not misusing sex.

The Brahmajala Sutra has this to say about precept number three:

A disciple of the Buddha must not engage in licentious acts or encourage others to do so. [As a monk] he should not have sexual relations with any female — be she a human, animal, deity or spirit — nor create the causes, conditions, methods, or karma of such misconduct. Indeed, he must not engage in improper sexual conduct with anyone. A Buddha's disciple ought to have a mind of filial piety — rescuing all sentient beings and instructing them in the Dharma of purity and chastity. If instead, he lacks compassion and encourages others to engage in sexual relations promiscuously, including with animals and even their mothers, daughters, sisters, or other close relatives, he commits a major offense.

This was written with heterosexual male monks in mind, but the same basic idea goes for anyone of any gender or sexual orientation, with the obvious modifications.

Some of the variations on this vow in English include, "Treating all beings with respect and dignity, I vow to take up the way of not misusing sex" (Boundless Way Zen Center), "Do not engage in improper sexual relations" (Kosen Nishiyama), "A follower of the way does not engage in sexual or sensual misconduct" (Dainin Katagiri), and "Not to engage in improper sexuality, but to practice purity of mind and self-restraint" (Philip Kapleau). Sometimes the precept is taken to mean "do not commit adultery," which, again, matches one of the Ten Commandments.

There are wordier versions too. Diane Eshin Rizzetto gives us "I take up the way of engaging in sexual intimacy respectfully and with an open heart. I take up the way of stepping into sexual intimacy not only naked in body, but in heart. And I take up the way of meeting the craving, as well as the fear of the craving; the desire for closeness as well as the fear of closeness; the greed for power as well as the fear of power; the escape as well as the union." And the Appleton Zen Center gives us "Be Loving — I am conscious and loving in all of my relationships. In sexuality, I discern the difference between love and lust and do not take advantage of other human beings. I transform the arising of lust into true loving."

But the grand prize for a lengthy version of this precept goes to the venerable Thich Nhat Hanh, who puts it like this: "Aware of the suffering caused by sexual misconduct, I am committed to cultivating responsibility and learning ways to protect the safety and integrity of individuals, couples, families, and society. I am determined not to engage in sexual relations without love and long-term commitment. To preserve the happiness of myself and others, I am determined to respect my commitments and the commitments of others. I will do everything in my power to protect children from sexual abuse and to prevent couples and families from being broken by sexual misconduct."

The reason for all this wordiness is that most of the Zen lineages that are active in the West derive from Japan — Thich Nhat Hanh being the exception among those I cited above. And in Japan, Buddhist monks stopped taking a vow of celibacy in the late nineteenth century. In places where the vow of celibacy is still taken by Buddhist monks and nuns, this precept is much more straightforward. Just don't have sex.

It's not that Buddhist monastics in those places think that sex in and of itself is immoral and wrong. After all, if the Buddha's parents hadn't had sex, the Buddha wouldn't have been born. Still, those Buddhist monastics who take vows of celibacy feel that sex gets in the way of their practice, and they want to focus exclusively on their practice.

I wrote a whole book about Zen Buddhist approaches to sexuality. It's called *Sex, Sin, and Zen*. There are other books on the subject of Buddhist sex, such as *The Red Thread* by Bernard Faure and *Lust for Enlightenment* by John Stevens. So rather than further addressing the subject of sex as it applies to this precept, I'd like to talk about the other ways of understanding it.

You'll notice that the versions of this precept used by both Nishijima Roshi and Kobun Chino Roshi don't mention sex at all. Rather, they talk about avoiding excessive desires and not attaching to fulfillment. In his "Commentary on the Precepts," Dogen also didn't mention sex. He gave this precept as "Do not be greedy" and commented, "The Three Wheels — body, mouth, and consciousness [or body, speech, and mind] — are pure and clean. Nothing is desired; go the same way with the Buddhas."

These teachers are not leaving out the part about sex just to be different. The Chinese characters used for this precept actually can be interpreted as something more like "don't have excessive desires" than "don't misuse sexuality." The first character means "vow" and the last one means "precept." The middle two characters both translate as "desire." The first one usually refers to a generalized sort of desire, while the second one carries more of a connotation of sexual desire — although it too can mean desire in general.

The Second Noble Truth of the Four Noble Truths is often translated as "The cause of suffering is desire." Nishijima Roshi objected to that translation because he said it is impossible to completely eliminate all desire. That's probably why he translated this precept using the words *excessive desire*.

Nishijima Roshi says, "We all have desire. Desire is an important factor in our life. But excessive desire is not the origin of happiness. It destroys our composure. Too much desire tends to make our life unhappy. So Gautama Buddha recognized the existence of desire but he warned against too much indulgence. He advised us not to desire too much."

In the book *Discovering the True Self*, Nishijima Roshi's teacher, Kodo Sawaki Roshi, said:

> Though people say, "Sawaki has very few desires," in fact that is not true. It's only that I persevere. If I give into my deep desires, I will hurt the Buddha, so I simply endure, that's all. Because I have many desires, I understand the deep desires of others. It's stupid not to realize the depth of one's desires. That's why I don't try to deny the fact. My desires follow a curve. They can be intense. While I have these intense desires, they lead me to the Buddha Way. Therefore, the more intense the desire the better. When my desires wane, so does my energy. So my ability to resist grows when my desires increase. That's the importance of our lives coming together with the Buddha way.

In *Embracing Mind*, Kobun Chino says:

> There is only you and Absolute Being, so there is basic confusion in having two objects as the Absolute. Yet, the ethical

meaning of this Precept is quite obvious. Adultery is a confused state. It causes separation from relating with whom
you really wish to relate. That is a kind of chasing after
many rabbits and not being able to catch one. The basic
problem is not objective, but, rather, subjective. The Absolute has many symbolic forms and images, which actually
represent what you were born as, and whom you are serving. The Absolute is this one, it is who we are. This is why
we keep following the life of no identity, in order to cleanse
our life. It is continually important to have an appreciation
for who and what formed you, which is watching your life.

He relates the precept to adultery, and by adultery I take him
to mean any kind of inappropriate sex. But what he really wants to
talk about is attachment and its relation to Absolute Being. He says,
"There is only you and Absolute Being." And he says that there is
confusion in having two objects as the Absolute.

He says that "the Absolute has many symbolic forms and images,
which actually represent what you were born as, and whom you are
serving." I am the Absolute, but born in this current form. The
world I see around me is whom I am serving in this current form.
The world is also a symbolic form of the Absolute, which is me.

What I call my "self" is really just a point of view. It's kind of
like when you're driving along a highway in a place with a lot of
interesting scenery, let's say Utah.

I drove through Utah a few years ago, and the scenery was
amazing. Some of it doesn't even look like it belongs on planet Earth.
Every so often you'll see signs on the highway telling you that a
"scenic viewpoint" is coming up. If you ever drive through Utah,
I recommend that you stop at as many of these as you can. I only
stopped for a few of them, and they were all incredible.

Each of these viewpoints is a place where you can stop and see
something really cool. But if we were more open to what life presents us, we'd realize that anywhere you stop to take a look at where

you are is pretty amazing. Even if it's just a random 7-Eleven or something. Just imagine how a creature from another planet would feel looking at a 7-Eleven. It would be astonishing and mysterious, full of wonderfully fascinating shapes and colors, and objects whose function our alien friend could only guess at, even though to us it looks like just another Slushee machine.

What we really are is a scenic viewpoint that the universe uses to observe itself. We might be one of those beautiful viewpoints like they have in Utah, or we might be a random 7-Eleven. But either way, we are each unique and valuable and provide the universe with a view of itself that it couldn't have without our being here.

But what or who is doing the viewing? To me, the only logical answer is that it is the universe itself looking out of your eyes and seeing the rest of its glorious form from one small but infinitely interesting perspective. Like when you're a kid and you look through the cardboard tube left over from an empty roll of paper towels, pretending it's a telescope. The entire universe has squeezed itself into your form just to get that point of view.

That's why Kobun describes it as "you and Absolute Being." He says, "The Absolute has many symbolic forms and images, which actually represent what you were born as, and whom you are serving." What you see when you look at the stuff around you are the symbolic forms the universe has taken. "Who you were born as" means what Zen people sometimes call "small self." As we've talked about, that's the self that most of us think we are. It's limited. It's tiny. It might even think of itself as insignificant. But it's not insignificant at all. It's the most significant thing that could ever exist. "Whom you are serving" means that which you perceive as external to you. It's also significant because it informs small self what it needs to do, and what it needs to be, for now.

Kobun says, "The Absolute is this one, it is who we are." This "one" he's talking about means what we think of as "me." What we think of as "me" is actually the limitless, timeless universe.

Kobun says, "We keep following the life of no identity, in order to cleanse our life." We have an identity in the conventional sense. That's important. And there's no need to try to deny or destroy our identity. But we can also live a life of no identity. This means that we live through our identity without accepting it as being our self. Our identity is just a function of who we are. It isn't the whole thing.

Kobun also says, "It is continually important to have an appreciation for who and what formed you, which is watching your life." The Absolute is who and what formed you and it is that — the Absolute — which is watching your life.

Appreciating this has given every moment of my life a deep significance, no matter what that moment happens to be. Even if it's just me in that 7-Eleven trying to pour myself a Slushee and finding out the machine is broken — even a moment like that has radiance and truth far beyond anything my small self can ever fully comprehend. But although I can't comprehend it, I can make an effort to accept and appreciate it.

In order to do this, I find that it is useful to avoid attaching to things. This means, as much as possible, I avoid ranking certain people, things, and events as more special than others. Doing so, I have learned to see every moment of life as equally the working of the entire universe. I try to appreciate every little bit of myself — as it manifests as a world external to me — fully and completely.

This seems the best way to try to fulfill my vow not to desire too much.

# 24. I VOW NOT TO LIE

THE BODHIDHARMA ONE-MIND Precepts version of the precept against lying is, "Self-nature is mysteriously profound. Unexplainable dharma. Not speaking even a single word is called 'no illusory words.'"

This is yet another of the Buddhist precepts that sounds very much like one of the Ten Commandments: "Thou shalt not lie."

Some of the ways this precept has been translated into English include, "I vow not to lie but to speak the truth" (Great Vow Zen Monastery), "A follower of the way does not speak falsely or deceptively" (Dainin Katagiri), and "Manifest truth — Do not speak falsely" (Taiun Michael Elliston).

There are also some wordier variations. Diane Eshin Rizzetto gives us, "I take up the way of speaking truthfully. I take up the way of honestly facing the distrust, uncertainty, and fear that propels my tongue to be disloyal to the truth of this moment." Boundless Way Zen Center's version is, "Listening and speaking from the heart, I vow to take up the way of not speaking falsely."

The Brahmajala Sutra says, "A disciple of the Buddha must not himself use false words and speech, or encourage others to lie or lie by expedient means. He should not involve himself in the causes, conditions, methods, or karma of lying, saying that he has seen what he has not seen or vice-versa, or lying implicitly through physical or mental means. As a Buddha's disciple, he ought to maintain Right Speech and Right Views always, and lead all others to maintain them as well. If instead, he causes wrong speech, wrong views, or evil karma in others, he commits a major offense."

In the conventional sense, it's bad to tell lies. But that does not mean you always have to say everything you're thinking. The answer to the question "Does this outfit make me look fat?" is always "Of course not!"

There is a big difference between telling a lie for personal gain or advantage and fibbing a little in order not to hurt someone. And, of course, there are many shades in between.

I recently heard about an argument between two famous Buddhist scholars over what you should say if you are hiding some Jews in your house when the Nazis come knocking at the door. One of the scholars said that, in such a case, the proper thing to do is to break the precept against lying and accept whatever karma that brings. The other said that you should tell the Nazis, "I have nothing to be ashamed of in this house."

The lesson I took from that is, if you're hiding from the Nazis, think hard before hiding in the home of certain Buddhist scholars! I side with the Buddhist scholar who said you should lie to the Nazis, by the way. I think there are times that you uphold the true meaning of the precepts by breaking the precepts.

Even so, trust between people is such a significant thing that a vow of honesty is written into the Buddhist precepts. Furthermore, intentionally saying something we know not to be true might sometimes seem expedient, but it always gets us into trouble. Even when no Nazis are involved. In order to devote ourselves to real Buddhist practice, we need to have as uncomplicated a life as possible. In order not to complicate our lives, it's best to always tell the truth.

Gudo Nishijima says, "We are living in the Universe. The Universe is the truth itself. Truth and honesty are bound together. If we want to find the truth we must be honest. If we are not honest we can never find our real situation in the Universe."

In his "Commentary on the Precepts," Dogen says about this

precept, "Since the dharma-wheel has been turning from the very beginning, there is neither too much nor too little. When a drop of sweet dew moistens all beings, reality and truth become revealed." Which is... confusing. I am honestly not sure how that relates to lying.

Kobun Chino seems to understand Dogen better than I do. Commenting on what Dogen said, he says:

> What is unreal and what is real is a very big subject for all of us. The life we live feels fantastic, but it feels like a continuous dream. Our experiences of the past twenty years, forty years, even seventy years, where are they? It feels like all are embedded in the present moment and the dynamic life we live. When we look into our past, the words we have spoken to ourselves and others show a narrow perspective. Even if we make our best effort not to lie, not to speak untruth, still we feel we have many times spoken illusory words. We are afraid we might still be doing this, and that this must still be going on.

The fact is, in some sense, we cannot help but tell lies — or at least nontruths. The truth is much too big ever to be put into mere words. Everything we say is an approximation of what's true, at best. Even in conventional terms, what's true is only ever partially true. If we want to refrain from all speech that could in any way be considered false, we couldn't speak at all.

Kobun continues, "It is very difficult to describe an actual thing in language. The word 'cat' is the word 'cat.' That word cannot become the cat, it merely points to something. If we can experience something together with another person, we do not need so many words. But communication can be complicated! When I say 'zafu' all of us understand it, but for people who don't know that a zafu is a black cushion, 'zafu' is just a sound. Also, 'zafu' doesn't point to something we don't know, but that invisible realm is important when we discuss communication."

By "invisible realm" he means those things that are not as tangible as cats or cushions. We often have to talk about things that no one else can confirm — our feelings, for example. Sometimes even I don't know if what I say about my internal states is true. If I say I'm depressed, for example, what you take that to mean might be entirely different from what I want to convey.

We're getting a little deeper here about the subject of speaking falsely than merely vowing not to shave a few years off our age or not to say we're "on our way" when we're really not. This gets into the very nature of communication. How do we avoid lying when everything we say is, in some sense, untrue?

This precept, like all the others, is a koan, in the sense that it's an impossible puzzle. The Bodhidharma One-Mind Precepts are intended to remind us of that, just in case we thought that following the precepts was easy and straightforward.

Honesty is one of the most significant aspects of Buddhist practice. The entire reason I got interested in Zen in the first place was that I could see that my first teacher was an honest person. I knew he wouldn't steer me wrong by saying things he knew were not true. That's why I kept with him when he started saying things I couldn't understand.

Teaching Buddhism requires saying things that are hard for most people to grasp. I would imagine I've already done plenty of that in this book. Nobody gets this stuff right away. I sure didn't! It takes practice to start making sense out of some of the weirder ideas you find in Buddhism. But nobody's going to commit to the difficult practice that's required unless they have some degree of faith that those who are doing their best to explain it are being honest.

This is why students of Buddhism are required to make a public commitment to honesty. The only way Buddhism can be transmitted is by honest people. A dishonest person could memorize every

Buddhist sutra and repeat them verbatim, and that wouldn't transmit Buddhism at all. If, for example, someone teaches Buddhism for personal gain or self-aggrandizement, students will pick up on that.

I've tried to be careful about the way I've taught Buddhism. I know I have made many mistakes, even so. I apologize for that! I'm trying to do better.

## 25. I VOW TO REFRAIN FROM INTOXICANTS

THE BODHIDHARMA ONE-MIND Precepts version of the precept about not using intoxicants goes, "Self-nature is mysteriously profound. In the truth of original basic purity, not to give birth to ignorance is called 'no selling wine, no drinking wine.'"

As you may have guessed from that, another version of this precept is "No selling of wine, no drinking of wine." Another version is "Don't live by selling liquor."

Nishijima Roshi, commenting on the version that says not to live by selling liquor, says, "This seems rather strange as a religious precept. I feel that the original concept might have been not to drink liquor. Perhaps as Buddhism spread from India to countries like China and Japan this precept was altered to suit local conditions. In those northern countries alcohol was considered an important aid to survival during the cold winter months. So personally I feel that it is important not to drink, but we should recognize the precept in the form that it has come to us from the past."

Some of the variations on this precept in English include, "A disciple of the Buddha refrains from taking or offering harmful intoxicants or drugs that delude body/mind" (Shunryu Suzuki), "A follower of the way does not intoxicate oneself or others" (Dainin Katagiri), and "Not to cause others to use liquors or drugs that confuse or weaken the mind and not to do so oneself, but to keep the mind clear" (Philip Kapleau).

The ever-reliable Diane Eshin Rizzetto has a wordier version that goes, "I take up the way of cultivating a clear mind. Fear holds the cup and I hide in the distortion of its shadow. The cup falls and sunlight blinds with painful brightness. I vow to stand with empty hands, tight chest, trembling, and tears. I vow to stand with eyes open to what is revealed. Who drops the cup?"

Ummm. OK, then!

Moving right along, the Brahmajala Sutra says, "A disciple of the Buddha must not trade in alcoholic beverages or encourage others to do so. He should not create the causes, conditions, methods, or karma of selling any intoxicant whatsoever, for intoxicants are the causes and conditions of all kinds of offenses. As a Buddha's disciple, he ought to help all sentient beings achieve clear wisdom. If instead, he causes them to have upside-down, topsy-turvy thinking, he commits a major offense."

Furthermore, abstaining from intoxicants can be a gift to others. The Buddha put it this way, "Furthermore, in abstaining from taking intoxicants, a disciple of the Buddha gives freedom from danger, animosity, and oppression to limitless numbers of beings. In giving freedom from danger, animosity, and oppression to limitless numbers of beings, he gains a share in limitless freedom from danger, animosity, and oppression." When you don't get drunk or high, the rest of us don't have to deal with your drunk/high ass annoying us or crashing your car into us.

Pretty much everyone agrees that, even though the Chinese character for *alcohol* appears in this precept, it applies to all forms of intoxicants. Still, whenever I comment about this precept on the internet I get arguments from people who claim that certain drugs — like LSD, psilocybin, DMT, and so on — enhance the meditative experience and so are exempt from this precept.

They are wrong. Those other drugs do not deserve to be exempt from the list.

Kobun Chino says, "We try not to intoxicate our body and mind, because if we go along with the heavy trip of intoxication, a very powerful life, or chemical, takes over our life. We don't know what was eaten, what was taken, or what was given. The unity of energy with other existences is very delicate, and if we are intoxicated, we lose the opportunity to unite with them."

During one of far too many pointless discussions I've had with someone who supports drug use as a way to gain spiritual insight, the guy I was talking to put forth the worn-out cliché that drugs are like taking a helicopter to the top of a mountain rather than climbing it. He said that you get the same breathtaking view as someone who has climbed the mountain. But, he said, you get there much quicker and more easily.

"You can't deny it's exactly the same view," the guy said. But, in fact, I would unequivocally deny that it's the same view. It's not. Not at all.

Let's say you met a veteran mountaineer with decades of climbing experience, a person who has written books on mountain climbing and routinely instructs others in the art of climbing. And let's imagine what would happen if you tried to convince this guy that people who take helicopters to the tops of mountains get everything that mountain climbers get, and get it a whole lot easier.

The mountain climber would certainly tell you that the breathtaking view a guy who takes a helicopter to the top of a mountain gets is not in any way, shape, or form the same view that a person who climbs the mountain herself gets.

To the mountain climber, the guy in the helicopter is just a hyperactive thrill seeker who wants nothing more than to experience a pretty view without putting any real effort into it. The helicopter guy thinks the goal of mountain climbing is to be on top of the mountain and that climbing is an inefficient way to accomplish this goal. He just doesn't get it. At all.

The helicopter guy misses out on the amazing sights there are to see on the way up. He doesn't know the thrill of mastering the mountain through his own efforts. He doesn't learn from the hardships and dangers involved in making the climb. And he'll never know the awesome wonder of descending the mountain back into familiar territory. All he's done is given some money to a person who owns a helicopter. He probably couldn't even *find* the mountain himself, let alone make it to the top. When there are no helicopters around, the poor guy is helplessly grounded.

If the helicopter guy claims that he has reached the same place as the mountain climber, the mountain climber knows — in ways the helicopter guy can't even fathom — that the helicopter guy is a fool.

To a mountain climber, the goal of mountain climbing is not the moment of sitting on top enjoying the view. That's just one small part of the experience. It may not even be the best part. To a mountain climber, every view, from every point on the mountain, is significant and wonderful.

Meditation practice is about the fullness of life, not about peak experiences that are over in a flash.

In his book *Embracing Mind*, Kobun Chino cautions us that even meditation practice can become a kind of intoxicant. When it does, you might start to treat spiritual experiences the way my friend who talked about helicopters thought of his experiences on drugs. Kobun says, "Many times we call on spiritual subjects in order to polish ourselves, but these can have the same kind of effect as wine. When some religion causes you to become excited, bringing you to a state of ecstatic excitement, you'd better think that this isn't the ultimate. Yet there are many religions which focus on an ultimate state. If zazen practice makes you feel like that, your zazen is not the right one. An intoxicated, agitated state is the opposite from great wisdom, opposite from a clear perspective on what this existence, this life, is all about."

It's important not to allow meditation to become an intoxicant.

But let's leave aside the whole matter of alcohol, drugs, and intoxication and dig into the Bodhidharma One-Mind Precepts version of the precept. It says, "Self-nature is mysteriously profound.

In the truth of original basic purity, not to give birth to ignorance is called 'no selling wine, no drinking wine.'"

In his "Commentary on the Precepts," Dogen gives this precept as "Do not be ignorant" and comments on it saying, "It has never been; don't be defiled. It is indeed the Great Clarity."

Not to give birth to ignorance... to Buddhists this is a tall order indeed. Because, according to Buddhism, ignorance creates the material universe. So let's get into that idea, shall we?

The prevailing belief in the culture in which I was raised is that I am a human being living in the material universe. A human being, said the people who taught me, is a kind of meat machine. The world it lives in is basically a bunch of rocks with a bunch of other meat machines crawling all over it, and some plants.

The machine that is me, I was taught, developed over the course of billions of years through a long process of evolution, which operates through random chance, natural selection, and survival of the fittest. The reason I feel that I am alive is that evolution provided me with a brain, whose function was to keep me alive long enough to reproduce. Scientific experiments and observations have proven this to be true, I was taught.

One of the things that attracted me to Buddhism right from the beginning was the fact that my teachers never attempted to deny this way of understanding things. Other religions did. They said that the prevailing view of my culture was bunk and that the truth was written in their holy books. The Earth was created by God in seven days six thousand years ago. I couldn't accept that.

But even though Buddhists don't try to fight against science, they say that the scientific way of understanding things is incomplete. They offered me a different view, without insisting that I replace what I'd learned from science with their version.

Buddhism has a lot of funny little formulas for understanding who and what we are. What's neat about them is that they don't necessarily go against the scientific understanding. You don't have to disbelieve science in order to accept them. At least I didn't feel like I had to.

But they do flip the scientific understanding of who and what we are on its head. That is to say, you can slot the scientific understanding of who and what we are into these Buddhist formulas if you want to. There's a place for evolution, natural selection, and even random chance in them. Sort of. Random chance may be the one idea the Buddhist formulas don't have a place for. I think they'd characterize what we call random chance as being the operations of something so complex that to the human mind it can only appear as random.

I'm getting ahead of myself here. Remember the Twelvefold Chain of Codependent Coorigination that we looked at a few chapters ago? Let's talk about that some more. *Pratityasamutpada* is what the ancient Buddhists called it. I love the sound of that. Pra-TEET-ya-sam-oot-pah-dah. Some people drop the *co-* and call it Dependent Arising or Dependent Origination. Sometimes they call it Conditioned Arising or Interdependent Co-Arising.

As we saw earlier, the whole darn thing starts with ignorance. When the writer of the Bodhidharma One-Mind Precepts asks us not to give birth to ignorance, he's asking us to roll things back all the way to the beginning. The material universe doesn't appear until step ten or eleven of the Twelvefold Chain — depending on whose interpretation you go by. Hell, consciousness doesn't even appear until step three!

The word *ignorance* is a poor choice for expressing this concept in English. Unfortunately, it's the most common one. *Ignorance* tends to imply that there's some fact or idea out there that everybody else knows except you because you've somehow failed to pick up on it; you've ignored it. That's not what the Buddhists are talking about here. The word in Sanskrit is *avidya*, and in Chinese it's *mumyo*. Both these words mean "lack of clarity." Probably the word *delusion* would be a better choice for translating the concept. The idea is that it's a fundamental misunderstanding of how things actually are.

Here's how Dainin Katagiri explains ignorance in the book *The Light That Shines through Infinity*:

> The first link is *avidya*, the very subtle vibration of mind that is called ignorance. Link two is *samskara*, the formative forces of karma; *vijnana*, human consciousness, is link three. *Samskara* accepts the movement of ignorance, nurtures it, and then human consciousness arises based on the creative forces of karmic energy. The functioning of *samskara* means that before your human consciousness appears, the energy that supports your life is already there.
>
> Once human consciousness appears, it is always looking for an object. So name and form appear as the fourth link, followed by the six sense realms, and then contact, sensation, craving, grasping, and being. In Sanskrit, grasping is called *upadana*, the acquiring of karma, and the tenth link, being, is called *bhava*, your very existence.
>
> The eleventh link is birth, the appearance of your present life, which exists for exactly one moment. Then, by your activity of living in that moment as a human being, you produce seeds of karmic energy that will mature in the future.
>
> Finally, in the twelfth link, one moment of life in the phenomenal world is passing away, and immediately a new moment of life is a rising. That new life appears based on the potential energy produced by causes and conditions created in the past.

The main point of the formula is similar to the point of the other formula we looked at earlier, the five aggregates. They're both trying to provide an alternative to the widely held notion that a human being is a single, immutable thing. They're both trying to let you know that a human being is actually a process or an activity of the universe.

A wave is a process that occurs within water. Waves are not

immutable things. Even so, we could speak about a wave as if it's a single thing because, for a time, it behaves like a single thing. We could even name a wave if we wanted. We could talk about when it came into existence and when it ceased to be — when it was "born" and when it "died." Yet the appearance or disappearance of a wave doesn't mean that some amount of water has appeared or disappeared. Humans are kind of the same. Humans are events that appear and disappear within the universe. But nothing is added when they appear or subtracted when they disappear. Not even the mind consciousness that we imagine to be in our possession.

These ancient Buddhist formulas are just highly intellectualized ways of pointing to that idea. They're fun to learn if you're into that sort of thing, but they're not essential for practice or even for understanding. When I say the formula has been useful to me, I mean that it helped me break out of my habit of understanding myself in the standard way as a single immutable individual.

Dogen writes about this formula in an essay called "Bukkyo," which literally means "Buddhist teachings." Actually, in contemporary Japanese, the word *Bukkyo* is usually translated as "Buddhism."

Anyway, about the twelvefold chain Dogen says, "Remember, if ignorance [or delusion] is the one mind, then action, consciousness, and so on are also the one mind. If ignorance is cessation, then action, consciousness, and so on are also cessation. If ignorance is nirvana, then action, consciousness, and so on are also nirvana."

All he's saying here is that whoever or whatever we are cannot be easily divided up into a neat little formula like this. He says it in a funny way, though. Because his understanding of who and what we actually are differs radically from the way most of us see ourselves.

The "one mind" is everything. It's the Universal Mind that includes all material and nonmaterial things. By "cessation" he means that when we cease doing any one of the activities in the twelvefold chain, all of them cease. Which makes sense. If you break one link in a chain, it's no longer a chain, is it?

Dogen also takes the opportunity to assert that there is no real difference between samsara and nirvana; that is to say, there is no mundane world to escape from in favor of a better world somewhere else. Right here and now, this is the Pure Land; this state you have right now is enlightenment itself.

Which is hard to believe sometimes, I know. Trust me, I know!

The way this relates to the precept about intoxicants is that the basic delusion by which we come into existence is a kind of intoxication. We're drunk on our own fundamental misunderstanding of things. The precept isn't just telling us not to chug beers, smoke pot, and drop acid. It is telling us not to do that, for sure! But it's also trying to point out that a kind of intoxication with ignorance is at the root of our suffering.

# 26. I VOW NOT TO DWELL
# ON PAST MISTAKES

THE BODHIDHARMA ONE-MIND Precepts version of the precept about dwelling on past mistakes is, "Self-nature is mysteriously profound. In the midst of unmistakable truth, not to speak of past mistakes is called the Precept of 'no speaking of past mistakes.'"

The more standard version of this precept is, "Don't discuss failures of Buddhist monastics and laypeople." The Brahmajala Sutra comments on the version of the precept that specifically mentions Buddhist clergy and says:

> A disciple of the Buddha must not himself broadcast the misdeeds or infractions of Bodhisattva-clerics or Bodhisattva-laypersons, or of monks and nuns — nor encourage others to do so. He must not create the causes, conditions, methods, or karma of discussing the offenses of the assembly. As a Buddha's disciple, whenever he hears evil persons, externalists, or followers of the Two Vehicles speak of practices contrary to the Dharma or contrary to the precepts within the Buddhist community, he should instruct them with a compassionate mind and lead them to develop wholesome faith in the Mahayana. If instead, he discusses the faults and misdeeds that occur within the assembly, he commits a major offense.

To me, the obvious problem with limiting the prohibition on criticism to monastics is that it can be used as a shield to protect monks and nuns from legitimate criticism. If I'm a monk or teacher, and you're a good Buddhist student, then you can't criticize anything I do. Which means I can potentially get away with a lot!

And this precept has, in fact, been used this way. Some less ethical Buddhist monastics from Asia seem to have been genuinely shocked when their Western students openly spoke out about their transgressions, thus violating this precept. But sometimes you have to speak out.

As we've seen, there are times when the precepts ought to be violated in order to maintain the true meaning of the precepts. When a Buddhist master abuses his students, for example, then speaking of that teacher's faults is necessary.

Nishijima Roshi commented on the standard version of this precept, saying, "As Buddhists we try our best to live and practice the Buddhist life. In doing so we often make mistakes. This is natural. Our mistakes come directly from our efforts. This may sound strange, but it is the fact in our life. So when we see the mistakes of others we should not be critical, for their mistakes are only the product of their efforts in this life."

Even though Nishijima Roshi used the version of the precept that seems to limit it to discussing the failures of Buddhist monastics and laypeople, in his comments he ignores this limitation and applies it to speaking of the faults of anyone. Most contemporary versions of the precept in English also do this.

Some other ways of putting it include, "See the perfection; Do not speak of others' errors and faults" (John Daido Loori), "I vow not to gossip about others' faults but to be understanding and sympathetic" (Great Vow Zen Monastery), and "A follower of the way does not slander others" (Dainin Katagiri).

The Appleton Zen Center's version is "Honor Silence — I remember the preciousness of silence. I see the perfection of others and refrain from gossip and frivolous conversation. I remain thoughtful and mindful of the effects of my speech." And Diane Eshin Rizzetto gives us, "I take up the way of speaking of others with openness and possibility. When I talk about others, who is speaking? Fear and shame inside push critical words outside. I vow to pause so the distress in the mind and body can speak."

Kobun Chino says, "The spirit of this [precept] is thinking before speaking or acting, and, instead, offering good actions, thoughts, and speech. These Precepts [this precept, the one before it, and the next one] are about words, the many sides of language. It is important to speak with fine timing and with truth from within. The true loving quality which appears with words is necessary if we wish to relate with other people."

In his "Commentary on the Precepts," Dogen says about this precept, "In the midst of the Buddha-dharma, we are the same Way, the same Dharma, the same realization, the same practice. Do not talk about others' errors and faults. Do not destroy the Way." At last! Dogen makes a comment I can understand!

I like the version of this precept that says "no dwelling of past mistakes" because it doesn't limit it to the mistakes of Buddhists or even of other people. You shouldn't dwell on your own past mistakes either.

Finding fault with others and even with oneself rarely helps very much. And dwelling on the mistakes of others or yourself is not a good thing to do. Once you've recognized a mistake and then made an effort not to make that mistake again, you don't need to dwell on it any longer.

Dwelling on past mistakes is a way of reinforcing your ego. The ego can be strengthened just as well by dwelling on what's bad about you as it can by dwelling on what's good. In fact, for some of us — myself included — dwelling on what's bad about ourselves reinforces the ego much more effectively than dwelling on what's good.

It's interesting that the Bodhidharma One-Mind Precepts version of this one just sort of restates the usual version of the precept. The other Bodhidharma precepts get all mystical. But this one doesn't. I remember Tim remarking on that the first time I heard him talk about the Bodhidharma One-Mind Precepts. Bodhidharma, or whoever really wrote the One-Mind Precepts, only adds "in the midst of unmistakable truth." But that addition is interesting.

In a sense, there are no mistakes. There are only actions. People can judge whether certain actions are right or wrong, and that's legitimate. But in another sense, action is just action. There is no right or wrong. In the Zen tradition, we stress the necessity of ethical behavior and emphasize the precepts. Yet we often talk about things in an absolute sense. And in an absolute sense there is no meaning to concepts like good and bad, right and wrong.

Dogen wrote extensively about this inherent contradiction. Probably the best place to see it in action is in his "Genjo Koan," where he says:

> When all dharmas [in other words, everything] are [seen as] the Buddha-Dharma, then there is delusion and realization, there is practice, there is life and there is death, there are buddhas and there are ordinary beings. When the myriad dharmas are each not of the self, there is no delusion and no realization, no buddhas and no ordinary beings, no life and no death. The Buddha's truth is originally transcendent over abundance and scarcity, and so there is life and death, there is delusion and realization, there are beings and buddhas. And though it is like this, it is only that flowers, while loved, fall; and weeds, while hated, flourish.

Although he doesn't specifically mention the contrast between good and evil or right and wrong, these are implied when he contrasts delusion and realization.

There is a contradiction in what Dogen is saying. He recognizes this — even emphasizes it. This is because that contradiction is an aspect of reality. When looking at things from one angle, there is right and wrong, good and evil, dark and light. Yet from another point of view these concepts don't make any sense. If there is any such thing as "enlightenment" it would be a state in which these contradictions can be held together without either one trying to force its way on the other.

In a practical sense, I try to understand my own mistakes as mistakes, and I try not to repeat them. But when I find myself dwelling on the many errors I've made in the past, I remind myself that the past cannot be changed. That is the undeniable truth. I try to remember that even making errors has helped me to understand something about the truth of life. In many cases, I would not have known that a certain action was wrong to do except through having done it. So while I do my best not to repeat my past mistakes, I also do my best not to dwell on them either.

This is, of course, easier said than done. When I do zazen, I often find that my mind regurgitates all the things I have ever regretted doing. I'm not alone in this. Even Shunryu Suzuki Roshi once said that zazen was like that for him sometimes. It's hard to let thoughts of past regrets go. As I already said, thinking about your regrets is a great way to enhance your sense of personal self, your ego. One good practical reason to act ethically is that, if you do so, you have less to regret and less to be ashamed about.

The only thing that has ever worked for me when I find myself dwelling on past mistakes is to follow Kosho Uchiyama's advice and "open the hand of thought." When I recognize that I've been dwelling on my mistakes, I do my best to let those thoughts go. I don't try to stop those thoughts or silence them. I don't judge the thoughts, and I don't judge myself. Or if I do, I try to allow even those thoughts of personal judgment to pass. Sometimes this means I have to keep noticing my metaphorical "closed hand of thought" and open it up over and over and over again. But if that's what has to be done, I just keep on doing it. Eventually it gets better.

# 27. I VOW NOT TO PRAISE SELF AND BERATE OTHERS

THE BODHIDHARMA ONE-MIND Precepts version of the precept against praising oneself while berating others is, "Self-nature is mysteriously profound. In the midst of equality, in the midst of identical dharma, identity of truth, not speaking of self and others is called the Precept of 'no praise or blame.'"

Nishijima Roshi, in speaking of the standard version of this precept, says, "Modern psychology tells us that most of us have some sort of superiority or inferiority complex. I think this is basically true, and because of these personal inclinations we are prone to praise or criticize ourselves and other people. But we are all human beings. If we recognize the true situation it is impossible to blame others for their faults, and praising ourselves is needless — it is a waste of breath."

Some other versions of this precept in English include, "A disciple of the Buddha abstains from praising oneself or slandering others" (Taiun Michael Elliston), "Not to praise oneself and condemn others, but to overcome one's own shortcomings" (Philip Kapleau), and "Realize self and other as one; Do not elevate the self and blame others" (John Daido Loori).

Some longer versions include this one from Appleton Zen Center: "Celebrate Others — I rejoice in the good fortune of others. I do not, through my thoughts, words, or action, separate myself from others through coveting, envy, or jealousy." And here's a really long one from Dianne Eshin Rizzetto: "I take up the way of meeting others on equal ground. Do I exist outside the realm of judgment and comparison with others? Do others exist when I spin in the realm of fantasy and belief? Insecurity, anger, and shame bar the way. I vow to let frozen breath, pounding heart, and churning stomach lead me through." Whoa!

The Brahmajala Sutra says, "A disciple of the Buddha shall not praise himself and speak ill of others, or encourage others to do so. He must not create the causes, conditions, methods, or karma of praising himself and disparaging others. As a disciple of the Buddha, he should be willing to stand in for all sentient beings and endure humiliation and slander — accepting blame and letting sentient beings have all the glory. If instead, he displays his own virtues and conceals the good points of others, thus causing them to suffer slander, he commits a major offense."

It seems a little odd that praising oneself would be important enough to get a whole precept about it. Bragging about yourself is annoying, but is bragging really on the order of what some of the other precepts cover, like killing and stealing?

In terms of social relations, though, it's often more than just irritating when someone praises him- or herself. These precepts were originally designed for monks living in close quarters and interacting with each other constantly. Bragging must have been enough of a problem for them that it rose to the level of being prohibited.

The One-Mind Precepts version gets a little deeper into why this was important. Again, it says, "Self-nature is mysteriously profound. In the midst of equality, in the midst of identical dharma, identity of truth, not speaking of self and others is called the Precept of 'no praise or blame.'"

In his "Commentary on the Precepts," Dogen said, "Buddhas and teachers realized absolute emptiness and realized the great earth. When the great body is manifested, there is neither outside nor inside in emptiness. When the Dharma-body is manifested, there is not even a single square inch of soil on the earth."

We're not just talking about bragging now. The very notion of the division between self and other is called into question.

Commenting on Dogen's commentary on this precept, Kobun Chino says:

> Like a scale, always the mind acts to put yourself high and others low. In Buddha Mind there is no such activity. The scale is always level. There are no others. There is no self. Others are self, and self is others, so comparing weights is impossible. Every Buddha and every ancestor realizes that he is the same as the limitless sky. When every Buddhist Ancestor realizes that he is the whole sky and whole great earth, when he appears with a great body, there is no inside or outside. If he appears as a true body, there is no soil on the earth. It means he is the earth itself.
>
> Dogen Zenji said there is no being proud of yourself and devaluing others, because there are no such others to devalue. When you devalue others, you are scratching at your body. When you are proud of yourself, you are scratching at the air.

I love the imagery he uses!

There are no others. There is no self. There is no one to compare to anyone else. Praise and blame make no sense if you can't compare anyone to anyone else. Another way to phrase this precept was suggested by my friend Emily Eslami, who said: "I vow not to compare myself to others or compare others to myself."

The idea of realizing yourself as the limitless sky or the entire earth might seem far-fetched. But we don't have to go that far to understand why comparing yourself to others is pointless. Let's say you're envious of your neighbor because he has a really nice house with a pool out back.

But if you looked into how your neighbor *got* that house and that pool, you'd find there was a lot of hard work involved, and maybe some luck. You'd also find that keeping that house from falling apart and keeping that pool clean eats up a lot of your neighbor's time and money. Your desire for that house and that pool probably don't take that kind of stuff into account. In the end, the only way you could ever have the things your neighbor has is to *be* that person. We all have our own lot in life, our own karma and past experiences and efforts. Things don't come out equally. Often life is unfair. But we can't trade places with anyone else, and if we really paid attention to the lives of others, we probably wouldn't want to.

Still, it's not exactly a sin to envy others. It just happens. I do it myself sometimes. Not long ago I was looking at the webpage of some Zen teacher whose students built him a big house to live in. I thought, "Jeez. My students never built me a house." But then I thought about the obligations that teacher must have now that he has that house. When people do something like that for you, it always comes with a lot of expectations and a price tag. Plus, that Zen teacher I was envying is really famous. I bet he gets bothered all the time by strangers who expect profound wisdom from him any time of day or night. Famous people often become the targets for people's fantasies and frustrations. I'm better off in my little apartment.

The point is that envy comes up sometimes, whether or not you want it to. And just like pretty much any other thought, thoughts of comparison between self and others are worthless. You're better off letting thoughts like that fade away without adding any energy to them. Nisargadatta Maharaj said, "Whenever thought says something, take whatever is urgent, necessary, and useful...and forget the rest....Thoughts consume your time unnecessarily, so you have to reject useless thoughts. If a thought complains about somebody, disconnect from that thought."

But it's not always easy to avoid these sorts of thoughts. They come unbidden, the result of old habits that haven't yet gone away. Whenever I find myself comparing myself to others, I try to remember how futile and illogical it is. Kobun's words "When you devalue others, you are scratching at your body. When you are proud of yourself, you are scratching at the air" are useful. It's a memorable image.

When Kobun talks right after that about realizing yourself as the limitless sky or the great earth, he's not just waxing poetic. You yourself, just as you are right now, are the limitless sky and the great earth. Whether or not you notice it.

I'm not going to try to prove that to you. There's no way I can do that. I'm just putting it out there. Maybe one day you'll remember I told you so.

# 28. I VOW NOT TO BE COVETOUS

THE BODHIDHARMA ONE-MIND Precepts version of the precept against coveting is, "Self-nature is mysteriously profound. In the midst of all-pervading truth, not clinging to any single form is called the Precept of 'no hoarding.'"

Gudo Nishijima Roshi gave this precept as "Not to begrudge Dharma or material possessions, but to give them freely." His comment about it is, "Our tendency is to want more than we have. We want more teachings; we want more things. But when we see our situation clearly we realize that we are part of the wide and glorious Universe. We have everything we need already. In such a situation it is natural to give. We want to share the teachings and what wealth we have with others. It is a natural activity of our true situation."

Some variations on this precept in English include, "Give generously; Do not be withholding" (John Daido Loori), "A follower of the way does not possess anything selfishly" (Dainin Katagiri), and "Do not be stingy" (Taizen Maezumi).

As far as longer versions go, the Appleton Zen Center gives us, "Be Giving — I give generously of myself, sharing freely my love, my gifts, my talents, and my abundance for the benefit of all. I do not selfishly withhold. I do not add any more suffering to the world." Diane Eshin Rizzetto, for once, keeps it short and sweet with "Not sparing the Dharma assets."

The Brahmajala Sutra says, "A disciple of the Buddha must not be stingy or encourage others to be stingy. He should not create the causes, conditions, methods, or karma of stinginess. As a Bodhisattva, whenever a destitute person comes for help, he should give that person what he needs. If instead, out of anger and resentment, he denies all assistance — refusing to help with even a penny, a needle, a blade of grass, even a single sentence or verse or a phrase of Dharma, but instead scolds and abuses that person — he commits a major offense."

In his "Commentary on the Precepts," Dogen says about this precept, "One phrase, one force, myriad phenomena. One Truth, one confirmation, All Buddha, All Ancestor. It has never been hoarded at all."

This is the last of the precepts that matches with one of the Ten Commandments, namely, "Thou shalt not covet." Some say that the Ten Commandments may have been created by a society that was transitioning from being nomadic hunter-gatherers into being settled farmers. If that's the case, then it makes sense to have a prohibition against not sharing. Of course, coveting something is a bit different from just refusing to share it. It can also mean that you long to possess it, which could lead you to break the precept against stealing. Coveting things can also promote resentment among people.

In the case of the Buddhist precepts, this one is usually interpreted as being not so much about coveting the possessions of others as about withholding what you have, or being selfish and stingy. It also refers to sharing the teachings. Buddhism is considered one of the "missionary religions," meaning its followers were expected to share the teachings rather than keep them to themselves.

Even so, the Zen form of Buddhism discourages proselytizing. You won't find Zen Buddhists knocking on your door to share the good news about emptiness. But other forms of Buddhism make greater efforts than Zen Buddhism to try to win new followers. Still, even in Zen Buddhism, while we don't try to make converts, we do try to share the teachings freely with anyone who is interested. This book is an example of that.

Also, as Nishijima Roshi points out in his comments, this precept is meant as an antidote to greed. We tend to want more than we really need. When we share what we have or give things away, we reduce our tendency toward greed, and it feels good.

Personally, I have a bad habit of being a collector. Over the years I've amassed several collections — a collection of bass guitars, a collection of CDs and records, a collection of Japanese monster memorabilia, and a massive collection of books. Every time I move I am reminded what a burden I have given myself.

During the time I've been writing this book, I've been getting rid of my collections. I gave nearly all my Japanese monster movie stuff to my friend Bob. I actually wanted him to take it all, but many of the items I had, he already owned. It was one of the happiest moments of my life when I gave that stuff to him. He will enjoy my collection much more than I did, and it's a lot of stuff I don't have to take care of anymore. Most of my instruments and my music collection are gone now too, and that feels nice. Books are harder to get rid of, but I found a place to donate them to, so most of them are gone as well, although I still have plenty of books left.

There's nothing intrinsically wrong with having stuff. Everyone has stuff. But it's good to recognize when it becomes a problem. I wouldn't call myself a hoarder, but the hoarder mentality is not difficult for me to understand. We collectors are just hoarders who are a bit more selective. It's funny not buying that kind of stuff anymore, but it feels good to have less. Every once in a while I remember something I used to own and regret not having it anymore. But that thought, just like all thoughts, lasts a little while and then fades away.

In early Buddhism, the monks were required to have no possessions other than their robes and their begging bowls. These days there are a few Buddhist orders that still follow that practice. The much more common practice these days, however, is to require monks to give up most of their possessions only while they are training in a temple or monastery. They usually don't get rid of their stuff entirely. They just store it somewhere while they're doing their training. Most Buddhist monks I know have fewer things than most other people I know, but I don't know any Buddhist monks who own only a robe and a begging bowl.

Kobun Chino says, "When you understand that everything was given to everyone in the beginning, a sense comes that there is nothing to limit as 'mine' and as 'not mine.' When you go to the mountain and see a flower blooming, and you pick it up, break it, and make it yours, this is attachment. If you let it be there for everything and everyone, this is what 'no attachment' is." I love that idea. Nowadays I take a kind of delight in spotting a really cool record at a store and then leaving it there for someone else to find.

The idea that everything was given to everyone at the beginning might be difficult to accept. There is clearly a lot of unfairness in the world. Some are born into unimaginable wealth, while others are born into desperate poverty.

Kobun continues: "When I say, 'Everything is given to you,' it sounds like everything belongs to you, and you may feel really good. But when I say, 'Nothing belongs to you,' you may feel bad. Even yourself doesn't belong to you! You are everything. This means you actually have no self to limit. Knowing this Precept is having this deep understanding. Every single thing we appreciate is all public truth and whole Dharma."

This is the other side of "everything is given to everyone." Some of us imagine that we own a limited portion of the universe. That is a mistake. *Nothing* belongs to you. Even if the law defines certain things as your possessions, that is a false idea. As Kobun says, even your self doesn't belong to you.

Think about it for a minute. My self does not belong to me. We all have duties and obligations to others. Even if we deny our duties and obligations or try to avoid them, we can't. They will find us. There are people who love and care about us. They need us to be there for them sometimes. Also, my image of myself is not the same as your image of me. Which one is true? Could the many images of me held by others be truer than the image of myself that I carry around in my own head? That is, if even my head is my own...

To take it further, what I think of as my personal self is really the possession of the entire universe. It does not belong to me at all. I didn't create it. I do not maintain it. I cannot destroy it. I don't even know it! I cannot predict what thought will come into my head next. Even that is out of my control. My so-called self cannot exist without the existence of everything else in the universe. Perhaps the entire universe cannot exist without my self either.

Kobun also says, "If you keep something, you may have had the idea that it was possessed by you, but it was not possessed by you. You become very poor by having this idea. Dogen Zenji said, 'When you open your hand, everything is in your hand. When you close your hand, the air is very limited.' Explaining this idea of possession in this very pure way, naturally you understand this Precept."

We come into this world with nothing, and we leave with nothing. And even in between, we possess nothing. So why even try to hold on to things that were never ours to begin with?

# 29. I VOW NOT TO GIVE WAY TO ANGER

THE BODHIDHARMA ONE-MIND Precepts version of the precept against getting angry is, "Self-nature is mysteriously profound. In the midst of the truth of selflessness, no measuring of oneself or giving rise to the thought of self and other is called the Precept of 'no being angry.'"

Nishijima Roshi's comment on the standard version of this precept is, "Many of us are prone to become angry. It seems a natural outcome of our personality, but in fact anger is not our natural state — it is not our natural condition. In Buddhism we seek to maintain our composure. To be composed is our natural condition. To be natural is the teaching of Gautama Buddha."

Some other contemporary ways of phrasing this precept include, "No indulgence in anger" (Robert Aitken), "A follower of the way does not harbor ill will" (Dainin Katagiri), and "Actualize harmony — Do not indulge in anger" (Taiun Michael Elliston).

The Appleton Zen Center adds some more words of explanation, giving us "Embody Compassion — I recognize and enlighten my greed, anger, and ignorance. I transform my negative emotions and act with equanimity, sympathetic joy, compassion, and loving kindness." Boundless Way Zen Center phrases the precept as "Transforming suffering into wisdom, I vow to take up the way of not indulging in anger." Diane Eshin Rizzetto again makes this one brief, giving us "I take up the way of letting go of anger."

The Brahmajala Sutra says:

A disciple of the Buddha shall not harbor anger or encourage others to be angry. He should not create the causes, conditions, methods, or karma of anger. As a disciple of the Buddha, he ought to be compassionate and filial, helping all sentient beings develop the good roots of non-contention. If instead, he insults and abuses sentient beings, or even transformation beings [such as deities and spirits], with harsh words, hitting them with his fists or feet, or attacking them with a knife or club — or harbors grudges even when the victim confesses his mistakes and humbly seeks forgiveness in a soft, conciliatory voice — the disciple commits a major offense.

In his "Commentary on the Precepts," Dogen says about this one, "It is not regress, it is not advance; it is not real, it is not unreal. There is illumined cloud ocean; there is ornamented cloud ocean." Which, I will grant you, is probably the strangest of his comments on any of the precepts.

And, of course, we have Yoda, who said, "Fear is the path to the dark side. Fear leads to anger. Anger leads to hate. Hate leads to suffering."

When I first started learning and practicing Zen, the precept about anger was the hardest one for me. Other people had a difficult time with the precept about sex or the precept about drugs. I wasn't really into sex and drugs, myself. But I indulged in a lot of anger.

I was one of those people Nishijima Roshi was referring to when he said, "Many of us are prone to become angry. It seems a natural outcome of our personality." He didn't know me when he wrote that, but he could have been talking directly to me. I didn't know how not to be angry. The idea that anger was not my natural state sounded absurd to me. As far as I was concerned at the time, anger clearly was my natural state and, as far as I knew, there was nothing I could do about it. Anger just flared up when it felt like flaring up.

I'd fly into a rage and start breaking things, or I'd just sit there being sullen and burning inside.

Zazen provided me a place to sit and watch my anger as it arose, as it burned, and as it eventually died away. I sat a lot of angry zazen sessions!

Nishijima Roshi always advised his students to suppress their anger. When I first heard this, it sounded not only absurd but positively unhealthy. At the time I thought that you shouldn't bottle up your anger; you should let it out or else you'd explode.

But then I began to look at anger a little more carefully. This I had ample opportunity to do, being such an angry person. When I really observed my anger, it became apparent that it wasn't some substance that built up inside me that I could "let out" and be rid of. There was nothing into which anger could be bottled. That something I called "me" and that something I called "anger" were completely indistinguishable. I started to see that the process of "letting anger out" was actually the process by which more anger was produced.

Suppressing anger is not the same thing as what most folks call "keeping it inside." For most of us, keeping anger inside is the act of reinforcing anger internally. To really suppress anger, you have to suppress the urge to wallow in the beautiful juiciness of anger.

It was hard to admit, but when I started paying attention I noticed that I actually enjoyed being angry, in a funny way. There's a wonderful rush of self-righteousness to it. Because, obviously, I couldn't be angry about something unless I knew I was right and the other person was wrong. I was angry because I wanted to be angry. Always, always.

Kobun Chino says, "If you become angry, you don't stop being Buddha. Anger appears, that's all. At that time you don't say to yourself that you shouldn't be getting angry. When you get close to fire, you don't say, 'It should be cold!'"

That's a good way of putting it, I think. Anger appears. That's all. Telling myself that I shouldn't be angry never did any good. It just made me angrier. The image of getting too close to a fire is useful. It wasn't that I needed the fire to be cold. I just needed to learn how not to get so close to the fire.

Kobun also says, "Usually this Precept is kindly explained: 'A disciple of the Buddha abstains from harboring hatred, malice, or ill will.' This realm [of anger] is very big, from very gentle anger to very developed rage, to the joy of hurting people. Anger changes from protective, to attacking, from negative to very positive."

Not everything we call anger is necessarily bad. You might say a certain person is "angry about the state of the environment," for example. That doesn't necessarily mean she's emotionally distraught over it or wants to hurt someone because of it. The word *angry* is often used in contexts like these to refer to a state of deep concern.

Sometimes anger is protective. One time it came to Nishijima Roshi's attention that one of the men who lived in the Zen house he established in Chiba Prefecture in Japan was being inappropriate with some of the women who lived there. I was there when he got the news. It was hard to say if he was angry, but he immediately took action. He went to the guy's room and, without mincing words, told him very firmly that he needed to move out. He didn't raise his voice at all, but it was clear he was serious. Once that was done, it was if it never happened. He didn't brood about it or even discuss the matter any further. He just got back to his regular duties. It was pretty impressive!

There are varieties of anger. The precept doesn't ask us to never be angry. It asks us not to give way to anger. It asks us not to make anger into ourselves.

Kobun says, "Anger is suffering, as you know. When someone gets very angry with you, his suffering is deeply concerned with you. He is letting you know how he exists. When he sees that you understand him, this anger disappears. When you see someone who is quite angry, when you really listen to him and completely understand his position, you, yourself, become angry. But, fortunately, anger does not stay. If you enjoy keeping it, it will continue. But, otherwise, it is always slipping off of you."

That's the thing with anger. Many of us enjoy keeping it. That was certainly the case with me. I wouldn't have defined what I was doing as "enjoyment" at the time. But I see why Kobun used that word. Anger was a way to define myself as an individual. If I was angry, then I was real.

The Bodhidharma One-Mind precept says, "In the midst of the truth of selflessness, no measuring of oneself or giving rise to the thought of self and other is called the Precept of 'no being angry.'" I measured myself with anger. But the real truth was that the self I measured with anger was a fiction. Anger appeared, but there was no self in it. I just thought there was.

Whenever I let go of anger, I had a fear that I might lose myself. It was like I needed anger in order to be me. And in a sense, that was true. The fiction I had created depended on anger to keep being re-created in my mind, moment by moment. Yet when I finally learned to let anger go, I did not disappear. Not only was I still here, but I felt relief, like I'd put down a heavy weight.

As always, the Buddhist precepts are advice about helping us have a better life.

# 30. I VOW NOT TO DISPARAGE BUDDHA, DHARMA, AND SANGHA

THE BODHIDHARMA ONE-MIND Precepts version of the final of the Ten Grave Precepts, the one against disparaging Buddha, dharma, and sangha, is, "Self-nature is mysteriously profound. In the midst of one Dharma, in the midst of one great truth, not to give rise to the thought of distinction between sentient beings and Buddhas is called the Precept of 'no abusing the Three Treasures.'" Sometimes the Three Treasures are called the Triple Treasure.

Nishijima Roshi's comment on this one is very straightforward. He says, "Buddha, Dharma, and Sangha are the foundation of Buddhist life. We must honor them, esteem them, and devote ourselves to them." I'll tell you a story about that later.

Some variant translations of this precept include, "No slandering of the Three Treasures" (Robert Aitken), "A follower of the way does not abuse the Three Treasures" (Dainin Katagiri), and "A disciple of the Buddha abstains from slandering the Three Treasures" (Taiun Michael Elliston).

Among the more detailed versions, Sojun Mel Weitsman gives us, "I resolve not to abuse the Three Treasures, my own true nature, by respecting the Buddha, unfolding the Dharma, and nourishing the Sangha." The Appleton Zen Center gives us, "Manifest this Way — I hold precious this Sangha and the sacred life we embody, especially these three treasures: This absolute purity of our Awakened Mind! (Buddha) This life filled with wisdom, compassion, and skillful means! (Dharma) This never-ending mystery of life unfolding!

All brothers, all sisters, all beings!" Gosh! Once again, Diane Eshin Rizzetto's version is short — "Not defaming the Three Treasures."

The Brahmajala Sutra says, "A Buddha's disciple shall not himself speak ill of the Triple Treasure or encourage others to do so. He must not create the causes, conditions, methods, or karma of slander. If a disciple hears but a single word of slander against the Buddha from externalists or evil beings, he experiences a pain similar to that of three hundred spears piercing his heart. How then could he possibly slander the Triple Treasure himself? Hence, if a disciple lacks faith and filial piety towards the Triple Treasure, and even assists evil persons or those of aberrant views to slander the Triple Treasure, he commits a major offense."

In his "Commentary on the Precepts" Dogen says about this precept, "Expounding the Dharma with the body is a harbor and a fish pool. The virtues return to the ocean of reality. You should not comment on them. Just hold them and serve them." I may have to revise my position about which of his commentaries on the precepts is the most confusing!

What I get out of Dogen's comment is that we should do our best to uphold the dharma. It's not necessary to express an opinion about it; we need to just do it. Or something like that. It's pretty weird. Maybe you had to be there ...

I said that I'd tell you a story about Nishijima Roshi's attitude toward this precept. Here it is. I wrote a piece on my blog many years ago called "Buddhism Sucks." At the time I didn't think Nishijima Roshi even read my blog. But he read that one and emailed me, saying, "We should never blame Buddhism." Japanese people who speak English tend to use the word *blame* in a funny way. I think he meant something more like *disparage*.

The blog was actually about how the thing that is called "Buddhism" these days is often not what I would recognize as Buddhism. Nishijima Roshi got that. It's just that disparaging Buddhism was a hard line that he felt a student of his should not cross. I didn't argue with Nishijima Roshi about the true meaning of my article. I just changed the title of the blog piece and told him I wouldn't blame Buddhism anymore.

The old man interpreted this precept quite literally, and I respected that. Even though I knew I wasn't really intentionally disparaging Buddhism, I had to admit that what I wrote could have been taken that way.

Another way to understand this precept was suggested to me by Leah Sokunin Sanford, who follows me on Patreon. She said, "I thought it would be useful to consider the act of disparagement itself, separate from its targets. I like looking up synonyms, and some of the synonyms for 'disparage' are pretty awful: 'belittle, vilify, disdain, scorn, impugn, ridicule, slander' — and there are lots more. Anyway, I thought the precept might also be about how the very act itself — of scorning or ridiculing — results in harm; about how such behavior adds to ignorance and misery, turning us away from clear seeing and the freedom of understanding."

I think that's a great point. Maybe the precept isn't just about not disparaging the Three Treasures but about not engaging in the act of disparaging anyone or anything. In fact, the Lotus Sutra contains a story about a bodhisattva whose name translates as "Never Disparage." His way of being a bodhisattva was that he never disparaged anyone or anything.

My friend Greg Fain, a practice leader at Tassajara Zen Mountain Monastery in California, was so moved by the story he even wrote a song about it! It's called "Our Hero Bodhisattva Never Disparaging (aka The Lotus Sutra Song)." The song's chorus goes:

> I would never disparage you or keep you at arm's length
> Where you only see your weaknesses, I only see your strength
> I would never despise you or put you down in any way
> Because it's clear to me
> I can plainly see
> You'll be a buddha someday
> I love you.

Getting back to the precept itself, Bodhidharma's One-Mind Precepts version goes, "In the midst of one Dharma, in the midst of one great truth, not to give rise to the thought of distinction between sentient beings and Buddhas is called the Precept of 'no abusing the Three Treasures.'" This is reminiscent of "Genjo Koan," in which Dogen says, "When the myriad dharmas are each not of the self, there is no delusion and no realization, no buddhas and no ordinary beings, no life and no death. The Buddha's truth is originally transcendent over abundance and scarcity, and so there is life and death, there is delusion and realization, there are ordinary beings and buddhas."

I know all that might seem really opaque and difficult. So let me switch gears here. I really like Kobun Chino's explanation of this precept. I think it's a good way to look at both the standard version and the Bodhidharma version of the precept. So forgive me for quoting him perhaps a bit too extensively in this chapter.

Kobun first explains the meaning of Buddha, dharma, and sangha, saying, "Buddha is Anuttarasamyak-sambodhi — supreme, complete awakening, itself. Dharma is Truth, itself, which has never been stained. There is no way to stain it. Sangha is the entire contents of supreme awakening, the harmonious manifestation of Truth in form."

Originally, *Buddha* just meant Gautama Buddha, the historical person who started Buddhism; *dharma* meant what Gautama Buddha taught; and *sangha* meant the people who followed that teaching. Here Kobun gives us the wider definitions of these terms that developed in the Mahayana schools of Buddhism.

*Buddha* is interpreted as meaning the awakened state rather than the historical person. *Dharma* is the truth itself rather than the historical Buddha's teaching. When Kobun says that the dharma can't be stained, he means that the truth is as it is, no matter what we think about it. The definition of *sangha* is much broader than merely the followers of Buddhism. It means the collective manifestation of the fundamental truth of all things. When anyone anywhere — Buddhist or not — takes right action, that person is part of the universal sangha, and that action is the manifestation of eternal truth.

Kobun takes things further in his definition of the Triple Treasure. He says, "The ground of the deeper meaning of Triple Treasure is shikantaza." As I said earlier, *shikantaza* literally means "just sitting." It's the form of zazen that Dogen taught.

Most forms of meditation involve concentrating on something or trying to attain some goal. Shikantaza is goalless. About shikantaza, Kobun once said, "Avoiding thoughts would be concentration, not meditation. Rather, we don't pay attention to thoughts. They pay attention to you, to make you realize what they are." So we're not even trying to rid ourselves of thought. We allow thoughts to pass and keep sitting. We don't even regard thoughts as belonging to us.

Defining the ground of the Triple Treasure to be shikantaza is pretty bold. Folks from other schools of Buddhism in which shikantaza is not practiced might object. But it is through the practice of shikantaza that we can come to understand our basic nature and the meaning of terms like *continuous awakening*.

Kobun continues his commentary on the tenth Grave Precept saying, "Bodhidharma speaks of this 'No abusing the Triple Treasure' as understanding that our essence of existence, continuous awakening, is nothing but our basic nature. He teaches that self-nature is profound, contained in one Truth. Not to give birth to the dualistic observation that you and Buddha are different existences, not to give birth to dualistic thinking about sentient beings and Buddha, that is called 'No abusing Triple Treasure.'"

When we understand that we are not different from Buddha, we act in accordance with truth. Again, the word *Buddha* here doesn't mean Gautama Buddha who lived 2,500 years ago in northern India. It means that we ourselves, just as we are, are the supreme truth itself. We are beyond the dualistic thinking that divides the world into subject and object.

Then Kobun says, "To think of the Triple Treasure as somewhere outside of you is the beginning of abusing, departing, from it. You are keeping yourself from it. If you understand Buddha and sentient beings as different beings, you are misunderstanding Triple Treasure and making the biggest mistake. You are cutting the Buddha's body and looking at his blood running!"

That's a pretty scary image! Kobun clearly wants us to take this seriously.

To emphasize this point Kobun says, "When you meet one little being, it might be a mosquito, or pine tree, or rock, to become Buddha with each of them is your practice. Do you understand? You become Buddha with each of them. This is communicating with a being that appeared for you, to make sure you are enlightened! It is also enlightened. This is how everything is actually happening but sometimes neither one knows what is going on. Sometimes both completely know what is going on."

To me, that is one of the greatest pieces of Buddhist literature ever committed to writing. Kobun didn't actually write that, as such. He spoke it out loud and it was transcribed by someone else. Still, it is Buddhist literature at its finest. Read it again and again.

That mosquito appeared for you to make sure you get enlightened. Your awful boss appeared for you to make sure you get enlightened. He is also enlightened. So is the mosquito. Maybe neither of you know it, but that doesn't change a thing.

There is no subject or object. Everyone and everything that appears to you is a manifestation of you. But it's not a manifestation of the small self that you think you are. It's not the limited, individualized self. It's a manifestation of your true self. Your true self is very large. Unlimited. In the macrocosm, there are universes without number. In the microcosm, every atom and molecule also contains limitless universes. Each one is infinite. And everything and everyone is contained within you.

You communicate with your true self in each encounter. Even

this encounter you're having right now with this book is an example of you communicating with your true self. It is you trying to bring yourself to a better understanding of what you really are. Which isn't to say this book is super special in that respect. It wouldn't matter if you were reading this book or the latest issue of *Motor Trend* magazine. Every encounter is an opportunity for awakening.

As Kobun says, "Sometimes neither one knows what is going on." Or as Dogen says, "You won't necessarily be aware of your own awakening." But sometimes both understand completely.

Then Kobun says, "If you believe in yourself as the creation of the absolute existence, whose presence is the only presence, then no problem! There is no separation between creator, creation, and created thing. You simply admit that you are an extension of the creation, a part of it, accepted by it. Eventually the effort becomes how to live within the intention of the creator. To find this out and follow this Way, is to live."

He tells you everything you need to know right there.

Kobun was fond of phrases like *absolute existence*. Sometimes he even called it God. You don't hear a lot of Zen teachers use the G-word, but Kobun did, and so did Kobun's student Tim, my Zen first teacher. As Kobun says, if you truly understand that there is no separation between creator, creation, and created, there is no problem. He says, "You simply admit that you are an extension of the creation, a part of it, accepted by it. Eventually the effort becomes how to live within the intention of the creator. To find this out and follow this Way, is to live."

"Simply," he says ...

It's not always that simple. But actually it is. The problem is that we complicate it rather than allowing it to be just as it is. I know I sure do! My biggest problem is how complicated I can make this simple thing. The trick is to learn to let go. I've been studying that trick for most of my life. Sometimes I even manage to pull it off.

# 31. DON'T BE A JERK

The Noble Eightfold Path and the precepts are the most obvious examples of ethical teachings in Zen Buddhism, but there are other interesting examples. Dogen believed that the most important teaching of Buddhism was "Do not do wrong." He wrote about this in an essay called "Shoaku Makusa." I wrote a book a few years ago in which I paraphrased that title as "Don't Be a Jerk." Others have translated it as "Refrain from All Evil Whatsoever" (Hubert Nearman), "Not Doing Wrongs" (Nishijima/Cross), and "Refrain from Unwholesome Action" (Tanahashi et al).

Dogen said that this idea of not enacting evil isn't something that some wise person came up with a long time ago. It existed before you and I or even Dogen got here. He says that "not doing wrong" predates the universe. People did not invent the idea of doing right and avoiding wrong, he says, but people can learn to align themselves with what is right and, in so doing, align themselves with the universe.

One of the most vexing issues for Western philosophy has always been the Problem of Evil. If God created the world, and if God is all good and all loving, then why is there evil?

There are all sorts of answers to this question. Some of these answers try to preserve the idea of an all-good God in a variety of clever ways. Some, for example, suggest that maybe God cannot prevent evil. But that would make him less than all-powerful. Others say that God allows evil to exist in order to test us. But this calls

God's pure goodness into question. Some of the Christian Gnostics even suggested that our world is under the rule not of God, who is nice, but of a sort of sub-God who is not very nice. But that begs the question of why the real God doesn't do something about the sub-God. And of course, some people think that the existence of evil is proof positive that God simply does not exist.

Buddhism doesn't have an all-powerful, all-good creator God in the sense that Christianity does. So a Buddhist doesn't need to explain the existence of evil in a way that preserves the existence of God or his goodness.

Dogen didn't look on evil as a thing that exists and sits around waiting for someone to do it. Rather, he believed that only action in the present moment is real. Sometimes the action we take is right, and sometimes it isn't. Evil only comes into being when people do the wrong thing. It's the same with good.

There are three broad categories of action, he says. Actions can be right, wrong, or neutral. It's tricky to try to define right and wrong. And yet, like US Supreme Court Justice Potter Stewart said about obscenity in 1964, even though it's hard to define, we know it when we see it.

Dogen recognized that there are similarities between right actions, no matter where or when they occur, and there are differences too, as there are with wrong actions. Eight hundred years later, Sam Harris coined the term *moral landscape* to describe a similar idea. Harris says that we can think of morality as a kind of landscape. Every landscape looks different from every other, and yet in each one there are high points and low points. Even when the shape of the terrain varies considerably, we can still recognize which points are high and which are low. Even when cultures and customs are different from each other, we can still recognize right and wrong.

Telling the difference between right and wrong requires balance, though. An unbalanced person can get very confused. And when you do the wrong thing, you become that much more unbalanced.

Learning to tell when you're becoming unbalanced is one of the ben-efits of zazen practice. You know the difference between right and wrong actions by how they make you feel.

A lot of people these days are looking for meaning and ethics, but instead they're finding Big Causes filled with moral posturing and slogans. When ethics are not balanced, things get weird. All sorts of unethical behavior can be made to seem justifiable when it's presented as a way to eradicate evil.

We humans are clever creatures. We can use our big, overdevel-oped brains to justify absolutely any action. We can use crafty words to explain our wrongdoings both to others and to ourselves in ways that make them seem reasonable and right. But we always know when we're wrong, even if we cannot consciously acknowledge it.

I know it sounds like a bold claim to say that we always know when we're doing wrong. So maybe I should modify it a bit. I always know when I am doing wrong. I assume I am not different from others in this, although I cannot offer you conclusive proof. So let's talk about me.

The fact that I always know when I am wrong was the source of a few days of pure horror for me when I was sitting at a Zen retreat in a temple called Tokei-in nestled among the peaceful tea fields of rural Shizuoka Prefecture in Japan one very hot and humid summer. As I sat there in the stillness, with nothing to distract me, I watched as my own mind justified wrongs I had committed in the past. The reasons I came up with were clever enough to convince any jury of my peers if I were ever taken to trial for the things I'd done. And yet I knew for a fact that I was lying to myself.

Up until that moment I thought that the only people who jus-tified what they knew to be wrong were monsters, like members of the Nazi Party or the Ku Klux Klan. Not that I'd done anything to match the atrocities committed by some of those people. But I saw my own mind making the same sorts of excuses I'd heard from peo-ple like that.

The moment I realized I was doing this, I was genuinely terrified of myself. It was as if every evil ever committed by humankind
might as well have been committed by me. I was honestly unsure if I
even deserved to live. My stomach did flip-flops for hours.

But I'd done enough zazen by then that I knew the drill. When
stuff like that comes up, the best thing to do is to continue sitting still.
So I sat still. Outside the temple a chorus of cicadas buzzed away.
Crows cawed. Someone coughed. Someone else adjusted his position and made the platform we sat on creak. My head slowly filled
with abject horror, and then it overflowed. I sat.

It's funny the kinds of things that happen in a zendo. If a stranger
were to walk into a room full of people doing zazen, she'd likely
think that everyone is just blissing out in meditation. Maybe she'd
imagine they're having beatific visions and probing into the true
nature of reality. In fact, a lot of us in there are just trying to hold
ourselves together and stay still while we freak out. Which is what
I was doing.

I had to make a lot of changes after that. It was probably twenty
years ago, and I am still far from finished in making those changes.
But to the extent that I have stopped justifying what I know to
be wrong, my life has been happier. It's not always easy, because
excuses are endless.

The trick in knowing that I'm making excuses is that excuses
always take work. I can feel the wheels turning up there in my head
while I make up justifications. When I notice that is happening, I
withdraw energy from the process. It then becomes impossible to
believe my own lies. I won't say I always do this with 100 percent
efficiency. But when I do, it works extremely well. I'm left with
only the bare recognition of my own action and no explanations or
excuses.

The process for doing this is watching my own mind play its
tricks without interfering — without helping it play those tricks or

trying to stop it from doing so. I just let it happen and watch. It's actually quite fascinating. That's shikantaza practice.

Buddhist ethics do not allow for excuses.

There is no external God we can appeal to who might accept our excuses. We cannot plead our case to anyone but ourselves.

I have to be unflinchingly honest with myself if I want to follow the Buddhist way of ethical action. Wrong action that results in personal gain can make me feel good in the short term. And when I say "personal gain," I'm not just talking about money. If I get some kind of pleasant sensory experience of so-called satisfaction from doing something wrong, that is also personal gain. That righteous feeling I get when I think I'm a hero who has vanquished an evil villain is one of the most devious of these pleasant sensory experiences. Even when that happens, there will always be some part of me that knows better. I can try to ignore that part. I can shove it way, way back to the darkest corners of my mind. But it will never go away. I'll always know I did wrong, no matter how skillfully I'm able to deny it to myself.

Dogen says that the essence of rightness, wrongness, or neutrality is nonappearance. He says that they are the state without excess and are real form. At the same time, he says, at each concrete place these three properties include innumerable dharmas.

That's Dogen's way of putting it, but as we know, it's not easy to follow Dogen sometimes. When Dogen says things like "nonappearance" or "the state without excess" or "innumerable dharmas," it gets confusing. So let me see if I can put it differently.

Nishijima Roshi always explained the meaning of "nonappearance" as instantaneousness. Here's how he put it in a blog he wrote: "Rightness, wrongness, neutrality, and so on, do not have any relation with appearance or disappearance because they are all real situations at the present moment." Instantaneousness means something that occurs spontaneously in this real moment.

"The state without excess" is a little easier. It means things just as they are, without anything extra added. Of course, it's always possible to add something extra, like an excuse or justification. Which is precisely the problem. Most of us habitually add excess to whatever we do by adding in the idea that our actions are the activities of a personal self.

Finally, Dogen says that rightness, wrongness, and neutrality "include innumerable dharmas." That just means that every activity of an individual is also the activity of the entire universe. Dharma, in this case, is a kind of catch-all term that means pretty much anything and everything. You can't even scratch your butt without the entire universe contributing to that action. I mean it!

Think about it. The very fact that there is a butt for you to scratch involved the entire evolution of the human species. And the evolution of the human species involved the entire evolution of life on Earth. And the evolution of life on Earth involved the entire evolution of the solar system. And the evolution of the solar system involved the entire evolution of the Milky Way galaxy. I could go on, but I hope you get the picture.

Your ability to make the movements involved in scratching your butt derives from energy patterns that extend far beyond anything you can possibly conceive. Your ability to move at all comes from the energy stored in the food you've ingested, which comes from the sun — because plant energy derives from the sun, and even if you eat meat, the animals you ate got their energy from plants. Even the sun's energy doesn't come from nowhere. It's the result of nuclear fission, which has to do with the force of gravity mashing the particles that make up the sun together. I'm no scientist, but I know it's an insanely complicated process. The fact that the sun has energy to contribute to you scratching your butt is attributable to processes that go back to the big bang, and probably far beyond.

That itch you feel has its own infinite history too. As does your desire to scratch it. As does everything about you and your butt. The point is that no matter what you do, literally innumerable dharmas are involved.

The good news is that there is a way to end all evil. And that is to simply refrain from doing what is wrong. Obviously this will not rid the world entirely of all evil action in one fell swoop. Good luck figuring out a way to do that! But the more people who commit to refraining from doing what they know to be wrong — even when they've got a damned good excuse to do it — the less evil will be present in the world.

It's like when Nishijima Roshi told me, "You can't fix your company. But you can make things a little better." He said that although I couldn't fix everything that was wrong where I worked, I could at least make a little difference.

That was some of the best advice I have ever received. It has so many applications.

You can't fix global climate change, but you can make a little difference.

You can't fix race relations, but you can make a little difference.

You can't fix the economy, heal the natural environment, undo centuries of human abuse and neglect; you can't be Superman and make the world spin backward so that time goes in reverse so you can prevent some disaster before it happened like he did in that one movie. You can't do any of that.

But you can make a little difference.

So make a little difference!

Watch carefully for your opportunity, and when it arrives, do that one positive, helpful thing that is available to you at that moment. Which is the only real moment that has ever existed.

Maybe no one will notice. Maybe even you yourself won't be able to see the difference you've made. But that's no reason not to make the effort.

Forget about being rewarded or even patted on the back for the good things you do. Just do what's right without any thought of compensation. Or if you do think of compensation, just put that thought aside. It doesn't mean anything. It arises out of habit. It doesn't make you a bad person or anything like that. It simply means you're normal. Forget about it if you can. And if you can't forget about it, don't worry. Just keep on working for good in your own small way.

Another odd thing that Dogen says is that right and wrong are time, and yet time is not right or wrong. Each action we take creates time. Time is not something apart from ourselves. Time is being. You and I are time. We'll get to that a bit later. For now, let's stick with this idea of not enacting wrong and see how it relates to time.

Every action we take affects the whole of the universe and the whole of time. We have a very limited view of ourselves. We imagine that we can do things in secret or on a small scale. This is an illusion. Every action we take is extraordinarily important. We have a tremendous responsibility. Everything we do affects everyone and everything else there is.

I might imagine I can do a small bad thing and that, as long as nobody else notices it, I can get away with it. But the very fact of me noticing it is the universe noticing it. I am the eyes and ears of the universe. So are we all.

I never get away with anything. When I think I do, I'm just fooling himself.

That can be really hard to believe sometimes. I'm always seeing people who do what I know to be very bad things who, nevertheless, end up rich, or famous, or powerful. Meanwhile people who are perfectly nice end up getting cancer and dying young.

But Buddhists are kind of funny when it comes to this stuff.

For one thing, what constitutes good fortune and bad fortune for regular people often doesn't work for Buddhists. Becoming rich, famous, and powerful is not always the best thing that can happen to a person. In fact, according to the Buddhists, it's usually the worst.

The richer, more famous, and more powerful you are, the less opportunity you're likely to have to encounter the Truth.

When Buddhists say this, they mean Truth with a capital *T*. But it also works for truth with a lowercase *t*. How do rich, famous, powerful people ever know who their friends really are or what people actually think of them? They've always got to wonder if people are just pretending to like them in order to get something from them. That's gotta be a hellish existence, no matter how many Lamborghinis and vacation homes in the South of France it allows you to afford.

As for the Truth with a capital *T*, what incentive does a rich, famous, powerful person have to do the hard work required to connect with their true self? They usually end up just indulging in the "finer things" until their bodies finally collapse from their own vices.

Maybe there are exceptions. I mean, Sting seems like a pretty spiritual guy, and he's rich as hell. He also seems like a decent fellow. The problem is, for a guy like Sting, even if he encounters a genuine spiritual teacher, how can he be sure that the spiritual teacher isn't just interested in his money and fame?

It's very tricky!

I feel my relationships with my own teachers were much better than the kinds of relationships with teachers that are possible for rich and powerful people. My teachers always knew they weren't ever gonna get anything of value from me, and I knew it too. That sort of thing was never even an issue.

The bottom line is, being rich and famous isn't the best thing that can happen to you. Nor is being dirt-poor necessarily always the worst. Don't get me wrong. Poverty can really suck. There've been times in my life when I was so poor that even scraping together $60 to rent a room in a dilapidated punk rock house was damned hard. I did not like it. When I lived in Kenya I saw poverty so crushing it was hard to imagine how people managed to live at all.

Still, the early Buddhists took a vow of poverty. They purposely relinquished everything they had and lived only on what they could beg for. They did this so they could be free from even the slightest bit of greed. A few Buddhists still do this, but it's not as common as it used to be. It's very rare in the West.

I've never taken the deliberate leap into total poverty that the early Buddhists did. But I know some people who have, and none of them ever regretted it. They discovered that they actually owned the entire universe.

But let's get back to what Dogen says about the matter of right and wrong.

When wrong is not done by someone, he says, evil doesn't come into existence. That's the bottom line. But it's hard for people to come to terms with this, and it bears repeating again and again. So he repeats it a lot in his essay.

According to Dogen, even if I lived in a place where I had all sorts of opportunities to do the wrong thing, and even if I lived at a time when everyone seemed to be hurting each other and taking unfair advantage of each other, even if all my friends were doing terrible things and I knew they'd never call me out for the bad things I did, and even if I ended up in circumstances where the easiest thing to do was also the wrong thing to do, I still have the power to overcome all that stuff by simply refusing to do what I know to be wrong.

Some people believe in Satan, who is an evil being who compels us to do bad things. But that always seemed to me like a lame excuse. Wrong has no fixed form. Wrong action is, itself, powerless. It has no voice of its own. It has no tools at its disposal. It doesn't even exist at all until one of us brings it into the world of our own volition, even when we always know — if often only in the most hidden regions of our subconscious — that we are doing the wrong thing.

You can choose to do wrong, or you can choose not to do wrong. The moment you understand that wrong action doesn't exist outside your own conduct at this very moment, you have realized a profound truth.

It's not like you get this realization once and then it's yours to keep forever. It comes up dynamically moment after moment. And yet, doing the right thing at this moment is simultaneously doing the right thing at every moment in the past, present, and future. This is because this very moment is the whole of time and the entirety of the universe.

Nishijima Roshi once told Jürgen Segelke, a German student of his, that every action is carved into the universe. Whatever you do in this real moment right now, he said, can never be undone.

Kodo Sawaki talked about a similar idea:

Ishikawa Goemon [a Japanese Robin Hood–like character who stole from the rich to give to the poor] once said, "Even once I have disappeared and all the sand has washed into the sea, the seeds of thievery in the world will never be exhausted." This is how he sings the praises of the thief's nature that penetrates heaven and earth. And yet as long as we don't act like Goemon we won't become thieves. It's also said that all things have Buddha nature and that it completely penetrates heaven and earth. But as long as we don't act like a Buddha we don't become a Buddha. Though you are inseparable from Buddha, only when you put Buddha's activity into practice are you a Buddha. And when you act like a fool then you're a fool. It's only in your approach to life that Buddha appears.

Dogen says that any teaching that doesn't sound like "do not commit wrong" is not the Buddha's right dharma. In fact, the very first sermon the historical Buddha ever gave was about not doing wrong. This was the sermon in which he delivered the famous Four Noble Truths and the Noble Eightfold Path. Dogen is on solid ground, then, in insisting that "do not commit wrong" is foundational to all Buddhism.

But Dogen isn't just invoking the authority of the historical

Buddha when he says that "do not commit wrong" is the most important teaching there is. He says that this teaching is the supreme state
of enlightenment put into words. This isn't just a human idea. It's
a universal truth. And I don't mean it's universal in the sense that
all people can agree to it. I mean that it's a truth that guides the
universe. Dogen says that it's "on the scale of the whole earth, the
whole world, the whole of time, and the whole of Dharma." And
remember that *dharma*, as used here, means the universe.

That part might be harder to accept. If you think of the universe as mostly made up of inert matter such as rocks, planets, stars,
quasars, gas clouds, and suchlike, it's hard to imagine how ethical
conduct could be a universal truth. The materialistic outlook is
incompatible with the idea that something like ethical behavior could
be significant on the kind of scale Dogen is talking about. But Dogen
is not speaking from the perspective of a materialist. To him, mind is
foundational to the very existence of the universe.

I'm tempted here to try to put forth some kind of evidence to
prove to you that he's right, or at least convince you that he might
have a point. I've seen books where the authors try to do that. But
even to me, a person who believes Dogen's view is correct, the sorts
of reasons people put forward to try to convince folks that the nondualistic way of understanding is correct usually leave me cold.

For example, they'll talk about how quantum physics supposedly proves that an observer is necessary for the existence of physical
reality. But years ago, my teacher Tim told me he had a friend who
was doing a PhD in physics. Both Tim and his friend had read a book
called *The Tao of Physics*, which was one of the first books to popu-
larize the idea that contemporary physics aligned with ancient Eastern spiritual traditions like Zen. These days there's a whole industry
of books like that!

Anyhow, Tim told his physicist friend that he felt like the author
of that book knew a lot about physics but didn't understand Eastern spiritual traditions at all. To which Tim's physicist friend said,

"That's interesting. Because I thought he knew a lot about Eastern spiritual traditions, but he didn't understand physics at all."

I prefer to stay out of those kinds of discussions. Anything I might say about physics will sound naive and uninformed to someone who really knows about physics. I'm not even sure I'm regarded as much of an expert on Eastern spirituality. All I can say is that I have practiced in the Zen tradition for a healthy amount of time and have come to accept Dogen's view that the entire universe is, in a sense, a single sentient entity. The idea that it might *not* be a single sentient entity doesn't even sound reasonable to me anymore. I can remember well the time when I doubted it, and so I fully understand why a lot of people think it's a crazy notion. With enough practice, I think anyone can understand why Dogen's view makes more sense than the so-called commonsense one.

# 32. SAME BRAD, DIFFERENT DAY?
## BEING-TIME

DOGEN HAD SOME weird ideas about time that might help make the weird ideas Buddhism has about ethics a bit clearer. He lays these ideas out in an essay in *Shobogenzo* called "Uji" ("Being-Time").

But before we dive into Dogen, I want to bring up something that one of Dogen's greatest fans said about this essay. In his book *Each Moment Is the Universe*, Dainin Katagiri said, "What we call the conscious world is nothing but a provisional picture of the world produced by our dualistic human minds. Is there anything wrong with our provisional pictures? I don't think so. If we think the world is just something imaginary or provisional, it appears to have no value and we become pessimistic. But remember, the conscious world is also time; our provisional pictures are beings in Buddha's world."

He explained this with an interesting example. "When you use the toilet, you don't believe it's a provisional picture in an imaginary world, because you can see the toilet right in front of you. But the toilet you see is a toilet fabricated by your consciousness. The real toilet is just like time — every moment it goes away. All you have to do is just use it, just handle the toilet as Buddha, and live with the toilet in peace and harmony. This is everyday practice."

"Uji" is Dogen's most famous piece of writing on the nature of time. Actually the word *uji* is kind of a pun. Normally, the Chinese characters used to write the word Dogen pronounced as *uji* are pronounced *arutoki* when spoken in Japanese. Japanese is written in a complicated combination of native Japanese syllabic characters that only have one pronunciation each and borrowed Chinese characters, which have fixed meanings but can be pronounced various ways, depending on context.

Anyway, when pronounced *arutoki*, it's just a very common word meaning "sometimes" or "at one time." Dogen noticed that if you read the Chinese characters differently the word could be understood as "being-time" or "existence-time." The first character can mean "to be" or "to exist," and the second means "time." He used this funny aspect of the Chinese characters as a way to get into expressing his idea that being and time are one and the same.

Normally we think that time is separate from our existence. We think that we move through time. I tend to imagine that the same Brad Warner who existed yesterday exists today. With any luck, the same Brad will still be around tomorrow. Same Brad, different day.

But Dogen says, "You should understand that even though there was a moon last night, the moon you see tonight is not last night's moon. Tonight's moon, whatever phase it appears in, is nothing but the moon of tonight. Although they say there is the moon, it is neither new nor old, because the moon inherits the moon."

Don't imagine that Dogen was some naïve, primitive guy who superstitiously believed the moon was swallowed up by a dragon every morning after it set and a new one was pooped out again the next night, or some such thing. He knew that, conventionally speaking, the same moon rose every night. He was pointing out that the sense we have of things being static and continuous existences that move through the dimension of time was a mistake.

We are not solid and stable beings who move through the dimension of time. Time is not separate from existence. What we are and what time is are the very same thing. The moon is an expression of time, just like we are. And time is an expression of the moon and of us.

The physicist Carlo Rovelli said something similar in his book *The Order of Time*. He titled one chapter "The World Is Made of Events, Not Things."

In that chapter he says, "The entire evolution of science would suggest that the best grammar for thinking about the world is that of change, not of permanence. Not of being, but becoming." He says, "The difference between things and events is that things persist in time; events have limited duration." He gives a rock as an example of a thing, as contrasted with an event. But, he says, "On closer inspection, in fact, even the things that are most 'thinglike' are nothing more than long events." A rock isn't a rock forever — even though it might seem like that to us humans. It starts off as a bunch of sand, gets compressed and melted, exists as a rock for a while, and eventually wears away into sand again. Even to say it started off as sand is wrong, because the sand wasn't always sand either. The molecules that make up each grain of sand have their own complicated history. Therefore, any given rock's existence as a rock is an event within the long, long history of its constituent parts.

Rovelli says, "Things in themselves are only events that for a while are monotonous." And he concludes the chapter in a very Dogen-like fashion by saying, "If by 'time' we mean nothing more than happening, then everything is time."

Dogen seems to agree with Rovelli. He wouldn't have said that each day he was the same thing, as in "same Dogen, different day." He believed that he changed from moment to moment, that he was an event, not a thing. He believed that his existence was not different or separate from the moments in which he existed, the same way that a wave is not separate from the ocean in which it occurs.

And yet, Dogen says, "the moon inherits the moon." We inherit the things we did in the past. As my teacher said, everything you do is carved into the universe forever. We have to be careful here and now, because what we do here and now can never be undone. That's where ethics becomes important. But let's keep looking at what Dogen says about time.

Dogen says, "The self arrays itself and forms the entire universe. Perceive each particular thing in this entire universe as a moment of time. Things do not hinder one another, just as moments do not hinder one another. For this reason, the whole world of time is arousing the way-seeking mind; the whole world of the mind is arousing time. The same is true with practice and attaining the Way. Thus, the self sets the self out in array and sees itself. This is the understanding that self is time."

That's how the quotation appears in Katagiri Roshi's book. Hee-Jin Kim, in his book *Eihei Dogen: Mystical Realist*, translates the first line of that section of "Uji" differently. His version goes, "You should examine the fact that my self unfolds itself and makes the entire universe out of it." Whoa!

We don't just live within time and space. We *are* time are space. Kobun Chino Roshi said, "Mind is captured by matter but when matter is not there, the mind recovers its nature, which is time and space itself. It is not just the concept of space, but actual space, actual time, without ignorance."

Nisargadatta Maharaj said:

Your being a person is due to the illusion of space and time: you imagine yourself to be at a certain point occupying a certain volume; your personality is due to your self-identification with the body. Your thoughts and feelings exist in succession; they have their span in time and make you imagine yourself, because of memory, as having duration. In reality, time and space exist in you; you do not exist in them. They are modes of perception, but they are not the only ones. Time and space are like words written on paper; the paper is real, the words merely a convention. What makes you say, "I am here?" Verbal habits born from assumptions. The mind creates time and space and takes its creations for reality. All is here and now, but we do not see it. Truly all is in me and by me. There is nothing else.

But let's return to Dogen. We've seen that phrase "arousing the way-seeking mind" that Dogen used before when I talked about people giving "Way Seeking Mind" talks. It's just a fancy way of saying what you're doing by reading this book. Like me, at some point you decided that you really needed to know what the world was and what life was all about. I couldn't tell you when this deep questioning of everything started for me. It seems like it was always there.

In any case, Dogen is saying the whole universe arouses this desire to understand itself. So even people who seem like they don't have any interest in this stuff actually do. They just haven't noticed it yet.

"The self arrays itself and forms the entire universe," Dogen says. The entire universe is just the self putting itself on display for itself to marvel at. I used to love my dinosaur toys when I was a kid. Sometimes I'd set them all up on a table or something just to see them all. That's the image that comes to mind when I read this. Only, the dinosaur toys and the "me" who looks at them are all the very same thing.

What we are as individuals is a bunch of different ways that the universal self uses to experience itself. Nisargadatta Maharaj's student Ramesh Balsekar says that "in the original state of unicity, or wholeness, no medium or instrument exists through which 'knowing' can take place." Or as Dogen puts the same idea in his essay "Inmo" ("It"), "We ourselves are tools that it [the universal self] possesses within this universe in ten directions." We are both the instruments or tools with which the universal self knows itself, and we are the state of "knowing" in the form of a person.

Dogen says, "The essential characteristic of being-time is this: while all existences in all the various worlds are interconnected, each existence is unique in itself, and precisely because of this, we can speak of personally experiencing the living reality of being-time."

In his commentary on this essay in the book called *Deepest Practice, Deepest Wisdom*, Kosho Uchiyama said, "What is living out right now, in every moment, this living reality of life before the division into self and all phenomena, is none other than me."

It's none other than me too, Kosho! And it's you, as well, dear reader. The universe wants to know all about itself. And to do so, it needs as many opinions as possible. Infinite opinions! Maybe you and I are just the universe's opinions about itself.

Dogen says, "The view of the common person today, and the causes and conditions of [that] view, are what the common person experiences but are not the common person's reality. It is just that reality, for the present, has made a common person into its causes and conditions."

Kosho Uchiyama's comments on this line are, "The unadulterated living quick of life as the all-pervading self has done nothing more than temporarily take the form of an ordinary person. In other words, all of us are just ordinary human beings, and the pure quick of life has taken on the appearance of an ordinary person."

Nisargadatta Maharaj expressed this same idea by saying, "Your being a person is due to the illusion of space and time. The mind creates time and space and takes its own creations for reality."

Most of us only understand the aspect of ourselves as ordinary human beings. When guys like Dogen and others say that we're manifestations of the universal mind, it doesn't mean they deny our existence as ordinary people. Both aspects are true.

In "Being-Time," Dogen says this in a real weird way (big surprise):

Celestial kings and celestial throngs, now appearing to the right and appearing to the left, are the existence-time in which we are now exerting ourselves. Elsewhere, beings of existence-time of land and sea are [also] realized through our own exertion now. The many kinds of being and the many individual beings which [live] as existence-time in darkness and in brightness, are all the realization of our own effort, and the momentary continuance of our effort. We should learn in practice that without the momentary continuance of our own effort in the present, not a single dharma nor a single thing could ever be realized or could ever continue from one moment to the next.

Dogen was fond of what we today sometimes call "purple prose." He even said that one of his greatest faults was that whenever he wrote he couldn't help but be elaborate and ornate. So don't worry too much about all that "celestial kings and celestial throngs" business. He's just talking about the stuff we encounter in ordinary life, both seen and unseen. Everything is a manifestation of being-time. Kosho Uchiyama explains Dogen by saying, "All things exist precisely because I personally experience them. He is saying that I myself am living through my personal experience of these things."

That is why we have to be so careful when it comes to ethics. The very existence of everything depends on me. I have a tremendous responsibility. And not just me. You too! You're also completely responsible for everything in the universe. So don't take your life lightly!

Dainin Katagiri says, "The unity of time and space, the unity of time and being, is operating dynamically, so you cannot separate them at all. You can really see this! When you open your eyes and see the world in the universal perspective, you realize this point."

He makes it sound like it's easy! But Dogen says, "To universally realize the whole universe by using the whole universe is called 'to perfectly realize.'" Which doesn't sound easy at all. And for most of us afflicted with this inborn need to realize the universe, it's not easy. We have to do loads of work.

But Dogen offers us a bit of encouragement, saying that "even a moment of half-perfectly-realized existence-time is the perfect realization of half-existence-time. Even those phases in which we seem to be blundering heedlessly are also existence."

Which to me means that we're all a bunch of dummies. And don't let anybody tell you different!

There are those among us who are great at pretending that we're not dummies, that we've got it all together and know what's up. But it's all an act. There's not a single person who doesn't have just as many doubts as you do, who isn't blundering as heedlessly as you are. There are just certain people who are good at hiding those doubts. Sometimes they get so good at hiding their doubts from others that they think they really don't have any. I always find it kind of sad when I encounter someone like that. They have more trouble than anyone else when it comes to discovering the truth.

Once, when I got very depressed about how remote the prospects were of my ever attaining anything like "enlightenment," I decided that instead of seeking enlightenment I'd dedicate myself to fully understanding delusion. That actually helped a whole lot. It focused my attention on the reality of this moment rather than on fantasies about the future.

Dogen says this kind of stuff a lot. Even when we seem to be blundering heedlessly, we're still just as much an expression of complete, unsurpassed, perfect enlightenment as we might be during some rarified moment of satori, or awakening. At *this* moment — right now — you are just as enlightened as anyone ever was or ever will be — including yourself at your much anticipated moment of Great Awakening.

I know that's hard to accept, because I know how hard it is for me to accept statements like that when I hear them from other teachers, or even when I type them out myself.

Life doesn't usually feel like a moment of Great Awakening. It feels like taking out the trash, or forgetting to pick up some bread on the way home. It feels like a traffic jam, or a long drawn-out meeting that didn't go anywhere at all. Or sometimes it feels good. You're having a great day with a close friend or a really good gig with the band. But even those times don't really match the kinds of fantasies people like us make up about Great Awakening.

Dogen had to make up his own way of talking about this sort of thing. Katagiri Roshi explains Dogen's ideas, saying, "Dogen Zenji says, 'the same-and-one-time-arousing-mind, the same-and-one-mind-arousing-time.' When you put Dogen's words together, it means that time is exactly timelessness and simultaneously mind.

Timelessness is arousing mind, and mind is arousing timelessness. There is no gap, no separation. When I try to explain simultaneity, my explanation is still just an idea created by the time process. But practically speaking, if you practice zazen exactly, you are right in the middle of simultaneity."

Katagiri Roshi continues, "Mind arousing time means, when conditions are arranged and the time is ripe, timelessness appears. At that time, forms appear as formlessness: trees are tree-less-ness, Katagiri is Katagiri-less-ness, and zazen is zazen-less-ness. Real time comes up with no gap, and zazen is a wonderful being creating cushions, people sitting next to each other, the sound of the cars, all completely as one. 24-hour time never leaves its own trace; it just becomes timelessness. That is arousing time."

Zazen creates cushions and people. I love that! Normally we think that people and cushions create zazen.

But even if you get to that place where you experience timeless time and infinite freedom, you can't stay there. You can't stay in the place where forms are formlessness and you are you-less-ness. If you try to do that, you'll end up in a weird mental place and no one will want to talk to you. You have to come back and be with the rest of us. Because that's your most sacred duty — to hang out with all of us who are still stuck in delusion. That's how we fulfill the vow to save all beings.

Ram Dass said that he once tried to stay high forever. He started off with a small dose of LSD, and after a few days he was drinking liquid LSD straight from the bottle. It takes only a drop of the stuff to get a normal person tripping balls for eight or more hours, and there Ram Dass was, guzzling the stuff like it was water! No matter how hard he tried, he couldn't stay high permanently. It always wore off.

The same is true of so-called enlightenment experiences. In one sense they occur outside time. Or, to put it another way, they show us the truth of what Dogen calls "being-time." They show us that we are time itself, not as an abstraction but as an undeniable fact.

But when viewed or understood in terms of time, even the experience of complete unsurpassed perfect enlightenment has a start and a finish. It comes, it stays for a while, and then it drops you off back here. You're changed forever by it. That's true. You'll never see things the same way as you did before. But even so, it drops you off back where you were before it started.

I've been asking myself why that is for a couple of decades now, ever since my own first experience of such a moment of awakening. The only conclusion I can come to is that *this* is where I need to be. *This* is where my duty is. *This* is where I want to be. I, as Absolute Reality, want me, as Brad Warner, to work in *this area*.

Sometimes Brad doesn't understand this. Sometimes he wonders if it's some sort of punishment for something he did in the past that he forgot about. But when I think about it some more, I don't think that's the answer.

I think it's because something needs to be done here. And the only way that thing is going to get done is for me to do it. I just wish I had a clear idea exactly what that thing is!

It seems to have something to do with meditating and talking to people. It's odd to me that something as simple as me, a fairly unimpressive person, meditating and talking to people would be deemed by the Great Cosmic Something to be valuable. But I can only suppose that it must have some sort of value.

And if that's so, I tend to assume that whatever you, dear reader, are doing here and now is also supremely valuable to the grand scheme of things. I think we are all here to work on whatever the thing is that the Great Cosmic Something wants us to work on. A big part of how we do that is by acting ethically and helping each other.

Katagiri Roshi calls the experience of understanding the true nature of the identity of Universal Self and the individual small self "illumination." Illumination is an important aspect of the work we're here to do. But it may not be the most important aspect.

It's a piece of the puzzle. If you've ever put together a puzzle and, at the end, realized you were missing a piece, it's really frustrating! There's a hole in the picture you've been laboring for days and days to put together. That's when you realize that every single piece of a puzzle is important. There are no pieces that are so trivial that the picture can be complete without them.

So illumination is a piece of the puzzle. But it's not the whole puzzle. The rest of the puzzle is your supposedly mundane life with all its little jobs and frustrations and its fleeting joys and sorrows. And you, just as you are, are also the one little piece that completes the grand puzzle that is the universe. Without your little piece, the entire universe can never be complete.

In any case, Dogen's view of time is unorthodox. He wrote:

> Existence-time has the characteristic of passage from moment-to-moment. It passes moment-to-moment from today to tomorrow, moment-to-moment from today to yesterday, moment-to-moment from yesterday to today, moment-to-moment from today to today, and moment-to-moment from tomorrow to tomorrow. The dynamic flow of moment-to-moment has the characteristics of time. While ancient times and present times do not pile up, nor do they line up, all of the well-known masters of the ancient past are time. Because the self and others are already time, practice and enlightenment are different times. Also, to enter into the mud and into the water is likewise time.

That stuff about going into mud and water refers to making an effort to help others. I didn't get that the first time I read it. Maybe you did.

When I first came across this passage, I had no idea what to make of it. Time passes from today to yesterday? The present influences the past? And yet, of course it does. The past is constantly changing as people's opinions and views change, and as they change their stories about what they've done. We tend to believe that what actually happened in the past remains fixed, no matter what people say about it. Dogen seems to be suggesting something much more radical here, though. Maybe the past isn't as fixed and constant as we believe it to be.

The past and the present don't pile up on top of each other. But each person who ever existed is also time. Maybe that's a clue to how things work in this universe of ours. Think about it this way. The nearest star to us is Proxima Centauri. It's around four light years away. Which means it takes the light of Proxima Centauri four years to reach us. When you look at the star, you're seeing it as it was four years ago. Some stars are so far away that what we can see of them is only what they looked like millions of years ago.

The light of the sun takes eight minutes to reach the Earth. So we don't even see the sun as it is right now. Or the moon. Or, if you think about it, anything else.

Because even when we're kissing someone we love, what we see of them is just a little displaced in time. It's such a brief fraction of a second that it doesn't make any practical difference. Still, we do not see them as they are right exactly now. You're not even seeing this book as it is now. You're seeing it as it was a fraction of a second ago.

Trippy, huh?

Zen masters of the past, says Dogen, are time. You and me are time too. Each of us is our own time. Maybe even the time of our own bodies is displaced from the time of our minds. You stub your toe and it takes an agonizing few seconds before you feel the pain, during which time you don't yet know how bad it's gonna hurt.

And yet we believe that there must be some sense in which now is now, some sense in which my now and your now are the same now. This is the simultaneity that Katagiri Roshi struggled to find words for. Remember how he quoted Dogen's way of putting it, "the same-and-one-time-arousing-mind, the same-and-one-mind-arousing-time." This is timelessness, he said, and simultaneously mind. There is no gap.

Philosophers trace Dogen's views of simultaneity back to the metaphysical outlook of the Huayan school of Buddhism. Huayan was a Chinese form of Buddhism that is credited with coming up with the idea of Indra's net.

Indra was the chief of the Indian gods, sort of a Zeus-like figure in ancient Hinduism. He lost some popularity as time went on, but his name could still be invoked to lend an air of grandiosity to a concept. The idea of Indra's net is that the universe is like a gigantic net with jewels suspended at each juncture. Each jewel reflects all the other jewels perfectly, like a mirror.

In the same way, all things in the universe reflect each other. You could even say they contain each other. Hee-Jin Kim puts it this way in *Eihei Dogen: Mystical Realist*: "The entire universe consisted of a creative process in which the multiplicity of things and events interacted with and interpenetrated each other without obstruction. . . . This non-obstruction was possible through the mediation of emptiness. This grand, cosmic process of interaction, interpenetration, and integration in all realms, dimensions, perspectives of the self and the world went on endlessly."

Which is some crazy stuff! It's nice to think about. But when I'm in the grocery store looking for dog food, I don't feel like I'm interpenetrated by everything in the universe, and I don't feel like I reflect all creation.

And yet, I do. I am only here as an extension of everything that ever was, is, or will be. I am one of the jewels in Indra's net, whether or not I know it. The entire universe and all of time and space flow directly through me. I am included in absolutely everything, and absolutely everything is included in me.

Our past and our future are part of us right now.

At the start of the essay "Being-Time," Dogen gives us a little poem. It goes like this:

Sometimes standing on top of the highest peak,
Sometimes moving along the bottom of the deepest ocean.

Sometimes three heads and eight arms,
Sometimes the sixteen-foot or eight-foot [golden body].
Sometimes a staff or a whisk,
Sometimes an outdoor pillar or a stone lantern.
Sometimes the third son of Chang or the fourth son of Li,
Sometimes the earth and space.

That's the translation by Gudo Nishijima and Chodo Mike Cross. The word they translate as "sometimes" is *uji*. So you could also translate this as "Being-time stands at the top of the highest peak…." "Three heads and eight arms" is a reference to an angry deity and represents times when we are not at our best. "Sixteen-foot or eight-foot golden body" refers to Buddha who, legend has it, was sixteen feet tall when he stood up and eight feet tall when he sat down. So it represents us at our best. "The third son of Chang or fourth son of Li" is a way of saying a really ordinary, unremarkable person. Like saying "any Tom, Dick, or Harry" in old-timey English.

All these and more are being-time. They are all beings and simultaneously time. Events in our lives, like standing on top of a high peak, are also being-time.

Dogen then says that people mistakenly think, "Sometimes I became [an angry demon with] three heads and eight arms, and sometimes I became the sixteen-foot or eight-foot [golden body of Buddha]. For example, it was like crossing a river or crossing a mountain. The mountain and the river may still exist, but now that I have crossed them and am living in a jeweled palace with crimson towers, the mountain and the river are [as distant] from me as heaven is from the earth."

The jeweled palace with crimson towers is Dogen's overly florid way of referring to the enlightened state. He's talking about someone making a hard spiritual journey from delusion and metaphorically climbing mountains and crossing rivers to at last reach the crimson towers of enlightenment.

Dogen says that the way of thinking he described above is not correct. He says the correct way to conceive it is as follows: "When I was climbing a mountain or crossing a river, I was there in that time. There must have been time in me. And I actually exist now, [so] time could not have departed. If time does not have the form of leaving and coming, the time of climbing a mountain is the present as existence-time. If time does retain the form of leaving and coming, I have this present moment of existence-time, which is just existence-time itself. How could that time of climbing the mountain and crossing the river fail to swallow, and fail to vomit, this time [now] in the jeweled palace with crimson towers?"

Each time swallows and vomits every other time. If we reach an enlightened state, our delusion doesn't depart. Being-time is not left behind. And if we are making efforts to get to an enlightened state, our delusional state right now also swallows and vomits our future enlightenment.

"We should not understand only that time flies," Dogen says. "We should not learn that 'flying' is the only ability of time. If we just left time to fly away, some gaps in it might appear. Those who fail to experience and to hear the truth of existence-time do so because they understand [time] only as having passed."

To me right now, as I sit here typing this, not knowing if it will ever be read by anyone, this means that there's hope. Although *hope* is sometimes thought of as a dirty word in Buddhist circles since it tends to suggest a wish for a future state. Still, hope is a real part of our lives.

Although I've had some experiences that one could call "enlightenment," it hasn't fixed everything in my life. And I haven't always lived up to the Truth that I once felt I had grasped. Yet, I still work at it. I think I always will.

There was a time that I imagined I could get a once-and-for-all enlightenment and just sit back in my crimson tower drinking cold root beer and gazing down with loving pity on those less enlightened than me. Maybe I'd beckon them to my tower, yet they would not hear. Poor fools!

Alas, that hasn't happened yet. And though I no longer hope for such a thing, I still hope that I can come to see more clearly than I do now. And I hope that I'll be able to communicate whatever I come to understand better than I have before. Because those who have been able to see such things and communicate them to me have been of such great help to me. In my worst moments, I can read their words or maybe even speak to some of them in person, and it makes the pain of life more bearable. The more people who can do that for others, the better this world is. So I try my best to be one of those people.

Dogen says, "The mountains are time, and the seas are time. Without time, the mountains and the seas could not exist: we should not deny that time exists in the mountains and the seas here and now. If time decays, the mountains and the seas decay. If time is not subject to decay, the mountains and the seas are not subject to decay."

You are time and I am time. And we ought to use this time to help each other out of all the messes we get ourselves into.

# 33. DOGEN'S WEIRD IDEAS ABOUT SPACE

WE'VE LOOKED AT Dogen's weird ideas about time. Now let's look his weird ideas about space.

The essay in *Shobogenzo* in which he most specifically addresses these is called "Koku," which can be translated simply as "space," although the word can also mean "empty space" or "empty sky." It's a common word that you can still find in Japanese-English dictionaries today, unlike some of Dogen's other chapter titles.

Dogen begins the essay by saying, "Provoked by the question 'What is right here?' the Way actualizes and buddha ancestors emerge." I love that line. Because it kind of says it all when it comes to Dogen's philosophy. He's not asking, "Is there a God?" He's not asking, "What is up in heaven?" He's not asking, "What happens after we die?" He's not even asking, "What is the meaning of life?" He's asking, "What is *right here*?" What is the deal with this incredibly strange place in which we find ourselves right now? That's his big question.

It's like what I said a few chapters back about driving through Utah and stopping at a 7-Eleven. If you don't think this place you are right now is incredibly weird, just try imagining what it would look like to an alien. What would some multilimbed eight-eyed being from the planet Zeta Reticuli 4 make of your bedroom, or the bus stop you're sitting at right now? It'd be the weirdest thing that alien had ever seen. And that doesn't even get you halfway to just how incredibly bizarre and amazing wherever you happen to be right now actually is. Why are you even here at all? Why is there something instead of nothing?

It is because our predecessors on the Buddhist path pondered this question of "What is *right now?*" that the Buddhist teachings have been passed along from generation to generation to arrive at you reading this book — not to mention me writing it. Isn't that neat?

And note that Dogen says, "The Way actualizes and buddha ancestors emerge." The way comes first, and in response, the people who teach the way appear. Weird, right? It's like when Katagiri Roshi said that zazen is a wonderful being that creates cushions and people to sit on them.

But Dogen's chosen topic for this essay is space, so he next introduces us to some traditional Buddhist ideas about that. In ancient forms of Buddhism, he tells us, they tried to classify different types of space. One Chinese sutra broke space down into twenty kinds, among which were internal space, external space, internal and external space, and space as space. This was based on the Buddhist idea of emptiness, which is often represented with the Chinese character for space. So you could think of these as twenty kinds of emptiness. Anyone who classifies emptiness into twenty types is a little strange. Right?

That Chinese sutra says that the six sense organs (the usual five, plus the brain as a sense organ for sensing thoughts) are transient, devoid of self, and therefore empty. They call this "internal space/ emptiness." The objects of the senses are also transient, devoid of self, and empty, and this is "external space/emptiness." The sense organs are similarly empty, and that's "internal and external space/ emptiness." Nonattachment to the emptiness of all that other emptiness is "the emptiness of emptiness itself," or "space as space." And the total emptiness of the universe in all directions is "universal emptiness." Those guys were serious about emptiness!

Remember, emptiness to a Buddhist doesn't mean a dark, black void. It means things just as they are, which is so vastly different from our ideas about them that they can be said to be empty. Even you yourself are nothing like what you think yourself to be. You and me and everyone we know are examples of emptiness. But we'll get to that in a minute.

Dogen says you can't classify space/emptiness into just twenty types or even eighty-four thousand types. Eighty-four thousand was the way people in those days said "a bazillion." It was thought of as a number so large as to be meaningless. There aren't just a bazillion forms of space; there are endless forms of space, Dogen says.

After laying all this on us, Dogen tells a story about two Zen masters named Ezo and Seido. But in this book I'm calling them Zen Master Moe and Zen Master Curly. You'll see why in a minute.

Zen Master Moe says to Zen Master Curly, "Do you know how to grasp space?"

Zen Master Curly replies, "Certainly!"

Zen Master Moe says, "Then how do you grasp space, wise guy?"

Zen Master Curly makes a motion like he's grasping at the empty space in front of him.

Zen Master Moe says, "That's not how you grasp space, you knucklehead!"

Zen Master Curly says, "Oh yeah? Then how do you grasp it, big brother?"

*Trivia time*: Did you know that Curly from *The Three Stooges* was Moe's little brother? The monks in this story were also brothers and in this part of the story Master Seido really does refer to Master Ezo as "big brother." Now back to the story.

Zen Master Moe sticks his fingers up Zen Master Curly's nose and yanks.

Zen Master Curly says, "Ow! Ow! Ow! That hurts! But now I get what you're saying!"

Zen Master Moe says, "You get it now! But you should've figured it out from the beginning, zucchini brain!"

Maybe you think I made that story up. But other than changing the names of the Zen masters and adding a couple of Three Stooges–style insults like "zucchini brain," that's the story, just the way Dogen tells it.

Then Dogen explains the story. Which ruins the joke. But he does it anyway. He says that when Zen Master Moe asks Zen Master Curly if he knows how to grasp space, he's really asking him about compassion. Which is a weird thing to say. But it relates to the Buddhist teaching that everything in the universe is alive, or more properly, everything in the universe is life. It also relates to Buddhist ethics, which are based on compassion.

Most people think of some things as being alive and other things as not being alive. In between those they think there are things that are more alive than others. For example, we think of people as alive and rocks as not alive. In between we tend to think of plants as being less alive than animals. Or at least we act like we do. We have fewer compunctions about killing or injuring plants than we do about killing or injuring animals. And among animals, we in the West regularly kill and eat pigs but are horrified when we hear about places where they kill and eat dogs — even though there's plenty of evidence that pigs are just as intelligent as dogs, if not more so. So we make distinctions even among different kinds of animals as to how "alive" we think of them as.

But Buddhism allows for no such distinctions. Not even between people and rocks. As Carlo Rovelli said, all seeming *things* in the universe are *events*. We call some events within the universe "beings," but maybe that's not how things really are. When Zen Master Moe asks Zen Master Curly about grasping space, he's asking him about making those kinds of distinctions and whether doing so is truly compassionate. Remember what Dainin Katagiri said about treating a toilet as a living thing?

In his book *Embracing Mind* Kobun Chino Roshi says, "We sometimes complain of pain in the legs, neck, or back [in zazen].

But know that pain is always there. You have just noticed it. It's not something you newly produced. Sometimes it shows up in other activities, such as when you walk on steep hills. When you stop climbing a mountain, the pain goes away, but you know it is still there. Although we call it pain, it is simply a force which came along with our existence. Maybe in this force there is always pain, if there is sense to feel it. When I touch my '*nyoi*' [a stick Zen teachers carry] to the floor, both my stick and the floor feel pain, but they don't say so."

It's a strange way to look at things. But Zen is a pretty strange philosophy. One of my pet peeves with current American Zen is it often tends to gloss over just how odd the philosophy can be.

Anyway, when Kobun says that the stick and the floor feel pain, he doesn't mean they're screaming in silent agony all the time, or that every time you touch any inanimate object you're hurting it. Rather, he's acknowledging the life that is present in all things. All things are manifestations of universal life. He's suggesting that even the stick and the floor may perceive the contact between them at some level. That level of perception is inaccessible to human perception, but it's real. What we call pain, Kobun says, is simply a force that came along with our existence. Maybe to exist as a thing separate from other things is itself pain. Maybe this is what the Buddha's First Noble Truth — often expressed as "All life is suffering" — really means.

Dogen explains the next line, where Zen Master Moe asks Zen Master Curly how he grasps space, by saying, "Space is one mass, which, once touched is then tainted. Since being tainted, space has fallen to the ground." It sounds odd. I know.

But saying that when space is touched it's tainted is just Dogen's way of saying that having an intellectual understanding of space is not the same as having a true understanding of the reality of space. Once space is "touched" by intellectual understanding, it's metaphorically spoiled, or tainted, and then metaphorically falls to the ground. He means that the understanding sort of "destroys space."

In other words, you replace the real experience of actual space with a concept of space, thus destroying real space. Still, Dogen acknowledges that such concepts are useful and necessary for human beings. Dogen wants us to understand that, at this point in the story, Zen Master Curly sees space only as a concept.

Dogen says that Zen Master Moe's words "How do you grasp it?" mean that even if you say that space is just exactly what it is, nothing more and nothing less, even these words have placed conceptual limitations on the actuality of space.

Then Dogen says that when Zen Master Curly made grabbing motions at the space in front of him, he was showing that he didn't really get what Zen Master Moe was trying to teach him. Dogen says that Zen Master Curly never understood the reality of space even in his dreams. But, says Dogen, Zen Master Moe didn't want to make things worse by trying to offer Zen Master Curly a verbal explanation. Reality is too profound and too eternal for mere words to describe.

So instead Zen Master Moe did the most compassionate and ethical thing possible in that situation. He stuck his fingers up Zen Master Curly's nose and yanked!

This brings up an interesting point about Buddhist ethics. Normally we'd think of someone yanking on someone else's nostrils rather than simply discussing the matter with them as being unethical. And in most cases it would be. Yet in this case, discussion would not have been adequate to convey Zen Master Moe's point. And so yanking Zen Master Curly's nostrils was the compassionate and ethical thing to do.

But you have to be really careful about this sort of thing. One of the problems with stories like this is that they can tend to give people who hear them the wrong idea. If you're not steeped in the standard Zen teachings of ethics that we looked at in earlier chapters before you hear these kinds of stories, you can get the impression that actions like Zen Master Moe's are acceptable all the time. But the precepts make it very clear that most of the time actions like yanking someone's nose are the wrong thing to do. The next few lines of Dogen's get into how Zen Master Moe's actions differed from the usual situations that most of us find ourselves in.

Dogen says, "Know that Zen Master Moe put his body into Zen Master Curly's nostrils. Space is one great big ball that bounces here and there." Zen Master Moe and Zen Master Curly ceased to be two distinct individuals at the moment Zen Master Moe yanked Zen Master Curly's nose. If you can't put your entire body into your friend's nostrils, you shouldn't be yanking his nose.

Both Zen Master Moe and Zen Master Curly knew at that moment that they were nothing but space itself. For the time being, space had coalesced into two people. But it was and still is space, exactly as it was before it solidified. If you don't get that, you're probably not ready to stick your fingers up someone's nose.

Dogen says, "The entire universe has no gaps to accommodate space." Space is not emptiness between one solid thing and another solid thing. Those solid things are also space, or emptiness.

Then Dogen says it wasn't that Zen Master Moe reached out to another Zen Master Moe, and it wasn't that empty space grabbed empty space. This is where Dogen gets his most Dogen-esque. He's denying even the explanation that he's about to give of what happened between the two Zen masters. He doesn't want you to get so comfortable with any explanation — even a good one — that you think it's the final answer.

Dogen then gives exactly the explanation he just denied. Once again he sounds like the guy from *Ancient Aliens* telling us, "I'm not saying it was aliens, but it was aliens." He says that before the moment his nose got yanked, Zen Master Curly had thought that Zen Master Moe was another person, someone separate and distinct from himself. But at that moment, Zen Master Curly realized that he had met himself. Thus Dogen contradicts what he just told us.

Why does Dogen do this to us? It's so confusing! And he does it all the time.

Here's my theory about why he does this. He wants us to understand that even the very best explanations are not the thing itself. It isn't aliens. But it's aliens.

Dogen then tells us that no effort was necessary to grasp space. But, he says, this story has resounded through the teachings of Buddhism like a thunderclap. Few practitioners, he says, have ever really understood what space actually is.

But our man Dogen has his own opinion on what Zen Master Moe did to Zen Master Curly. He says that he would like to say to Zen Master Moe, "Before, when you grabbed Zen Master Curly's nostrils, if you wanted to grasp space, you should have grabbed your own nostrils, and you should have understood how to grasp your own fingers with those very same fingers." Which is a pretty difficult thing to do! Like seeing your own eyeballs and not just a reflection of them in a mirror.

Dogen admits that Zen Master Moe does know a thing or two. But, Dogen says, "Even a good player at grasping space needs to research the interior and exterior of space, needs to research the killing space and making space come alive, and needs to know the lightness and weight of space." He says that Zen Master Moe should know that the dialogues of the ancient Zen Masters were examples of "grasping space."

Dogen is saying that this kind of behavior — sticking your fingers up someone's nose and yanking — isn't for everyone, and that usually you can just explain things without having to resort to such tactics. That's why he brings up the ancient dialogues. Dogen adds this explanation because he doesn't want us to go around imitating Zen Master Moe. If we don't know the lightness and weight of space, we should not attempt the kind of thing Zen Master Moe does in this story.

Dogen sums up this section of the essay saying, "My late master, Tendo Nyojo, the eternal buddha, says: 'The whole body like a mouth, hanging in space.' Clearly, the whole body of space is suspended in space."

He's quoting a poem by his teacher about a wind bell. The poem goes,

> Whole body like a mouth hanging in space
> Not asking if the wind is east, west, south, or north
> For all others equally, it chatters intuitive wisdom
> Ting-a-ling-ting-a-ling-ting-a-ling.

Dogen pushes this poem one step further, saying not only that we are bodies hanging in space but also that even our bodies are nothing but space itself.

Modern science seems to agree. Most of our bodies are empty space between our atoms and molecules. And even those atoms and molecules are themselves ultimately not solid things but patterns of formless energy. And even that energy itself may be a manifestation of empty space. We've learned that empty space is full of potential energy. Again, as Dogen says, the universe has no gaps to accommodate space.

Lawrence Krauss, author of the book *A Universe from Nothing: Why There Is Something Rather Than Nothing*, said in an interview that "nothing is unstable. Nothing can create something all the time due to the laws of quantum mechanics."* When he says "nothing is unstable," he doesn't mean that there are no unstable things. He means that nothingness is unstable.

He says, "Empty space is a boiling, bubbling brew of virtual particles that pop in and out of existence in a time scale so short that you can't even measure them. Now, that sounds... like counting angels on the head of a pin; if you can't measure them, then it doesn't sound like it's science, but in fact you can't measure them directly."

I don't pretend to understand the science and mathematics that led Professor Krauss to this conclusion. But the idea comes pretty close to the way Buddhists have understood space or emptiness for

---

\* NPR, *Talk of the Nation*, January 13, 2012.

a few thousand years. I find that intriguing. I think the Buddhists have a clearer understanding of this than scientists do, because scientists are still trying to study emptiness as an object apart from themselves. Buddhists like Dogen, Tendo Nyojo, and Zen Masters Moe and Curly have the insight that allows them to include themselves in the emptiness they study.

# 34. SOME MORE ABOUT SPACE

DOGEN'S ESSAY ON space is in two parts. Part two begins with another story. It goes something like this.

There once was a Zen priest named Ryo. He was a very smart guy who gave a lot of lectures about one of his favorite Buddhist sutras. One day Ryo paid a visit to a Zen master named Baso, who is also known as Mazu. It's that thing where Japanese people pronounce Chinese characters differently from how the Chinese pronounce them — the Chinese pronunciation in more like *Mazu*. But since I learned this story from a Japanese source, I tend to say Baso.

Anyway, Baso asked Ryo what sutra he lectured on. Ryo said, "The Heart Sutra!"

Now, in order to follow this story, you need to remember that the character for *heart* in the title the Heart Sutra is also the character used for *mind*. We in the West make a big distinction between heart and mind. We often use the word *heart* to refer to the emotional component of our psyche and *mind* to refer to the rational part. In Chinese and Japanese there's no such distinction. Also remember that *mind* in Buddhist terms often refers to something much larger and more universal than the individual human mind.

Baso asked Ryo, "With what do you lecture?"

Ryo said, "I lecture with my mind (heart)!" I'm having him say mind here rather than heart because I think it gives more of a sense of what he meant.

Baso said, "They say mind is like a leading actor, the will is like a supporting actor, and the six kinds of consciousness are the accompanying cast: how are these able to lecture on the sutra?"

Ryo replied, "If mind is unable to give the lecture, space (emptiness) is hardly able to give the lecture, is it?"

Baso said, "Space itself is indeed able to give lectures."

Ryo got all cocky, thinking he'd tripped Master Baso up and made him say something stupid. He turned and, swinging his sleeves arrogantly — like they did in those days — started to walk out.

As Ryo was leaving, Baso shouted after him, "Hey, Ryo!"

Ryo turned.

Baso said, "From birth to death it's just like this!"

At that moment Ryo got it. He had a major insight into the nature of life, the universe, and everything. He went off into the mountains to meditate, and no one heard from him ever again, or so the story goes.

Dogen comments on this, saying that every great Buddhist teacher of the past has lectured about sutras in exactly this way. What lectures on sutras, Dogen says, is always empty space. Without being empty space, he says, not even one sutra can be spoken of.

Given that we are ultimately just transmutations of empty space, when we talk about anything it's just space talking to space about space. Dogen didn't know the contemporary scientific understanding that our bodies are mostly empty spaces between particles that are not solid at all but energy. At least he didn't know it as a scientific theory.

But scientific theories are descriptions of reality. A scientific description is based on complicated mathematics and detailed observations, often with the aid of machines like microscopes and telescopes. Dogen's description is based on deep personal experience and detailed observation of his own body and mind.

Nowadays we have a tendency to think that descriptions based on mathematics and machines are better than descriptions based on personal experience. After all, personal experience is often biased or mistaken. But science is reliable, we think. In my neighborhood lots of people have signs on their lawns saying, "In this house we believe science is real." Science is evidence based. It's peer reviewed, tested, and all that good stuff.

I'm not going to say that point of view is wrong. After all, it's served us well. It's given us better medicine and sanitation, it's taken people to the moon and brought them back alive. It's even given me the laptop I'm using to type these words. Science is good!

But when it comes to something like describing the deepest aspects of reality, science can only tell us so much. This is because science is always based on a separation between the observer and what is observed. Dogen was working in an area where the distinction between observer and observed had melted away.

And when seen from that place, Dogen says, we are all just space. Which, ironically, is the sort of idea science seems to be getting to in its own way.

In his book *The Grand Delusion: What We Know and Don't Believe*, Katagiri Roshi's student Steve Hagen says that science is fundamentally flawed because it is based on the belief in substantiality, the belief that the things — and people — of this universe are made of substances like particles.

He says:

> If particles were actual things, then it would be reasonable to assume that they have specific positions in space that change in time as they move. But quantum theory doesn't allow this. And, though there are instruments that seem to reveal tracks that these "particles" ostensibly follow, upon close scrutiny the "tracks" show themselves to be discontinuous, appearing not as unbroken straight or curved lines, but only as a series of, say, bubbles in a bubble chamber. At no point is it obvious that anything moved through the chamber leaving such "tracks" — especially given the bizarre ways in which many of these phantom "things" would have had to move.

Hagen adds:

> If particles comprise matter, then it would be reasonable to
> assume that in a total vacuum there would be no subatomic
> activity. But quantum theory correctly predicts that a Gei-
> ger counter placed in a total vacuum will still click — i.e.,
> detect "matter." In other words, "matter" cannot consist of
> whatever it is we think we mean by the term "particle." If
> particles were real, objective things, then it would be rea-
> sonable to assume that they exist. But here's what happens
> when two observers view the same vacuum: If one person
> is at rest in relation to the vacuum, while the other is accel-
> erating in relation to the vacuum, the former will see a cold
> vacuum, while the latter will see a warm gas of particles. So,
> are particles real or are they an illusion? Are they Some-
> thing or are they Nothing?

Hagen says quite a bit more, and I highly recommend the book.
I have to admit, though, the science parts are way above my pay
grade. But intuitively, what he's saying makes good sense to me.

Getting back to Dogen, next he says, "Whether it's the Heart
(Mind) Sutra or the Body Sutra, it's always spoken about by space."
Or to put it another way, whether a sutra is expounded with the mind
or expounded with the body, space is what expounds the sutra. This
is a little play on words because, as I mentioned earlier, the word for
*mind* and the word for *heart* are the same in Chinese and Japanese.

Dogen says, "Both thinking and non-thinking are also realized
and actualized with space." Here he uses one of his favorite words,
*genjo*, which appears in his most famous essay, "Genjo Koan." I've
translated *genjo* as "realized and actualized." The word is a compound of a character meaning "reality" and a character meaning "to
be" or "to become." This second character is often translated simply
as "is."

What he's saying here is that even our deepest internal experience is also space. Our thoughts and even our lack of thoughts are space itself. Body and mind are both just space, or emptiness. This is hard for us to grasp. But he's saying that everything we are and everything we experience are nothing but space. Which is a really strange thing to say.

Here is what I think Dogen means. We are not a being that observes a universe outside itself. Rather, we are the process of the universe observing itself, like in a mirror. We are one way that the universe tries to figure out what it is. We are the universe's curiosity about itself. We are a process — a fluid, ever-changing, moving process. We are an event rather than a thing. We mistake ourselves to be individual beings, but we're really not. We are space trying to come to terms with what space is.

People who believe in God tend to think that God knows everything. But maybe he doesn't. Or maybe the reason he knows everything is we keep him informed.

And this explanation, like all explanations, falls far short of the mark. But there ya go! Every attempt we make at explaining the unexplainable is fundamentally mistaken. Yet we've got to keep trying, or else nothing ever gets done!

Let's get back to what Dogen says about space, because we're almost to the end of it. He says that learning wisdom with a teacher and learning wisdom without a teacher is space. And he says that the development of the intelligence that you were born with and the development of the intelligence that you learned from others is space. And he says that becoming a Buddha or becoming a teacher of Buddhism are also space.

So whatever you learn, whether you were born knowing it or you got it from someone else, is space. Even becoming a Buddha is space. It's all space. It's all emptiness.

But let's be careful here. He's not saying that everything is worthless just because it's all emptiness. That's what the nihilists say. And Dogen was not a nihilist. There is tremendous value to empty space. After all, everything in the universe, including me and you, is just a permutation of empty space.

Next Dogen quotes Vasubandhu, one of the greatest and most highly respected teachers of Indian Buddhism. Vasubandhu is generally considered one of the originators of the so-called Mind Only — Yogacara or Vijnanavada — school of Buddhism.

The quote from Vasubandhu that Dogen gives us goes, "The Mind is the same as the world of space, and it reveals the reality that is equally space. When we are able to realize and verify space, there is no right and nothing wrong."

Again, the Mind he's talking about here isn't the individual mind. It's the great big Mind, which is all things and all phenomena.

That stuff about there being no right and nothing wrong is a dangerous idea when it gets into the wrong hands. It's important to understand that in the everyday world there is right and wrong. That's why Buddhists are so concerned with ethics. Yet looked at another way, things are just what they are, and characterizing them as right or wrong is not really possible. Let's put a pin in that discussion for now and get to the rest of what Dogen has to say about space.

He says that when a person faces a wall — meaning while a person sits zazen, of course — that person meets the wall and the wall meets the person. Here in the practice of zazen, he says, is Mind as fences and walls, and Mind as withered trees.

Dogen often says, "Mind is fences, walls, tiles, and pebbles." Instead of saying something vague and general about Mind being everything, he gives specific examples. It's not always fences, tiles, walls, and pebbles. Sometimes it's other things. He doesn't want us to get lost in generalities but to look at specific things we see every day and understand them as examples of the Mind he's talking about.

So when you face the wall in zazen, you're facing yourself. Not just mentally but physically as well. The wall you are staring at is just as much you as the you who sits there staring at the wall. So the wall, in a sense, meets you. When he says "here is Mind as fences and walls" he's saying that we can concretely experience Mind as a wall by facing a wall. "Withered trees" is probably a reference to the person sitting, who might feel like nothing more than a withered tree while sitting there.

This, by the way, is why we sit zazen with eyes open rather than closed. If we closed our eyes, we'd be saying that what we are is our internal experience rather than the external world. Dogen said that there is no fundamental separation or difference between the internal and the external.

Then Dogen says, "For those who can be saved by another body, [buddhas] manifest at once a body and preach for them the Dharma that reveals the reality that is equally space." That thing about "those who can be saved by another body" is a reference to the Lotus Sutra, in which it says that the bodhisattva of compassion manifests herself in whatever form is needed by whoever is in need of compassion. What the bodhisattva of compassion reveals to that person is that reality is space, that reality is emptiness. This refers back to the Heart Sutra, which says that form is emptiness and emptiness is form.

Then Dogen says, "Being used by the twelve hours, and being in control of the twelve hours, are both the time when we are able to realize and verify space." Days, in Dogen's day, were reckoned as having twelve hours, so we'd say twenty-four hours where he says twelve. What he's saying here just refers to the actuality of living through real days. Living a normal life with twenty-four hours in each day is the realization and verification that reality is space/emptiness. This is true whether or not we know it.

Then he says, "A big stone being big, and a small stone being small is no right and nothing wrong." The thing about big and small stones is a reference to an old Buddhist sutra, but that doesn't really matter. The idea is that things exactly as they are — big rocks are big and small rocks are small — is an example of "no right and nothing wrong."

From one point of view there is right and there is wrong. But from another, maybe right is like a big rock and wrong is like a small rock. They're all just events in a vast, ever-changing universe.

As I said, this can be a dangerous idea in the wrong hands. Charles Manson, apparently, was a big fan of those parts of Hindu and Buddhist philosophy that say there is no right or wrong. But Charles Manson, of course, was completely wrong in his understanding of those ideas. His understanding was one-sided. Dogen's point of view is not.

Dogen wants us to understand that completely contradictory ways of understanding things can be equally true. He is not trying to replace our ethical understanding of right and wrong with an understanding that there is no right or wrong and therefore that ethics don't matter. Remember that he also strongly emphasizes ethics in his writings. He wants us to be very clear about the value and necessity of ethical behavior. But he also wants us to be able to see things from the point of view that transcends the categories of right and wrong.

Finally, Dogen ends by telling us to "investigate the fact right now that empty space is the treasury of the true dharma eye and the fine mind of Nirvana."

The word for "treasury of the true dharma eye" in Japanese is *Shobogenzo*. And the subtitle of his book *Shobogenzo* translates to "the fine mind of Nirvana." So this is like one of those cheesy moments when a character in a movie says the title of the movie *in the movie*. Dogen actually does this a bunch of times in *Shobogenzo*.

What he's asking us to do is to use the teaching he's given us as a way of understanding the world we experience. It's just a point of view. So it's not reality as it is, which is beyond all points of view. But he offers it to us as a better point of view than the usual one.

# 35. SUPERCONSCIOUS STATES AND MIRACLES

SPEAKING OF SPACE, lots of people think that Zen practice is all about spacing out or going into special states of consciousness. But it's really not.

This is not to say that such extraordinary states don't happen within the practice of zazen. They do, sometimes. The problem comes when we use the achievement of such altered mental states as a standard to measure the effectiveness of the practice. I'm often asked if zazen is "effective." When I press people on what they mean by effective, they often say they mean whether the practice produces extraordinary states of mind.

We already talked about this in an earlier chapter when I got into the matter of the different levels of *jhanas*. But it's a crucial point, so I want to try looking at it from another angle. Because I find myself measuring my own zazen against how I think it ought to be, even after years and years of being told that that's the wrong way of looking at things.

There's an essay by Dogen called "The Samadhi That Is the King of Samadhis" ("Zanmai O Zanmai"). *Samadhi* is usually defined as a special kind of state achieved through meditative practice. In Dogen's telling, the king of all samadhis is zazen. But he's not saying that the king of all samadhis is a superconscious state that can be attained by practicing zazen. No. Zazen is *itself* the king of all samadhis. This means any kind of zazen — including zazen where you feel like it's been a complete waste of time.

Dogen says, "Sitting in the full lotus posture is just the samadhi that is king of samadhis, and is just experience and entry. All samadhis are the followers of this, the king of samadhis. To sit the full lotus posture is just to set the body straight, to set the mind straight, to set the body-mind straight, to set Buddhist ancestors straight, to set practice and experience straight, to set the brain straight, and to set the lifeblood straight. Now, sitting our human skin, flesh, bones, and marrow in the full lotus posture, we sit the samadhi that is king among samadhis."

Dogen uses the term *kekka fuẓa*, which literally translates as "full-lotus posture." But you don't have to worry if you can't twist your legs up into that posture. There are other ways to do zazen. Referring to the physical posture is just his way of indicating zazen as a concrete, physical thing that you do rather than some sort of special state of consciousness.

One way of understanding how zazen — no matter what state of consciousness occurs while doing it — is samadhi itself is by relating it to another piece of writing by Dogen called "Mystic Powers" ("Jinzu"). That's my teacher's translation of the title. Sometimes the title is translated as "Miracles." Both are perfectly good. Actually, I tend to prefer the translation "Miracles" myself. Apologies to Nishijima Roshi.

In this chapter Dogen recounts some of the miracle stories in Buddhist literature. I like this chapter because the very first time I ever raised my hand in Tim McCarthy's class on Zen Buddhism was to ask if there were any miracle stories in Buddhism.

The reason I asked that particular question was that I was really starting to get into religious stuff in a big way. I was interested in talking to anyone who I thought might have some insight into such matters. So maybe a week or two before I asked Tim that question, I'd had a conversation with a guy at the little booth that the Campus Christian Ministries had set up on the second floor of the Kent State University Student Center next to the cafeteria. I remember the poster behind him was a parody of the poster for the movie *Raiders of the Lost Ark*. In the style of the logo for that film it said "REPENT and Turn to God." The word *repent* was written really big in the same style of letters as the word *raiders* in the movie poster.

One of the things that Campus Christian Ministries guy told me was that Jesus performed miracles. I asked him why he believed that. What was the evidence? He told me that he believed Jesus performed miracles because several of Jesus's disciples refused to recant their stories of the miracles they'd witnessed, even when being tortured to death. They chose to die rather than deny what they'd seen with their own eyes.

Therefore Jesus performed miracles. Therefore he was divine. Therefore everything he said was correct. And therefore I should believe it.

I couldn't follow that logic. On the one hand, the story that Jesus's disciples chose to die rather than recant was compelling. Later, I found out there's actually no concrete evidence of the disciples choosing to die rather than to recant the stories of Christ's miracles. The stories of that happening are even less well attested to than the stories of the miracles themselves. But I didn't know that at the time, so we'll leave it aside.

But even if Jesus walked on water and raised people from the dead, how did it follow that therefore everything he said was correct? I couldn't work out the connection. I guess the logic is that only God can do things like that. But how do I know that only God can do those things? Maybe Jesus was an alien or something. I'm sure the guy from *Ancient Aliens* would say that's a possibility.

This especially perplexed me when it came to the ethical teachings of Christianity. Does the advice to love your enemies as well as your neighbors, turn the other cheek when struck, and so on depend on the person who said it being able to do magic tricks? Why?

As we've already seen, Buddhist ethics don't depend on such claims. And to be fair, neither do Christian ethics, according to a lot of Christians. I don't think the guys from the Campus Christian Ministries at KSU were the most authoritative sources! But I had no clue about Buddhism when I started taking that class on Zen Buddhism. So I wondered if the Buddhists used the same sort of logic as the guys from the Campus Christian Ministries.

Tim said that there were a few such stories associated with the Buddha. He mentioned one in which the Buddha supposedly flew up into the air and shot water from his mouth and sprayed fire out of his butt. Or something like that. The story is kind of unclear about where the fire came out of. It just says "the lower part of his body." Sounds to me like the worst case of gas anyone ever had. But Tim also said that lots of Buddhists don't believe those stories and that the truth claims of Buddhism are not tied to whether or not Buddha could perform miracles.

In any case, that story of Buddha flying is one of the miracle stories that Dogen mentions in his essay on miracles that I referred to above.

He also mentions a few more stories like that. But then Dogen talks about another sort of miracle. He talks about the miraculous power of chopping firewood and carrying water. Lest we start thinking of that as exotic, remember that chopping wood and carrying water was something the monks living with Dogen had to do every single day. That's how they got their drinking water and cooking fuel. In today's terms that's like talking about the mystical power of adjusting the thermostat and turning on the faucet. He's talking about the most mundane and ordinary action he could think of.

Dogen also tells us a story about two monks and their masters "performing miracles." It goes like this.

Once, while Master Dai-i was lying down, [his student] Kyozan came to see him. Dai-i just then turned so that he was facing the wall.

Kyozan said, "I'm your disciple. Don't show me your butt!"

Dai-i started to rise. Kyozan by then was leaving, but Dai-i called him, "Hey, disciple!"

Kyozan came back. Dai-i said, "Let me tell you my dream."

Kyozan lowered his head, ready to listen.

Dai-i said, "See if you can divine the dream for me."

At that, Kyozan went out, fetched a bowl of water and a towel, and came back. Dai-i washed his face. After washing his face, he sat for a short while, and then Dai-i's other student, whose name was Kyogen, which sounds confusingly similar to Kyozan, came along.

Dai-i said, "Me and Kyozan have just practiced a mystical power that is truly amazing. It is not the same as the small powers of the Lesser Vehicle."

Kyogen said, "I saw it all."

Dai-i said, "Then, disciple, you must try to say something!"

Kyogen immediately went out and brought back a cup of tea.

Dai-i praised them, saying, "The mystical powers and the wisdom of you two disciples are far superior to those of [Buddha's famous and celebrated disciples] Shariputra and Maudgalyayana."

Dogen goes on to explain that what Dai-i's students did was an example of the Great Miracle, as opposed to small miracles like the Buddha flying through the air spraying fire out of his butt and water out of his head. The reason that the seemingly much less impressive actions of Dai-i's disciples are called an example of the Great Miracle, Dogen tells us, is that it is only within the Great Miracle of ordinary life that minor miracles like Buddha's flying through the air can occur.

Dogen says, "The great mystical power entertains small mystical powers, [but] small mystical powers do not know the great mystical power. 'Small mystical powers' are 'a hair swallowing the vast ocean,' and 'a poppy seed containing Sumeru.' [These are other examples of miracle stories in Buddhism.] Again, they are 'the upper body emitting water, the lower body emitting fire,' and suchlike."

He also says, "When we look at wizards, they have something that resembles the powers of Buddha, and when we look at a buddha's forms of behavior, they have something that resembles the powers of a wizard; but we should know that even if [what a wizard shows] is the forms of behavior of a buddha, that is not the mystical power of Buddha."

The mystical power of a Buddha, Dogen says, is the power of not being impressed by the kinds of "mystical powers" displayed by wizards. Take that, Gandalf!

This is the way I understand Dogen's insistence that zazen itself is samadhi, whether or not it seems like a superconscious state. It's the same as the way that everyday life, mundane as it may seem to be, is the Great Miracle, as opposed to one of the small miracles that so impress a lot of people.

This universe, just as it is right now, is a kind of miracle. It's real in ways that "small miracles" can't hope to be. Your ordinary state of mind is part of the Great Miracle, exactly as it is.

Dogen says:

> The reason the five powers and the six powers are called small mystical powers is that the five powers and the six powers are tainted by practice and experience, and they are confined to and cut off by time and place. They exist in life [but] are not realized after the body. They belong to the self [but] are beyond other people. They are realized in this land but are not realized in other lands. They are realized in unreality but they are unable to be realized in real time. This great mystical power is not so: the teachings, practice, and experience of the buddhas are realized as one in [this] mystical power.... Without the mystical power of buddha, the establishment of the mind, training, bodhi, and nirvana of all the buddhas could never be.

We tend to look at the universe that we're sitting in right now as kind of mundane. There's a brick wall behind me, and some books on the table, and my dog Ziggy Pup lying on the floor in front of me. I'm a guy with glasses writing on a laptop. Yeah, yeah ... big deal.

I want miracles! Turning water into wine or flying through the air with fire shooting out of my butt or something flashy like that. But Dogen says the only place that these minor miracles — these kinds of magic tricks and things — can take place is within the Great Miracle that is existence itself. So don't worry about the minor miracles. Pay attention to the Great Miracle.

For Dogen, samadhi is sitting very quietly and noticing that actual existence as it is, in the so-called mundane world, is really extraordinary. Really amazing. Gravity is an amazing thing. Oxygen is incredible. Water, soil, dogs, cats, ugly people, soggy corn flakes, garage doors... it's all amazing! And yet we pass right by it looking for something else. That's our big mistake.

This mundane existence is something special. We use zazen practice to engage with the specialness that already *is*, the samadhi that already *is*, the super consciousness or whatever you want to call it that is already here right in front of our noses and is already amazing. The reason for behaving ethically is that we don't want to mess up this Great Miracle.

# 36. WHO WALKED MY DOG?

ONE OF THE things an experience of samadhi is supposed to answer is the question "Who am I?" I'd like to take a look at that question. The answer might be different from what we tend to imagine it is. In fact, it may challenge our very concept of what constitutes an answer.

In a neat conversation between Nisargadatta Maharaj's student Ramesh Balsekar and Leonard Cohen, Balsekar says:

> But, when the ego gets weaker and weaker and weaker, then it has to ultimately die, finding out "Who is doing anything? Who is seeking anything? Who is to get anything?" You see? That is why I said, the only Sadhana [spiritual practice] I recommend, is to find out at the end of the day, how many actions that I remember having happened today, were *my* actions, and how many just happened?
>
> And I dare say that an honest analysis will make the ego come to the conclusion that no actions were *his* actions, or *her* actions! And if this happens day after day — it may start with the end of the day, but it will be found that this analysis happens many times *during* the day! Until towards the end, an action happens and the analysis that it was not my action, happens almost simultaneously; so that with the firmest possible conviction, with unconditional acceptance that I do nothing, the question arises, not intellectually "Who am I?"

but from the very depths of frustration — it can be said, frustration of the ego — "If I have not been doing, if no act is my action, who is this *me* I've been so concerned about?"

Ramana Maharshi used the words "Who am I" because in English there is a marvelous distinction between "I" and "me," but in the Tamil language and most other languages I am told, this distinction is not there. So when Ramana Maharshi said, "Find out who am I," he really meant, "Who is this me I'm so concerned about?"*

Ramana Maharshi was a twentieth-century Advaita Vedanta teacher whose works I have turned to from time to time ever since I started studying Zen. Because I read Ramana Maharshi's stuff early on, the question "Who am I?" has been part of my Zen practice since the beginning, and still is. I don't sit and chant it in my head like a mantra. But I often direct my attention to that question. I think it's pretty much the same thing as Dogen's admonition that during zazen one should turn the light around and shine it inward. To shine the light inward is to silently ask, "Who am I?"

Even so, reading this conversation between Leonard Cohen and Ramesh Balsekar really helped me understand that question a lot better. Balsekar is correct. The English language does make a distinction between *I* and *me*. The dictionary definition for both words is the same. They're personal pronouns used by a speaker to refer to him- or herself.

But in actual usage, the question "Who is this *me* I've been so concerned about?" is different from "Who am I?" When I think of "I" it seems sort of abstract, like a concept. So the question "Who am I?" seems to be asking me to come up with a logical answer. Lots of people work with it that way, looking at every way they might define

---

* In *janeadamsart*, September 28, 2014, https://janeadamsart.wordpress.com/2014/09/28/a-resonance-between-two-models-leonard-cohen-ramesh-balsekar.

*I* and rejecting them all. "Who is this *me* I've been so concerned about?" seems to cut to the heart of the problem.

Some Advaita Vedanta teachers are fond of likening life to a movie. They say that the events of our lives as individuals are like a movie projected on a screen. The screen is reality. The movie is just a pattern of light dancing across that screen. We are not the movie. What we are is more like the light that shines through the film, unaffected by it but producing the images on the screen. It's a useful metaphor because sometimes when we watch a movie, we get so involved that we forget it's a manufactured thing. We identify with the characters and feel their emotions.

You don't hear many Zen folks using that particular movie metaphor. But Dogen likens life to a dream, which is something the Advaita Vedanta folks do a lot as well. In an essay called "Expressing a Dream within a Dream" ("Mu-chu Setsu-mu"), Dogen says, "The pervasive disclosure of the entire universe is the dream-state. This dream-state is just 'the clear-clear hundred things' —and it is the very moment in which we doubt that it is so; it is the very moment of confusion. At this moment, it is to dream things, it is to be in things, it is to preach things, and so on. When we learn this in practice, roots and stalks, twigs and leaves, flowers and fruit, and light and color are all the great dream-state, which is not to be confused with dreaminess."

Let me take that apart a little bit. "The clear-clear hundred things" is an expression Dogen uses a lot. It just means actual things in the real world. In his notes on this chapter, Nishijima Roshi defines "to dream things" as referring to the mental side of reality and "to be in things" as referring to the material side of reality. He says "preaching things" — which can also be translated as "manifesting things" — suggests the reality that, in the state of action, is "manifested as concrete things."

I like that Dogen says reality is also "the very moment when we doubt it is so; it is the very moment of confusion." Dogen does that sort of thing a lot. He says that even doubt about the truth is part of the truth.

He also says that the dream state he is referring to is not to be confused with dreaminess. He is stressing the difference between what he's saying and what Western philosophers call idealism. Yes, the material world is illusion. But that doesn't mean it's all in our minds. At least not in the way we usually mean it when we say that something is "all in our minds." We're not just imagining it — again, at least not in the way we usually mean when we talk about imagining things. Yet the world "out there" is not at all what we think it is. And we ourselves are not what we think we are. So any guess we make based on the idea that we and the external world are separate things cannot possibly be correct.

Dogen addresses the difference between what he's saying and the idealistic point of view, saying, "People who prefer not to learn the Buddha's truth, when they encounter this 'preaching a dream in a dream,' idly suppose that it might mean creating insubstantial dreamy things which do not exist at all; they suppose it might be like adding to delusion in delusion. [But] it is not so. Even when we are adding to delusion in delusion, we should endeavor just then to learn in practice the path of clarity of expression on which the words 'delusion upon delusion' are naturally spoken." In his footnotes Nishijima Roshi explains this by saying, "Master Dogen understood delusion practically as a momentary state that we should clarify by our effort."

I know. It's confusing!

He's trying to point out that, on the one hand, the world we live in is like a dream or hallucination. But Dogen won't ever just stop there. It might be enough for someone else to say that life is a dream and leave the listener thinking, "Oh! I get it! *That's* what life is! Life is a dream!" Not our Dogen, though. Whatever mental image you try to replace your initial mistaken ideas about reality with is also wrong, according to Dogen, even if it's the mental image he just suggested.

This is what makes Zen so incredibly obnoxious. Just when you think you've figured out what a Zen teacher is saying, he'll tell you that you haven't figured out anything!

But let's circle back to the question: Who is this *me* I've been so concerned about?

Just a few minutes ago, I took a break from writing to go out and walk Ziggy Pup. I decided to use the opportunity to try to figure out who this "me" was who was walking the dog.

To other people on the street, I'm sure we looked pretty ordinary. Just a guy out walking his dog. I don't know if anyone Ziggy and I encountered on that walk made up any stories in their heads about me based on my Godzilla T-shirt and my hat with a picture of one of the Sleestaks from the old kids' TV show *Land of the Lost*. Maybe they did. But if so, none of those stories would be very accurate.

In any case, that's just what I am externally. Internally, though, what am I when I walk the dog?

As I walk, I have thoughts, memories, daydreams. Am I my thoughts? I used to identify with them very strongly. I thought of thoughts that passed through my head as belonging to me. I believed they were produced by me.

But do I actually choose to think certain things and then summon those images up? I guess I can do that to a certain extent, sometimes. But most of the time it feels like what I think is not really in my conscious control. I often think about things that I would prefer not to think about. Whose fault is that?

I can no more predict my own next thought than I can predict your next thought, dear reader. Whatever "I" am does not seem to be in control of thought. So how can this "I" that I believe I am be the thing that creates thought?

A lot of us believe that our thoughts are our own creation. But when I've looked at my own thoughts, that doesn't seem to be the case. If you slow things down by doing a practice like zazen, you can actually watch thoughts sort of bubble up from who knows where. They start off very vague and unformed, and then they sort of firm up and take a more definite form, like Jell-O does when you put it in the fridge. Sometimes they turn into sets of words. Like colorful Jell-O words!

I identify with some thoughts, the ones that feel like they come out of what I think of as my personality. Other thoughts that appear in my mind don't seem related to my self-image, and I barely acknowledge them. I didn't even realize I did this until I'd done lots of zazen.

In any case, my thoughts are not "me." Even when I think of them as having been created by "me," it doesn't seem like they *are* "me." I mean, who is this "me" that I imagine creates "my" thoughts? Some invisible and silent thought maker? Many times while doing zazen, I've tried to find the invisible and silent thought maker, but I've never succeeded.

If I am not thought or even the thought maker, I must be something else.

Let's get back to my walk with Ziggy Pup. I was out there to do a job, to guide the dog around the neighborhood to pee and sniff the leftover pee of other dogs, and to get some exercise for both of us. As I rounded the corner near the end of the block where there's a fountain, we saw little Gigi, who is a neighborhood dog that Ziggy loves to play with a lot, and Gigi's person. While Ziggy and Gigi chased each other around, I had a little chat with Gigi's owner, who is my wife's mom's friend.

When I meet other people walking their dogs, I sometimes ask them how old their dogs are, what their dogs' names are, and stuff like that. Our conversations are mostly pretty trivial and shallow. But shallow and trivial conversations aren't necessarily a bad thing. I enjoy them a lot, in fact. It's good to talk to other people in any capacity, I think.

Occasionally, I ask other dog walkers about themselves, and they ask me about me. We tell each other what we do for a living, where we came from, maybe some interesting places we've gone or things we've done. In short, we talk about our pasts.

Is that what I am? My past? Was it my past who was walking Ziggy? Was that "me"? Was "me" the guy who wrote a bunch of books about Zen? Was "me" a guy from Ohio who grew up partially in Africa and then lived in Japan for a long time? Was "me" the bass player in a band that nowadays only gets together about once a year because the rest of the guys live in Ohio and I live in California? Is the trajectory that this body and mind have taken "me"?

Let's consider that for a bit. I suppose you could say that every experience I've ever had played some role in my walking the dog today. So in some sense, maybe my past walked the dog.

You could say, for example, that because I was born in a certain time and place, and made a specific set of decisions throughout my life, I ended up in just the right place to walk Ziggy Pup on a random Thursday afternoon. Because I chose to take a teaching job in Japan in the early '90s and then quit that job, I ended up working for Tsuburaya Productions, the folks who make the superhero show *Ultraman*, and they sent me to work at their Los Angeles office, which subsequently closed, leaving me adrift in LA, and this eventually set off a chain of events that led me to meet my wife, who decided to rescue a dog from a shelter, and — voilà! — there I was walking that dog.

Things could have been different. Or so we are prone to believe. You could say that if I hadn't taken that teaching job in Japan or made any of a number of other decisions I wouldn't have ended up walking that dog. Based on that idea, you might say that I could have had some other very different life. Most of us believe that sort of thing. We imagine that our lives could have been different from the way they are. I'm not so sure I believe that, though.

I used to believe that. In fact, I'd often get very worked up about how things might have been. I used to find myself in places I didn't want to be, cursing the fact that I wasn't somewhere else.

Then I noticed that, no matter where I was, that was where I was. The idea that I could be somewhere else simply was not true. I can't be anywhere other than exactly where I am. Where I am and who I am seem to be inseparable.

Life got a lot better when I finally came to terms with that. It's not that I never wish I was somewhere else. Those kinds of ideas still come up sometimes. But I know that where I am is just where I am. If I want to be somewhere else, I have to get off my ass and go there. The reason that I'm not somewhere else is always the same: I'm not there because I am here.

But why am I here? This is not so clear, actually. As we've seen, you could say I am here because of the trajectory my life took in the past and the decisions I made — ethical and unethical. It's simple cause and effect. I accept that. But I can't actually trace the entire trajectory of my life, even though it seems like it ought to be accessible in my memories.

But in fact, all my memories are pretty iffy. Sometimes I think I remember a situation clearly, and then I meet someone else who was there at the time and they tell me I'm completely wrong about significant details. In my first book, *Hardcore Zen*, I told the story of how Zero Defex, the band I was in back in 1983 (and that I'm still in today), got attacked by a bunch of angry rednecks at a bar in Dover, Ohio, where we were booked to play a show. About ten minutes into our set, all hell broke loose. Bottles were flying. Chairs were flying. I ran away and hid in the ladies' room.

When writing *Hardcore Zen*, I wrote the story of that night from memory. At the time I wasn't in touch with anyone else who'd been there. Years later, I made a movie about the hardcore punk scene in Northeast Ohio in those days called *Cleveland's Screaming*. As part of making the movie, I talked to many of the other people who were also there that night in Dover. They pointed out a whole lot of things

I'd forgotten. I realized that much of what I said in my book was totally wrong.

A few years ago I found a diary I'd kept during one of the first Zen retreats I went on with Nishijima Roshi at Tokei-in, the temple in Shizuoka, Japan, where we did most of our retreats. In the diary I wrote about some locals taking a bunch of us foreign Zen students for a ride in the back of a pickup truck to go look at fireflies. I don't remember that at all. But it's there in that diary in my own handwriting. Weird.

Even when it comes to very recent events, it's mostly a blur. I could tell you what I had for breakfast today — a banana and peanut butter smoothie — and I know I made a video for my YouTube channel a couple of hours ago, and then worked on writing this book. But there are lots of details that are lost forever. More than I'll ever know.

My memories, therefore, are not a particularly reliable guide to what actually happened in my life. I can recount my life story — I do it a lot these days in interviews — but I know I'm probably getting it wrong, as in the case of my book *Hardcore Zen*. That stuff with the rednecks who attacked us in that bar was only part of it. I think we all do this. We fill gaps in our memories with purely made-up stuff, and then we don't really know which parts actually happened.

I'm not even sure I was ever actually born. I know that probably sounds kooky. But I have no memory of my own birth. My mom remembered it. But then again, what she remembered was the moment she pushed me out of her body. That was on what they call my "birthday." But was that the day I came into existence? Surely I was already alive before then, at least for some time. When exactly did I start? There are loads of political debates about that question. But nobody really knows the answer.

Even if I could pinpoint the exact moment when something identifiable as my individual human life began, was that really the beginning? Was I alive as something else before then? Even if you don't believe in reincarnation, maybe you could say that before my conception I was alive as a sperm and as an egg. If so, I was two individuals who merged into one!

So who the heck was walking Ziggy Pup?

Was it my future? Was it all the things that I worry might happen to me? Was it all the things I look forward to? Those are just thoughts. They come and they go. And as I said, my thoughts do not seem to be "me." I worry about my future sometimes, just like anyone else. But worrying about my future has only limited value. If I were to look at my bank balance and see that there wasn't enough for next month's rent, then worry might be appropriate. But in most cases, worries about the future are far more abstract and far less practical.

There are literally infinite ways a person might die, for example. And some of them are really scary. But what's the sense in imagining speculative scenarios of my death? Or imagining what it would be like if nobody ever bought my books and I went broke? Or imagining any of an infinite variety of other things that might happen? Yet lots of us waste far too much mental energy on such imaginary scenarios. Thankfully, I seem to have finally learned not to follow those sorts of thoughts very far when they come up. It took a lot of hard Zen practice to get there, though!

When you do zazen for long periods, it seems like the brain starts churning up all kinds of random memories and fears and stuff like that. At first it can be extremely distracting. But after a while you just get sick of it. My friend Greg, that guy from Tassajara Zen Monastery who wrote the song I quoted a few chapters ago, said that it's kind of like a piece of gum you keep chewing even after all the flavor is gone. Eventually you realize that you need to just spit it out.

OK. So if that isn't "me," then was the "me" who walked the dog my experience of walking the dog? Was "me" my experience of the sunshine on my face, the earth and concrete beneath my feet, the feeling of the leash in my hand, the sight of Ziggy's furry butt waddling about four feet in front of me? I've learned to keep a sharp eye on him, since he's escaped from his harness a couple of times. As I walked Ziggy, there seemed to be a human-shaped *something* with eyes and other sense organs who experienced the walk as a physical being participating in a physical event.

Was that "me"? I'm sure other people would define it that way. They might say that Brad Warner, a physical being, took his dog, Ziggy Pup, for a walk. Simple! But what was the "me" who subjectively experienced that?

I honestly do not know. There's a story about Bodhidharma, the Indian Buddhist master who brought the Zen form of Buddhism to China. The story goes that the emperor wanted to meet him. So Bodhidharma went to the palace. The emperor told him about all the Buddhist temples he'd built and asked Bodhidharma what merit he had acquired by doing so. Bodhidharma said, "No merit." Then the emperor asked him about the highest truth. Bodhidharma said, "There is only vast emptiness, nothing holy." So the emperor asked Bodhidharma who he — Bodhidharma — was. Bodhidharma said, "I don't know."

If the emperor of China had invited me to his palace and asked me who walked Ziggy Pup, I'm not sure I'd have the guts to answer like Bodhidharma did, but the most honest answer is the one he gave, "I don't know."

I subjectively experienced a walk with a dog. Or at least that's how I'd describe it. I feel like the same person who walked the dog is typing this right now. The person who is typing this certainly has specific memories of that walk with Ziggy Pup that no one else has. Presumably, these memories could be verified by whatever surveillance cameras might have caught parts of the walk or by people who witnessed the walk, if anyone would recall such a mundane thing. If I had committed a crime during that walk — like if I'd failed to pick up Ziggy's poop — then the person who is typing this now would be considered the guilty party.

But is it "me" who walked the dog? In conventional terms, that's what I'd tell someone who asked who didn't want a long philosophical discussion about the nature of the self. But, honestly, I am not sure.

When I get worked up about "me," what am I getting worked up about? As I said, I might start worrying about things that might happen to "me" in the future. But I'm not sure if future me will experience any of the things I worry about. And I'm not sure if, even if future me did experience those things, it would be anything like what the me of right now imagines. Lots of things in the past that I anticipated would be horrible turned out just fine, while lots of things that I looked forward to ended up being kind of crappy.

Whatever can be thought is just a thought. My most terrifying fears are just secretions of my brain. My most joyful anticipations are nothing more than energy bopping around in my head. My deepest regrets are just brain farts.

I might get worked up about my past, about things I did and that I regret having done. But again, who did those things? As I said, if I'd done something criminal, a court could determine me to be guilty. Which is one reason why I avoid doing anything illegal. But even though I haven't broken any major laws, I still have regrets. Everyone does. But once we do something, we can never go back and undo that thing. As my teacher said, once we do something it's carved into the universe.

In some sense, all those past things I did — the unethical ones I regret, the ethical ones I'm proud of, and the neutral ones I've utterly forgotten — are sitting here now typing out this book. Maybe some of the things I regret the most made me a better person somehow. Maybe some of the things I take pride in having accomplished aren't really all that great.

But are they "me"? Are they the *something* that watches my fingers type these words? Are they the *something* that watches thoughts form into words? Are they the *something* that abides even in deepest, dreamless sleep and who somehow reacquaints itself with the life trajectory of Brad Warner every morning after having not been anyone at all for most of the night? Or after having been someone else in a dream?

The fact is, I don't know "me" at all.

When I look at it this way, "me" seems to be made up mostly of memory and imagination. When I describe me in conventional terms, all I'm really describing is my iffy memories of my past and my imaginary and usually mistaken ideas of my future.

Yet something was out there walking the dog. Something real. And something real is typing this right now. And it's not just memory and imagination. Maybe what I'm writing is based on memory and imagination. But the me who is writing it seems to be something else.

When someone yells, "Brad!" I respond. When I respond to my name, a certain feeling comes with that. It's a far more definite feeling of *me-ness* — if there is such a word — than when I simply think of myself as me.

There's an old Zen story that relates to this. It goes something like this. A guy named Go-ei visited Sekito Kisen, who was a very famous Zen master, and said to him, "If you can say something I agree with, I'll stay here and study with you. If not, I'll leave."

Sekito didn't respond.

Go-ei figured he'd bested Sekito and walked out of Sekito's temple, swinging his sleeves widely with pride, as folks did back in those days. We've seen that move before!

When Go-ei was almost at the temple gate, Sekito yelled, "Hey! Go-ei!"

Go-ei turned his head.

Sekito said, "From birth to death it's just like this!"

Go-ei immediately awakened to the truth and later became a renowned master.

Usually this story is explained by saying that Go-ei was trying to play an intellectual game with Sekito. Then Sekito made him suddenly aware of the real situation at that very moment and he was awakened to the truth. Which is fine if you like explanations like that. I'm not so sure that's the best explanation, though.

This was one of the first koan stories I ever heard. I never forgot that last line, "from birth to death it's just like this," but I forgot the rest of the story. It took me ages to find it again. What strikes me about the story is the way Go-ei came to his awakening when he heard his own name followed by "from birth to death it's just like this."

The moment he turned his head, Go-ei was face-to-face with reality.

Nobody called out my name when I was walking Ziggy Pup this afternoon. There were no Zen masters standing at the bus stops I passed waiting to awaken me to the truth of the universe. Even if there had been, I wonder if I'd have gotten it. Moments of awakening seem to happen on their own terms. You can't force them. And the specific trigger that works for one person at one time probably won't work for anyone else ever again.

Names are interesting. Ziggy responds to his name. So he must have some feeling of identification with his name. I even had a cat who responded to his name. There must be something very primal about that sort of identification. It is a shock to discover that the same thing you identified with your personal name is also the basis for the entire universe, that the entire universe is made exclusively of the very thing you've always identified with your personal name.

In an essay called "Buddhas Alone Together with Buddhas," which we'll be spending some time with later in this book, Dogen says that "if we look at the mountains, rivers, and earth while one human being is being born, we do not see this human being now appearing through isolated superimposition upon mountains, rivers, and earth that existed before [this human being] was born." Does a person appear into a universe that was already there before she or he was born, or does the universe arise simultaneously with the person who perceives it? After all, even in conventional terms, a newly born person isn't made of anything that wasn't already there. No new elements have suddenly popped into existence.

Does the me who walked Ziggy Pup also include the street on which I walk, the sky above, the hills, the trees, the cars whizzing by, the planet whose gravity embraces my body and doesn't allow it to fly away, the sun that provided the energy that created everything I ever ate and that makes up my body and everything my mother ate that made up the body I was born with, the stars that exploded a zillion years ago, producing the elements that made up my mom's body and then mine, the galaxy in which we all spin, and the universe whose mysterious and utterly inexplicable appearance made it all possible?

I cannot see any possibility that it's otherwise. Everything I am depends on all those other things. I depend on the entire universe for my very existence. In a very real sense I *am* the entire universe.

In his essay "Inmo," Dogen says, "The situation of the supreme truth of bodhi is such that even the whole universe in ten directions is just a small part of the supreme truth of bodhi: it may be that the truth of bodhi abounds beyond the universe. We ourselves are tools that it possesses within this universe in ten directions. How do we know that it exists? We know it is so because the body and the mind both appear in the universe, yet neither is our self."

*Inmo* is an ancient Chinese word that just means "it" or "what" or "something." Sometimes people translate it as "suchness," but I never liked that translation. What does the word *suchness* even mean?

When Dogen says that "we ourselves are tools that *it* possesses," the word translated as "it" is *inmo*. Maybe Dogen would say that the me who walked Ziggy Pup was a tool used by the entire universe in ten directions, a concrete expression of the supreme state of bodhi, which abounds even beyond the universe.

So if neither body nor mind is me, am I consciousness?

This is one popular solution to the problem of "me." Lots of people say that what we really are is not body or mind, but consciousness.

Nishijima Roshi used to like to say that "reality exists in the contact between subject and object." Often consciousness is defined as the contact between subject and object. He followed that up by stating that if we say that the world is only mind, we have to also say that the mind is only the world. This comes up in his introduction to an essay by Dogen called "The Triple World Is Mind Alone" ("San-gai Yui Shin"). The phrase *triple world* means "the entire universe." Those ancient Buddhists had a lot of cute ways of saying "the entire universe."

In English we often make a distinction between mind and consciousness. And in some cases that can be a valid and useful distinction. But in this case we can read the Japanese word that Dogen uses, *shin*, as mind or as consciousness. It's a word we've talked about before in this book. As I said before, the Chinese character for *shin* is a pictogram that represents the shape of the human heart. So if you wanted to, you could translate the title of Dogen's essay as "The Triple World Is Heart Alone." But nobody does that.

Was it consciousness alone that walked Ziggy Pup?

That's an intriguing possibility. There really isn't any way to prove that it wasn't. There's an entire school of Buddhism known sometimes as Vijnanavada and sometimes as Yogacara, which is often referred to as Consciousness Only Buddhism. Even after having read a bunch of stuff about this form of Buddhism, I have a hard time understanding exactly what Yogacara Buddhists believe with regard to consciousness.

Sometimes it seems like they believe that consciousness is the only thing there is, as the name Consciousness Only would seem to imply. Other times it seems like they sort of sidestep the whole question of whether or not consciousness is the only thing that exists and instead say something like, "Even if it's not the only thing that exists, consciousness is the only thing we can ever know, so we might as well focus our study only on consciousness." Which would be another perfectly valid way of understanding the name Consciousness Only.

Dogen was not part of this school of Buddhism. That essay, "The Triple World Is Mind Alone," seems to be a criticism of what Dogen felt were misunderstandings on the part of those who advocated the idea that consciousness was the only thing in the universe.

I'm not Dogen, though. I have a lot of trust in his opinions on things, but I can't simply defer to him and leave it at that. He might have been wrong. Or he might have been right and I have misunderstood him. Therefore I have to look into this for myself. Which is what Dogen clearly advocated, that we look into this stuff for ourselves.

So... was it consciousness that walked Ziggy Pup? Certainly every sensation that I associate with having walked Ziggy Pup could be considered a thing that appeared within consciousness. Thoughts and physical sensations appeared in consciousness. In fact, the entire world appeared there. I can't prove that anything outside consciousness produced any of those sensations.

For me the trouble happens when I start to think of consciousness as *my* consciousness. Is consciousness *mine*? There is a strong tendency to imagine that consciousness is the possession of "me." There is a strong tendency to believe that every entity has its own consciousness, separate from the consciousness of every other entity. This tends to create the impression that my consciousness is eternally distinct from every other consciousness in the universe. But the very idea of a "me" who owns or creates "my consciousness" is questionable.

What if there is only one consciousness? What if that one, singular consciousness just appears to be a bunch of distinct individual consciousnesses?

If consciousness walked Ziggy Pup, then consciousness must be something far bigger than my consciousness or Ziggy Pup's consciousness. It must be consciousness that encompasses the entire universe in all directions and in all times and all places.

Some people would call that "God." So let's look at that possibility. Did God walk Ziggy Pup?

Don't get me wrong, I don't think I'm God. I'm certainly not God in the sense of being the old white man with the long beard who sits up in the clouds smiting the Peloponnesians or whatever it is that God does up there.

But one of the ways some folks like to characterize the universe is to say that God is all of us, and all of us are God. In his book *The Book on the Taboo against Knowing Who You Are*, Alan Watts says:

> God... likes to play hide-and-seek, but because there is nothing outside God, he has no one but himself to play with. But he gets over this difficulty by pretending that he is not himself. This is his way of hiding from himself. He pretends that he is you and I and all the people in the world, all the animals, all the plants, all the rocks, and all the stars. In this way he has strange and wonderful adventures, some of which are terrible and frightening. But these are just like bad dreams, for when he wakes up they will disappear.
>
> Now when God plays hide and pretends that he is you and I, he does it so well that it takes him a long time to remember where and how he hid himself. But that's the whole fun of it — just what he wanted to do. He doesn't want to find himself too quickly, for that would spoil the game. That is why it is so difficult for you and me to find out that we are God in disguise, pretending not to be himself. But when the game has gone on long enough, all of us will wake up, stop pretending, and remember that we are all one single Self — the God who is all that there is and who lives for ever and ever.

This is Watts's explanation of his understanding of one of the ideas you find in the Advaita Vedanta tradition. It's not too different from what some people in the Zen tradition say as well.

If this is the case, then I am me and I am Ziggy Pup too. Ziggy walked himself, and so did Brad. God split himself up into Brad, and Ziggy, and the other dog walkers, and the street, and the planet, and the galaxy, and the whole shebang. It's all just God playing hide-and-seek with himself. The Sufis say that God is a mirror that shattered itself so that it could see itself.

I'm fond of this way of understanding things. It makes far more sense to me than the common view that each and every thing is an individual unto itself. The separation we feel from each other is clearly an illusion.

Only, why can't I see past that illusion? From time to time, in my Zen practice, I have had glimpses beyond it — clear and unambiguous peeks into a kind of existence in which I am both one small part and the entire thing. Yet I keep getting drawn back into what I know for certain to be a kind of twisted hallucination — the hallucination of being a thing apart from the rest of creation. Why?

This is a hard question to answer. It's a lot like the guy in a koan called "One Bright Pearl," which we'll look at in the next chapter. The short version of the koan is that this guy who'd been practicing Zen for a long time stubs his toe real bad on a rock and then says, "I've heard that the body and the mind are both unreal. So where is this pain coming from?"

You don't need to stub your toe on a rock or suffer some other sort of painful incident to ask this question. I ask it of myself quite often. I know for certain that the body and the mind are an illusion, yet why do I suffer so much pain because of them? Even if the pain isn't an obvious physical or psychological pain, you can still ask this question.

For the moment my answer would be that the pain exists whenever I believe that I am this body and this mind. Pain seems to be fused with that belief. When I turn away from that belief, I turn away from the pain as well.

One thing I firmly believe is that once you have established your aim to the truth, you will get the truth. The truth is more powerful than anything that stands in its way. My own bad habits are no match for the truth. Recognizing my bad habits and abandoning them brings my actions more in line with the rule of the universe. This makes more of the truth available.

If you start out on this path, you will get to the end.

Only, there is no end.

Which is fine because there is no you to get there anyhow.

# 37. ONE BRIGHT PEARL

IN THE LAST chapter I mentioned one my favorite Zen stories, "One Bright Pearl." Dogen wrote one of his greatest essays about it. I'd like to take some time looking at that old story because it's meant a lot to me over the years.

Recently I came across a passage in Kobun Chino's book *Embracing Mind* in which Kobun tells his own version of the story. It's not quite the orthodox version. But I love it. Here's how he tells the story:

> There is a story about one of [Zen Master] Seppo's disciples whose father was a fisherman in the Yangtse River, and this young man was his helper. Every day they caught a huge carp or something in the big river. One night the moon was bright so they set up night fishing, but the father slipped and went into the water; maybe a big fish caught the hook and pulled him down.
>
> So he was drowning from the slippery river bank. The son tried to save him, and threw out his bamboo poles and fishing tackles, trying to save his father, until he, himself, was slipping, so finally he had to let the poles go. His father sank in the moonlight.
>
> The son's mind was kind of screwed up at that moment and he ran to the monastery of Seppo, "Snow Peak, Seppo Gisan," a very famous Rinzai teacher. After years of practice

with Seppo, the disciple, whose name was Gensha, told Seppo, "I'm no good. I must go away from this place," so he began to climb the mountain, until, in the dark, he kicked a sharp rock.

When he held onto his toes, they felt warm and yucky, "Oh, no, it hurts!" And he said to himself, "This body and mind do not exist, I know, but where is this pain coming from?"

He sat there thinking, "Wait a minute! What did I say?" So he started to climb back down the path, back to Master Snow Peak. "I was wrong, so I came back."

When the Master asked him why he had returned, he answered, "Bodhidharma hasn't come to China. The Second Patriarch hasn't gone to India." This was a strange statement, since Bodhidharma came to China. Everyone knew that. And Huiko [Bodhidharma's student] had gone to India. What he meant was that Bodhidharma didn't need to come to China and Huiko didn't need to go to India. Seppo recognized something underneath this statement, so Gensha stayed there in Kose, west of the Yangtse, and taught many people, maintaining that this entire universe is nothing but a bundle of light.

Pain is sometimes a good thing, you know!

The version of the story that Dogen tells in *Shobogenzo* doesn't mention the part about Gensha's father's death, but that's part of other versions of the traditional story. Also, instead of saying that the universe is a bundle of light, Dogen's version says it's one bright pearl, hence the name of the story. Otherwise it's pretty much the same story in different words.

Oh, and by the way, calling the story "One Bright Pearl" in English is probably a mistake. The word translated as "pearl" is a more general term meaning something more like "jewel" than specifically a pearl. According to Shohaku Okumura, it's most likely a reference to the idea of Indra's net, which I talked about earlier. At each intersection of the net is a jewel. Each jewel perfectly reflects all the other jewels. It's a symbolic representation of the interconnectedness of all things.

In his book *Commentary on the Song of Awakening*, Kodo Sawaki says that Gensha's cryptic statement about Bodhidharma and Huiko means that "the entire universe was a single transparent jewel, the jewel symbolizing unity. In consequence it was useless to go anywhere — there was nothing to seek nor anything to flee."

Anyway... I'm just gonna keep calling the story "One Bright Pearl," because that's the name I learned it under and it's the most common way of referring to the story in English.

I mentioned the story of "One Bright Pearl" at an event I did with Stephen Batchelor, author of *Buddhism without Beliefs*, *Confession of a Buddhist Atheist*, and many other books about Buddhism. In response, Batchelor bought up an argument known in Western philosophy as the "Appeal to the Stone."

This argument is credited to Samuel Johnson, an eighteenth-century British philosopher. James Boswell, in his book *The Life of Samuel Johnson*, tells the story like this: "After we came out of the church, we stood talking for some time together of Bishop Berkeley's ingenious sophistry to prove the non-existence of matter, and that every thing in the universe is merely ideal. I observed that though we are satisfied, his doctrine is not true, it is impossible to refute it. I never shall forget the alacrity with which Johnson answered, striking his foot with mighty force against a large stone, till he rebounded from it, 'I refute it thus.'"

The two stories are similar, but there's an important difference. Upon kicking that stone, Samuel Johnson satisfied himself that material things exist independent of anyone perceiving them. But kicking a stone didn't convince Gensha that the Buddhist philosophy of Mind Only was wrong. Rather, it confirmed to him that it was true, and Gensha became a renowned teacher of that philosophy. Weird, huh? Let's see what we can do with that.

The very end of Dogen's commentary on "One Bright Pearl" goes (spoiler alert!), "The mind is not personal; why should we be worried by attachment to whether it is a bright pearl or is not a bright pearl, as if what is born and passes away were some person? Even thinking and worry is not different from the bright pearl. No action nor any thought has ever been caused by anything other than the bright pearl. Therefore, forward steps and backward steps in a demon's black-mountain cave [a symbol of ignorance and confusion] are just the one bright pearl itself."

The mind is not personal.

Let's dig into that statement a little bit. Because I think most of us conceive of our mind as the single most personal thing there could ever possibly be. Our thoughts are our own, and nobody else's. Nobody knows what I'm thinking unless I deliberately tell them. Well... maybe that's not always true. I might make a Freudian slip and accidentally say something that lets people know what I'm secretly thinking. Or my facial expression could announce my unspoken thoughts. Still, even that sort of thing can't reveal everything I'm thinking.

But as we have discussed, thoughts are only a teeny, tiny part of what Buddhists mean when they use the word *mind*. Thoughts are the superficial activity taking place on the surface of the mind. Thoughts are attached to personhood. I imagine that I am a person, and I imagine that I must therefore have personal thoughts.

But is this true? When I examine it for myself, as I did when I walked Ziggy Pup, I have to wonder if my thoughts really belong to an entity I can call "me." I seem to have some limited capacity to think what I want to think, but most of the time I have no control over what pops into my head.

When I do zazen, I watch what takes place when thoughts appear.

Some thoughts are stickier than others and stay around for a while, and others just flash into existence and disappear immediately.

In the Advaita Vedanta tradition there's a name for the stages by which a thought appears, matures, and finally becomes something that you can put words to. The first step is called *para*, or source consciousness. Most people are completely unaware of thoughts at this stage of development. Next comes *pashyanti*, or thought emanation. At this stage, the thought begins to take on a form. Most of us aren't aware of this stage of the process either. Then there's the stage called *madhyama*, in which the thought appears in the mind. This is the first part of the process that an ordinary person notices. The final stage is called *vaikari*, which means "language explodes out." This is where the thought becomes a set of words. We mistakenly believe these thoughts to be produced by a self.*

In zazen you can become aware of the earlier parts of the process of thought formation. It was really strange when I started noticing this. Thoughts in those early stages of development are vague and unclear. They're not necessarily about anything. As we read earlier in this book, Uchiyama Roshi calls thought the "secretions of the brain," and at that early part of their development, thoughts feel more like a kind of primordial ooze than like anything I'd call a thought.

While doing zazen, I noticed that I have a habit of sorting through my thoughts and trying to make them align with my personality. I accept some of them as good and reject others as bad. If I have a lot of "bad thoughts" — ideas about unethical actions I could take to harm others, for example — I might get distressed about what sort of person I am even to be having such thoughts. Sometimes that distress leads to even more of those "bad thoughts."

It was useful to learn through the practice of zazen that those

---

* Nisargadatta Maharaj, *Prior to Consciousness*, ed. Jean Dunn (Durham, NC: Acorn, 1990), 24.

"bad thoughts" were not my own. But then again, neither are the "good thoughts." Thoughts are all just thoughts. None of them are mine. None of them are me. Understanding that made a huge difference in my life.

Also, I can always interrupt the process of dwelling on thoughts, whether good or bad, by removing attention from thought. It took me quite a while to notice that this was even possible. But once I noticed it, and worked with it, it wasn't so hard to do. There is always something else going on. Maybe there are birds chirping, or the noise of cars passing by, or an ache in my legs, or any of a million other sensations happening at the same time as my thoughts. So I can always turn my attention to one of those things instead of my thoughts. I can even turn my attention to the great silence that underlies all thought and sensation.

I've found that one of the most consistently useful ways to interrupt a flow of thoughts while doing zazen is to adjust my posture. The body follows the mind. If the mind gets active, the body responds to that activity. Maybe my shoulders tense up, or maybe I slouch forward or backward, or my teeth start to clench. The specific bodily reactions change, but there's always some kind of bodily response.

So I fix that. I open up my chest, or I drop my shoulders, or I unclench my teeth. Whatever reaction the body does in response to thought, I undo that reaction and get back to the proper zazen posture. If I'm having a day where thoughts are particularly active, I might have to do this dozens of times in a single half hour of zazen. If that's what needs to be done, though, I just do it.

When I do it, the thoughts that were bugging me just kind of fly away, like flies being shooed away from a pile of Ziggy Pup's poop. Sure, they might fly right back. And then I have to start the process again. But sometimes they don't come back. And there's this nice quiet space where even the idea of "me" no longer exists. In fact, that quiet space never goes away. It's just that sometimes thoughts come in and fill it up, and sometimes they don't.

Even so, that quiet space is always there. No matter how many noisy thoughts land on top of it and buzz around it, the quiet basis is always present. The more I learn to keep attention on that quiet space rather than on the noisy thoughts that try to obscure it, the better I feel.

The mind is not personal. My mind is not me. I may call it "my mind," but it's not mine at all. Gensha must have noticed this when he stubbed his toe on that rock. His body wasn't himself and his mind wasn't himself either, but still he felt great pain. The pain was the bright pearl, which is the universe. The universe was Gensha and is you.

In his book *Commentary on the Song of Awakening*, Kodo Sawaki tells the story of Gensha and the rock and says that when Gensha stubbed his toe, "he understood that the absence of character is neither empty nor non-empty." This, Sawaki said, is "the true face of Buddha."

By "absence of character" Sawaki means that Gensha transcended any view of himself as an individual person. He stopped worrying about his personality the way I worry when I sort through my thoughts trying to align them with who I imagine myself to be.

Shohaku Okumura relates this phenomenon to the Twelvefold Chain of Codependent Coorigination that we looked at a few chapters ago. He says, "Gensha's experience of pain is one example of 'contact,' one of the important links in the Twelvefold Chain, a Buddhist teaching of dependent origination. Because of 'contact' between sense organs and their objects, we have various sensations such as love and hatred, and grasping and clinging; then our life becomes unstable, moving up and down between success and failure in the cycle of samsara."

But contact is actually an illusion. Okumura writes that when Gensha says, "The body and mind do not exist, where does this pain come from?" it's not really a question but a statement. Okumura says that this was Gensha's "exclamation of his realization of the reality of form-and-emptiness. Here were not two or more separate, independent things, therefore there was no 'contact.' The pain was not only in his toe or in his mind or in both; the entire universe was nothing other than pain."

Okumura says, "When we see the interconnectedness of all beings there's no contact. Because I think I am not some particular object and that object is not me, I have contact with that object. Yet self and object are interconnected, existing only in relationship with each other and with all other beings and things, so there's actually no way contact can exist; everything is already connected."

Remember that Dogen takes a much wider view of what mind is than most people. In an essay called "Mind Here and Now Is Buddha" ("Soku Shin Ze Butsu") he says, "An ancient ancestor said, 'What is fine, pure, and bright mind? It is mountains, rivers, and the earth, the sun, the moon, and the stars.' Clearly, 'mind' is mountains, rivers, and the earth, the sun, the moon, and the stars. But what these words say is, when we are moving forward, not enough, and when we are drawing back, too much."

What he means by that last sentence is that we usually just ignore the fact that mind includes everything (moving forward, not enough) or we do the opposite and overthink it (drawing back, too much).

Dogen continues, saying:

Mind as mountains, rivers, and the earth is nothing other than mountains, rivers, and the earth. There are no additional waves or surf, no wind or smoke. Mind as the sun, the moon, and the stars is nothing other than the sun, the moon, and the stars. There is no additional fog or mist. Mind as living-and-dying, coming-and-going, is nothing other than living-and-dying, coming-and-going. There is no additional delusion or realization. Mind as fences, walls, tiles, and pebbles is nothing other than fences, walls, tiles, and pebbles. There is no additional mud or water.... Because the state is like this, "mind here and now is buddha" is untainted "mind here and now is buddha." All buddhas are untainted buddhas. This being so, "mind here and now is buddha" is the buddhas [themselves] who establish the will, undergo training, [realize] bodhi, and [experience] nirvana.

Remember that when he says "buddhas themselves" he means you and me. You've already "established the will." I know because you're reading this book. Maybe you're even "undergoing training." The rest will come. That much is certain.

The next part of the story of "One Bright Pearl," as Dogen tells it, is that Gensha, after he becomes a great Zen master, teaches that the universe is one bright pearl, or in Kobun's words, "nothing but a bundle of light." One day a monk asks Gensha, "How should I understand this teaching?"

It's a good question. If someone just says to you "the universe is one bright pearl," you might ask how that could possibly be. There are certainly aspects of life that do not seem like one bright pearl. All sorts of nasty things happen all the time. In fact, the experience that caused Gensha to make that statement in the first place might be one of them.

When Gensha said the universe is one bright pearl, he wasn't speaking from the point of view of someone who'd always had a nice, cushy time and was exclaiming, "Life is great!" to all us poor saps for whom life isn't always that great. Quite the opposite. Gensha was known for his hard, dedicated practice. He went to Seppo's temple after witnessing the death of his father, whom he couldn't save from drowning, so he must have been grieving terribly and questioning the meaning of life at the deepest level.

Gensha took his monk's vow of poverty so seriously that he had only one robe made of woven grass that he continually repaired. That's pretty serious! Yet he experienced a dark, dark moment when he thought that all his dedicated practice had been useless. The agony he felt that night was much more than that in his toe! How can stubbing your toe on a sharp rock in the dark after giving up on a practice you've dedicated your life to be characterized as one bright pearl?

When the monk asked him how to understand the teaching of one bright pearl, Gensha answered, "The whole universe is one bright pearl. What is the use of understanding?"

Understanding would mean trying to capture the bright pearl in words. And you can't do that. It's like how you can't explain baseball in a book to someone who has never played baseball, and how you can't explain what Zen is in a book about Zen to someone who has never done zazen. It just is what it is. Even if you could understand it intellectually, what good would that do? An intellectual understanding might be the kind of thing you could write a term paper on for an Eastern philosophy course, but it wouldn't be good for much else.

Later on, Gensha went up to that monk and said to him, "The whole universe is one bright pearl. How do you understand this?"

The monk said, "The whole universe is one bright pearl. What is the use of understanding?"

Gensha said, "I see you're struggling to get into a demon's cave in a black mountain."

Gensha was saying that the monk understood his words, but he didn't understand their meaning. The demon's cave he was struggling to get into was the cave of intellectual understanding. He was looking in the wrong place. But it wasn't a hopeless situation, and it wasn't nearly as scary as the image of a demon's cave in a black mountain might make it seem. Gensha was pointing the way out for the monk. All the monk had to do to get out of that cave was to stop trying to grasp Gensha's words with his mind. The story doesn't say whether or not the monk figured it out. But I'm guessing he did.

When Gensha's teacher, Seppo, asked Gensha why he came back to the temple after stubbing his toe that night, Gensha said, "I can't be deceived by anyone." That part isn't in Kobun's telling of the story, but it's in Dogen's version. According to Okumura Roshi, it means that "the separation between subject and object has ceased to be."

Gensha realized that direct experience was the only way of understanding the dharma. The statement "this body and mind do not exist" is well established in Buddhism and considered to be a statement of fact. And yet understanding those words only with the intellect can lead you to the wrong conclusions. It can lead you, for example, to believe that stubbing your toe on a rock shouldn't hurt.

That night on the path out of the mountain, Gensha finally reconciled the teaching that the body and mind don't exist with the real facts of his actual life. He saw that the teaching he'd received had been true after all, even in the midst of his terrible pain. He could not be deceived, nor could he deceive anyone else.

Dogen says that the point of Gensha's assertion that the universe is one bright pearl is that "the whole universe in ten directions is not vast and great, not meager and small, not square or round, not centered or straight, not in a state of vigorous activity, and not disclosed in perfect clarity."

Of course we all know that the whole universe ("in ten directions" just means the entire thing in all directions) is vast and great. I just looked it up, and *Wikipedia* tells me that the universe is 93 billion light years across. I don't know if the universe is square, round, centered, or straight, but 93 billion light years is most assuredly vast and great!

But there's an old Zen saying that when the room is ten feet wide, the universe is ten feet wide. It means that even if the universe is 93 billion light years across, if your personal experience is a ten-foot-wide room, then the entire universe might as well be ten feet wide. That's what Dogen is referring to here. He's saying that the universe is neither objectively 93 billion light years across nor subjectively ten feet wide. Both views, the objective/materialist view and the subjective/idealist view, are mistaken.

The rest of what Dogen says about it not being square or round and all that can be understood as his saying that whatever way you use to try to understand the universe is always going to be mistaken.

Then Dogen says, "Because it is utterly beyond living-and-dying, coming-and-going, it is living-and-dying, going-and-coming." This is typical Dogen. He's not saying it's aliens, but it's aliens.

Living and dying and coming and going are facts. We live and then we die. People come into our lives and then they go away. You can't hold on to anything. Impermanence is one of the most important teachings of Buddhism. Nothing lasts.

And yet, not to be all coy or anything, but *nothing lasts*. That is to say, the state we call "nothing" may be the only thing that really lasts. The universe is utterly beyond living-and-dying, coming-and-going, because it is nothing. It's not nothing in the sense of being absent of things. There are plenty of things in the universe. It's nothing in the sense that it is utterly beyond any description we could possibly come up with to explain it.

When Zennies talk about emptiness, this is what they mean. Or at least it's part of what they mean. They mean that real things are always much more than — or "beyond," in Dogen's words — our names and our concepts of them. They are so far beyond any way we can describe them or think of them that we could say the entire universe is vast emptiness. As Kodo Sawaki put it, emptiness is "neither empty nor non-empty."

Then Dogen says, "Because it is like this, the past has gone from this place, and the present comes from this place." "The past has gone from this place" makes sense. We know that the past is gone. But another way of translating that line is, "The past departs from this place." It is here, in the present moment, that we create the past. We think we had breakfast an hour ago. We may even be able to prove it. But at the same time, the breakfast we had an hour ago is nowhere to be seen. Well, I guess if we barfed it up, we could see what we ate. But that's not what I mean. I mean that the activity of past breakfast eating cannot be found, only its aftereffects. The past is a total mystery.

The present comes from this place. The only real time is now. But by the time we recognize now, the "now" we recognized is already the past. The present moment is a total mystery.

Then Dogen asks us, "When we are pursuing the ultimate, who can see it utterly as separate moments? And who can hold it up for examination as a state of total stillness?" The first question refers to a core idea in Buddhism that each moment is a separate universe unto itself. The word *moment* here refers to the Buddhist concept of a *kshana*, which is the smallest period of time possible. According to Dogen in an essay called "Shukke Kudoku" ("The Merit of Leaving Family Life"), there are 6,400,099,180 *kshanas* in each day. How he determined such a thing is a matter way beyond my pay grade, so I don't worry too much about that part.

The next thing Dogen says in his essay "about one bright pearl" is really interesting: "The [phrase] 'the whole of the ten directions' describes the ceaseless process of pursuing things to make them into self, and pursuing self to make it into something."

As I said, "the whole of the ten directions" is another way of saying "the entire universe." So Dogen is saying here that the entire universe is the process of pursuing things to make them into self and pursuing self to make it into something. That is a pretty bold claim!

Dogen explains this saying, "Because of the pursuing of things and making them the self, the universe in its entirety is unceasing. And because its own nature is prior to such activity, it is beyond grasp even through the essence of the activity."

We pursue external things, trying to make them into self. We try to gain possessions and positions and praise and fame, all to add to our small sense of self and thereby make it bigger. Or we try to gain experiences. In reality, though, we are already infinite exactly as we are. We can't add anything to our own infinity.

We also try to make self into something. We try to make the

ever-changing impermanent self into something solid and permanent. Again, this is impossible.

But we don't have to worry if we can't see that we and the universe are really one bright pearl. Dogen says, "There is no reason to worry that you are not one bright pearl because in confusion you think, 'I am not the pearl.' Worrying and doubting, grasping and rejection, action and inaction are all but temporary views of small measure. Moreover, this is only one bright pearl appearing as small-scale notions."

Dogen also says, "Both you and I, not knowing what one bright pearl is and what it is not, have had a great many thoughts and non-thoughts about it which have come to form definite ideas. Yet when, thanks to Gensha's words, it is made known and clarified that even our bodies and minds are one bright pearl, then the mind is not I.... Even if there is worry and confusion, it is not apart from one bright pearl. It is not a deed or thought produced by something that is not one bright pearl. Therefore, both coming and going in the demon's cave in the dark mountain are themselves nothing but one bright pearl."

It's an optimistic way to end the essay. Maybe that's why I like it so much. And once again, Dogen says that even our confusion about the ultimate nature of reality is part of the ultimate nature of reality.

## 38. DOGEN'S LETTER TO HIMSELF
### Buddhas Alone Together with Buddhas, Part 1

IN THE YEAR 1288, thirty-five years after Dogen died, someone sat under the southern eaves of the guest quarters at Eihei-ji, the monastery that Dogen established in a remote mountainous region of Japan, and copied an essay Dogen had written many years earlier called "Yui Butsu Yo Butsu." My teacher translated that title as "Buddhas Alone Together with Buddhas." We no longer have Dogen's original. But that copy still exists.

Whoever copied the essay did not sign his or her name. But it was probably one of the senior monks who had practiced with Dogen and with his successor, Ejo. Ejo himself passed away eight years before the essay was copied. Maybe it was Ejo's successor, Tetsu Gikai, who copied it. We don't really know.

We also don't know when Dogen wrote the essay. We don't know if he considered it complete. We don't know if it was composed as a sermon to be delivered aloud or if it was composed to be read silently by individuals.

When reading the essay, I sometimes get the sense that Dogen was writing to himself. He seems to be trying to put words to a feeling he has, or perhaps an understanding he has come to, that he wants to convey as clearly as possible. Yet he knows that what he wants to say will be difficult for others to understand and accept. So he's trying to get it down in a way that he himself can understand when he reads it back before he goes on to present it to anybody else.

The essay "Buddhas Alone Together with Buddhas" is one of

his most profound pieces of writing. It strikes at the very heart of his understanding of what it is to be a human being. Yet it isn't one of his "greatest hits." In fact, I don't know of any commentary on it in English, so I guess that's up to me.

Although this essay doesn't directly and specifically address matters of Buddhist ethics, it does address the Buddhist understanding of who and what we really are. And as I've been saying, that understanding underpins all the Buddhist ethical teachings.

The title of the essay presents some problems for English translators. *Yui* means "only" or "solely." *Yo* means "and." Nobody really disagrees there. It's the other word Dogen uses twice in the title that hangs people up. It's the word *Butsu*, and it means "Buddha" or "Buddhas." Because there are no true plurals in Japanese, it could be interpreted either way.

As I said, my teacher Gudo Nishijima and his student Chodo Cross give the title of this essay as "Buddhas Alone Together with Buddhas." That's the title I like best. Kazuaki Tanahashi and Ed Brown gave it the title "Only Buddha and Buddha." You'll see that Nishijima and Cross take the word *Butsu* as plural, while Tanahashi and Brown read it as singular. Hubert Nearman splits the difference and calls his translation "On 'Each Buddha on His Own Together with All Buddhas.'" The reason Nearman quotes the "Each Buddha... etc." part is that the title Dogen gave to his essay is a quotation from the Lotus Sutra.

Part of what separates Mahayana Buddhism from the earlier types of Buddhism is that the Mahayana Buddhists believed in multiple Buddhas in addition to the historical Buddha. In fact, the Lotus Sutra was one of the earliest pieces of writing to put forth this idea of multiple Buddhas. This is why I think Nishijima and Cross were correct in reading the word *Butsu* as plural rather than singular. This reading of the word as plural also affects how certain other lines of the essay are interpreted, so it's not a trivial distinction.

The thing is, though, that making a distinction between the

singular and the plural is kind of what this essay is all about. Dogen is talking about how the entire universe is both a bunch of individual things and one single unified whole. Yet most of us fail to perceive it as a single unified whole. And the reason we fail to perceive it that way is that we insist on making a distinction between singular and plural. We don't see how things can be both ways at once. We don't understand that Buddha is really Buddhas. We don't understand that we are all plural as well as singular. We don't understand that each one of us, as discrete individuals, is also the entire universe.

Back when I was living in Japan and studying with him, Nishijima Roshi used to encourage me to "write about Buddhist philosophy." It was very difficult to pin him down as to exactly what he meant by Buddhist philosophy. It wasn't that he wanted me to write some kind of textbook of Buddhist philosophical ideas. Rather, he wanted me to put the Buddhist philosophy I had experienced into words. This was important, he said, because "people like to have explanations."

I think this essay by Dogen is his response to people's desire to have explanations.

Experiences of awakening or enlightenment or satori or whatever are not common. But they are more common than most people realize. A lot of us have little moments where we become momentarily aware that things are very different from the way we had imagined them to be and the way we were taught they are.

But our society teaches us that such moments are unreal, false, mere hallucinations. The real way to understand the world we live in, they say, is the one that they broadcast twenty-four hours a day, seven days a week, through all forms of mass media and social media. It's the one that will get you to buy more Pepsi-Cola and Nike shoes, it's the one that will get you to hate the people with what the folks who run those broadcasts think are the "wrong opinions," it's the one that will get you to worry about whether your hair is right or if you'll ever find true love.

But that's a load of crap. Reality is so much different from that image that you can hardly even compare the two. You are not that small! But if you knew you were not that small, you probably wouldn't want to buy all the garbage they try to sell you.

Dogen even addresses this in his essay. I mean, he doesn't refer to Pepsi-Cola and Nike. But he does talk about our fear of being small. I'll get to that in a bit.

Just so we're all on the same page, the full quotation from the Lotus Sutra is, "Buddhas alone, together with buddhas, are directly able to perfectly realize that all dharmas are real form. What is called 'all dharmas' is form as it is, nature as it is, body as it is, energy as it is, action as it is, causes as they are, conditions as they are, effects as they are, results as they are, and the ultimate state of equality of substance and detail, as it is."* This was Nishijima Roshi's preferred translation. A number of other translations of the Lotus Sutra have appeared since then. But I think this one will do for our purposes.

Let's dig into what Dogen says about it.

Right from the outset, what he says is contentious: "The Buddha-Dharma cannot be known by people." Because of that thing with plurals in Japanese, Tanahashi and Brown have Dogen say, "Buddha-Dharma cannot be known by a person."

This goes against the Buddhist ideal that the Buddha-Dharma *can* be known by people. I mean, what would be the point of teaching Buddhism to people if people couldn't understand it? Why would the Buddha have even bothered? I don't think Dogen is making some kind of ultimate statement. I think he's trying to categorize those who understand the Buddha-Dharma in a special class of people who aren't people anymore because they are buddhas.

To that end, he says, "Because it is realized only by buddhas, we say that 'buddhas alone, together with buddhas, are directly able

---

*    *The Threefold Lotus Sutra*, trans. Bunno Kato, Yoshiro Tamura, and
Kojiro Miyasaka (Tokyo: Kosei, 1975), LS 1.68.

perfectly to realize it.'" That's the quotation from the Lotus Sutra that he wants to talk about in this essay.

Then comes a line that I like better in the Tanahashi/Brown translation than in the Nishijima/Cross version. Their version goes, "When you realize the Buddha-Dharma, you do not think, 'This is realization just as I expected.'" Nishijima and Cross have Dogen say, "When we perfectly realize it, while still as we are, we would never have thought previously that realization would be like this." The meaning comes across much more clearly in Tanahashi and Brown's translation.

The point is that realization is nothing like what anyone would imagine it to be like. Dogen spends some time digging into this idea. He says that it's not useful to imagine what realization will be like. But of course, anyone who gets into a practice that involves the promise of realization is not going to be able to help but imagine what it might be like.

Dogen does give us an out, though. He says it doesn't mean that it's bad to think about what realization might be like and that our thinking had no power in it. On the contrary, he says that even our past mistaken thoughts about realization were realization itself. It's just that we were looking the wrong way.

Then Dogen says, "Whenever we feel that we are useless, there is something that we should know; namely, that we have been afraid of becoming small." I absolutely love that line. We are the biggest thing in the universe. Bigger even, since we are the universe itself, and much more than that. Yet we feel useless sometimes because we fear becoming small.

Just after this Dogen delivers another of my favorite lines. After telling us that realization is nothing like we could imagine it to be, he says, "Delusion, remember, is something that does not exist. Realization, remember, is something that does not exist."

In other words, that thing we define as "realization" doesn't exist. And even our delusions are not really delusions. We are deluded even about delusion.

Then Dogen talks about a state he calls "untainted" or "unstained," depending on whose translation you're reading. This is an idea that comes up in Buddhism a lot. We are aiming at an ability to see things as they are without our perceptions being tainted or stained by personal ideas or wrong views. It's not easy!

To lead into this he says that when the supreme state of enlightenment is a person, we call it "buddha." When buddha is in the supreme state of bodhi, Dogen tells us, we call it "the supreme state of bodhi," aka "enlightenment."

When the supreme state of enlightenment is a person... let's ponder that one for a bit.

Dogen calls our commonsense ideas about personhood into question. We generally assume that a person is a human being, and that that human being has certain attributes. A Buddha, then, would be a person who has the attribute of being enlightened.

But Dogen is talking about "when the supreme state of enlightenment is a person." That's a whole different way of looking at things. Then he adds that when a Buddha is in the supreme state of bodhi, we call it the supreme state of bodhi. So we can look at it either way. We can look at the supreme state of bodhi as a state that a Buddha is in, or we can look at the person who is a Buddha as a manifestation of this supreme state of bodhi. Both ways are equally valid.

Dogen says, "If we failed to recognize the feature of the moment of being in this truth, that might be stupid. That feature, namely, is untaintedness." So we're dummies if we can't see this. But then again, I'm kind of a dummy. So I want to see what Dogen has to say about it.

Dogen says that being untainted is not about forcing yourself to be aimless and free of attachment. Nor does it mean having no aim at all. This is one of the many, many times Dogen addresses his own initial big question, the one that got him to study Buddhism in the first place. As a child he had heard that all people have Original Enlightenment, that we're enlightened already just as we are. So little Dogen asked his elder teachers why they did all kinds of meditation and study and other practices. No one could give him a satisfactory answer until he met his teacher Tendo Nyojo (aka Tientong Ryujing), who told him to just drop off body and mind.

Which doesn't sound like an answer to the question at all, I know. But to Dogen it was.

Be that as it may, Dogen's answer here seems a little more directly connected to the question he asked as a child. He says, "Actually, without being aimed at, or attached to, or detached from, untaintedness exists." The state of untaintedness is always there, whether or not we aim for it, whether we attach to it, and whether we completely fail to even so much as wonder if it exists.

This is a really important point. People strive to make themselves into something other than what they are without understanding that the purity they seek is already present. And yet that striving is not without value. In fact, it's absolutely necessary.

Dogen has a lot to say elsewhere on this matter. For example, in another of his essays he tells an old story in which a Zen master sees his student meditating and asks him what he's doing. The student says, "I'm trying to make myself a Buddha."

The Zen master picks up a tile off the floor and begins rubbing it with his sleeve. The student asks him what he's doing. The Zen master says, "I'm trying to make this tile into a mirror."

The standard interpretation of this story was that it was as futile to try to make yourself into a Buddha by meditating as it was to try to make a tile into a mirror by polishing it.

Dogen, being contrarian like he always was, says that you *do* make a tile into a mirror by polishing it. In other words, as Shunryu Suzuki Roshi said, "You're perfect just as you are, but you could use a little improvement."

Getting back to the essay we've been looking at, Dogen then

says that when we meet people we try to fix their features in our minds, and that when we see anything we tend to mentally embellish it a bit. Even our understanding of seasons like spring and autumn, he says, isn't the reality of those seasons. It's a mental picture built up of our past experiences during those times of the year. But, he says, "even if we try to be other than ourselves, we are ourselves."

He then says that that which is accumulated has no self and that no mental activity has a self. And he reminds us that we are not the five aggregates. Another way of saying *aggregates* is *accumulations*, which is how it relates to the previous sentence. We looked at the five aggregates, or skandhas, earlier. They are form, feeling, perception, impulses, and consciousness. The Buddha said that our true form is not an indivisible individual soul but the coming together of these five things. But then Dogen says that even the five aggregates are not what we really are.

Right after saying that, Dogen delivers another one of my favorite lines in the essay. He says, "Thus, the colors of the mind excited by a flower or the moon should not be seen as self at all, but we think of them as our self." I wrote a whole chapter about that line in my book *Sit Down and Shut Up*. And then he says, "If we consider what is not our self to be our self, even that can be left as it is, but when we illuminate [the state in which] there is no possibility of either repellent colors or attractive ones being tainted, then action that naturally exists in the truth is the unconcealed original features."

Let me see if I can put that in different words. We see, hear, and experience lots of things —Dogen's examples are flowers and the moon. Those are nice examples. I'm sure you can think of plenty of not-so-nice examples of things you've seen, heard, or otherwise experienced. Whatever we encounter "excites the colors of our mind," as Dogen puts it. We have a specific reaction to them that is uniquely colored by our sense of who we are as individuals. People often react in vastly different ways to the same experiences, even when they're standing right next to each other. It all depends on your previous experiences.

But however we react to what we experience, we tend to take that reaction to be our *self* reacting to whatever it is. That's how we describe it. "I saw that play and I was moved to tears." "I was disgusted by that sandwich." Whatever my reaction is, it's an example of me. I can define myself by the way I react to things. For example, *End of the Century* is my all-time favorite Ramones album, even though lots of Ramones fans hate it. So I can define myself, in part, as one of the rare Ramones fans who loves that record. And that would not be a lie.

There are reasons I like that album that are unique to my life trajectory. For one thing, it was the first Ramones album I ever bought. I'd read a few articles about them, but I didn't know what they sounded like until the first time I put that record on my dad's turntable. They did not play the Ramones on the radio in Ohio in those days. I was also sixteen years old when I got the record, and some things mean more to you when you're sixteen than they do when you're older.

Many years later, that album is still my favorite, even though I totally understand why other Ramones fans don't feel that way about it — especially if their first Ramones album was one of the earlier ones.

It's weird how we get into all kinds of disputes with each other based on aspects of our personal preferences that are shaped by totally arbitrary stuff we had no choice at all about. Even our religious and political preferences are shaped by all kinds of arbitrary and meaningless happenings in our lives. Yet we get really worked up about that stuff. Sometimes we get dangerously worked up! If we examined ourselves and discovered how arbitrary our opinions and beliefs really were, we'd probably waste a lot less energy defending them.

That stuff is not our real self. Our real self is something quite entirely different. Even so, says Dogen, we can just let that be. Still, we can "illuminate the state of untaintedness." In Hubert Nearman's version, Dogen describes this as "illumin[ating] the condition where there is no color that repels us nor any that attracts us." Or as one old Buddhist poem says, "when no like or dislike appears." I take that to mean that we can focus our attention, not on the false sense of personal self with its opinions and views, its likes and dislikes, but on the untainted state in which our personal opinions are of no importance. When we do that we can discover the very basis of our being.

In that way "our unconcealed original features are revealed." Our unconcealed original features are who and what we truly are before we make a lot of false assumptions about who and what we are. We'll get into this idea more as we go along.

## 39. YOUR TRUE BODY IS THE UNIVERSE
### Buddhas Alone Together with Buddhas, Part 2

FURTHER ON IN the essay "Buddhas Alone Together with Buddhas," Dogen says that "in death there are instances of living; in living there are instances of being dead; there are the dead who will always be dead; and there are the living who are constantly alive."

I think we all know people like that. Sometimes people, in the face of almost certain death, rise to the occasion and become alive for the first time. There are others who, although technically alive, live as though they might as well be dead. Those who have passed on before us will always be dead, and regardless of any belief we might have about an afterlife, it's clear that we're not going to encounter them again, at least not in the way we encountered them when they were alive. But the best type to be is a person who is living and is constantly alive.

We don't even have to force ourselves to be this way. This is just the way we are no matter what we do, whether or not we know it. The Buddha is a great example of a person who was constantly alive. In a very real sense, he lives even now. I don't mean that he's up there in Buddha heaven looking down upon us unfortunate mortals — although I wouldn't categorically rule out that possibility. What I mean is that he poured everything he had into establishing a way for others to discover the truth he had found for himself. And that way exists even today.

Woody Allen once said something like, "I don't want to achieve immortality through my work. I want to achieve immortality by not dying." Whatever you might feel about Woody Allen, I think this joke is worth looking into. A lot of us want to live forever in the literal sense.

I think about this sometimes myself. I've written books that have remained in print. I can be reasonably confident that people will still be reading them after I pass away. Hell, for all I know you — yeah, I mean *you* sitting there on your couch in your underwear — you might be reading this book after I'm long gone. *Hi there!* It's weird having a dead guy talk to you, right?

Anyway, in the past I would have thought, like Woody Allen, that if that happened, the real me would be dead and the book you're reading would not, in any meaningful way, be a manifestation of my being alive.

Now I'm not so sure. I don't think I begin and end at the borders of my skin. I don't believe that I am my body, and I don't believe that I am my mind. I seem to be something much bigger than that. By reading the words I wrote when I was alive after I'm dead — if that's what you're doing — you are bringing to life something that is more truly me than my body or even my mind ever was or could have been.

Weird, huh?

Don't think about it too much.

The idea that we are much more than we think we are is expressed by Dogen, who quotes an old Zen master named Chosa Keishin, who said, "The whole great Earth is our Dharma body." The phrase "whole great Earth" (*dai-chi*) means the entire universe, not just this one little planet.

But, Dogen warns us, the dharma body should not be hindered by the dharma body. That's his cute way of saying that we shouldn't confuse our ideas about what the dharma body might be with the actual dharma body.

So what's a dharma body? I'm glad you asked!

Traditionally, the dharma body — or *dharmakaya* in Sanskrit — is one of the three bodies of a Buddha. The other two are the physical body — or *nirmanakaya* in Sanskrit — which is Gautama Buddha's regular old body. The other one is called the reward or enjoyment body — or *sambhogakaya* in Sanskrit.

You don't have to buy into all this mumbo-jumbo. I'm not sure how much I buy into it. But I want to go into it so that you can follow the rest of what Dogen says. The physical body is the easy one. So we'll leave that one be. For me, the concept of the reward/enjoyment body is the hardest to get my head around. Even the concept of the dharma body is easier for me to understand than the idea of the reward/enjoyment body.

Apparently the idea of the reward/enjoyment body of the Buddha is that, once a person fulfills her/his Buddhist vows to save all beings and the rest of that, they get a reward body. One example of a Buddha who got his reward body is Amida Buddha, the Buddha worshipped by members of the Pure Land sect. They believe that Amida Buddha lives in the western heavens and helps those who placed their faith in him attain Buddhahood there after they lead a good life on Earth.

I think a lot of Pure Land Buddhists would argue with that little capsule explanation and say it's a bit more complicated than that. Which it is. But I'd rather let a Pure Land Buddhist explain the nuances of Pure Land Buddhism to you and just move along to what a dharma body is.

The dharma body is a Buddha's "truth body." It's what gives rise to the other two bodies. It's the eternal truth of the universe manifested in physical form. The concept originates in the Lotus Sutra, as does the quotation "Buddhas alone together with Buddhas." It is the supreme state of absolute knowledge and enlightenment.

Old Chosa Keishin talks about how the whole great earth is *our* dharma body. So he doesn't reserve the idea of the dharma body just for special people like Gautama Buddha. You and I have a dharma body too. And it's the entire universe!

Dogen then quotes another old Zen master who said, "The

whole earth is the real human body; the whole earth is a gate of liberation; the whole earth is one eye of Vairochana Buddha; the whole earth is our Dharma body."

Vairochana Buddha is the primordial Buddha, the Buddha of Emptiness. He supposedly came along way before Shakyamuni Buddha. He's not a historical figure. He's more of a concept. Although some Mahayana Buddhists would surely argue that Vairochana Buddha is more real than Shakyamuni.

Anyway, Dogen comments on this statement by the old Zen master by saying that the "real body" he's talking about is our actual body. And by "actual body" he means "the whole earth." And by "whole earth" he means everything there ever is, was, and will be. He says this isn't just imaginary. Then he says that if someone should ask why they never noticed that the whole earth was our real human body before, he'd just say, "Give me back my words that the whole earth is the real human body." Or, he says, we could answer that the person who's asking this already knows it to be true because it's so obvious.

Dogen is being kind of a tough cookie here, and a bit cranky. He won't accept our protestations that we don't know what he's talking about. He gets like that fairly often.

Dogen did the hard work that was necessary to discover that things were not at all the way he had imagined they were. He saw that most of humanity had the wrong idea about what this world was and who they were as part of it. And once he saw that, he also discovered it was incredibly obvious. It was so obvious, in fact, that he could not possibly have missed it, and neither can we.

Once you've caught on to how things really are, you're never going to be able to go back to your previous worldview. It's just too absurd! The ideas you previously had about yourself and the universe — ideas that you once thought were common sense — now just seem ridiculous. You'll still be able to engage in life as if it works the way most people think it does. After all, most of the people you interact with don't know any better, so you'll basically have to do that, whether or not you want to. But you'll know better. Sometimes it gets tiring to pretend things really are the absurd way most people imagine them to be. I guess that's how Dogen felt when he wrote that line.

Anyway, after the part where Dogen gets cranky at his imaginary questioner, he starts talking about that matter of the earth being a gateway to liberation. He says there is not the slightest gap between the earth as a gateway to liberation and the present moment. Nearman, in his translation of this essay, adds a footnote here that says, "What physically exists is inseparable from time and mind." I like that.

Dogen says that this gateway to liberation is limitless and unbounded. Yet, he says, if we seek to enter or pass through that gateway to liberation it would be utterly impossible.

"Why is that so?" he asks. Then he answers his own question, saying that it's impossible to enter a place that doesn't exist.

Now, that is some pure Dogen right there. He pulls this kind of crap all the time. He tells you something in the strongest and most certain terms and then, a sentence later, he takes it all back. He's not saying it's aliens, but . . .

Then he just moves right along to the next topic!

But I can't just leave it at that. I've worked with Dogen for long enough that I'm pretty sure I get what he means here. Even so, I can see how someone newly coming to his work would just throw up her hands and go watch *Ancient Aliens* instead.

But Dogen is serious here. And he's saying exactly what he means to say. He wants us to know that it is true that the whole earth is a gateway to liberation. Yet at the same time, he wants us to recognize that any ideas we might have about liberation or gateways to it are mistaken. This is a little bit of a callback to the very beginning of the essay, in which he told us, "When you realize the Buddha-Dharma, you do not think, 'This is realization just as I expected.'"

It's the same deal here. If you think you know what it means to say that the entire earth is a gateway to liberation, and that you are therefore ready to pass through that gateway, you're probably just imagining a place that doesn't exist.

Then Dogen takes up the line from the poem about the whole earth being the solitary eye of Vairochana Buddha. As I mentioned earlier, Vairochana is a legendary Buddha who is the embodiment of the concept of the dharma body. When Dogen says that something is an "eye," he means that it is a point by which someone or something perceives or experiences things. To say that the whole earth is an eye of Vairochana Buddha is like saying that the whole earth is a means by which the universe experiences itself.

But why is it just a solitary eye? Most statues I've seen of Vairochana give him two. Dogen goes on about this point for quite a while. It's worth reading the whole thing. But I'll try to summarize it.

He says that in the state of Buddhahood there is just one eye. By this he means that a Buddha is not confused about reality. He sees clearly the one single truth of all things.

That being said, Dogen tells us that eyes may be of many kinds. The human eye is just one of them. Again, an eye in this sense is a point of view, a way of perceiving and understanding things. The human way — the human eye — is one among many. That's not something most people would argue with. My dog Ziggy Pup certainly doesn't perceive the world exactly the way that I do. Nor, for that matter, do a lot of people I know.

Dogen also mentions the eighty-four thousand eyes of compassion of the Kannon, Bodhisattva of Compassion. Kannon is said to be aware of all suffering everywhere, which is why she has so many eyes, and so many ears as well.

In any case, this is still just a way of indicating that the universe is full of eyes with which to perceive itself. Yet a Buddha has just one eye, meaning again that a Buddha sees the single unified truth of the whole. Dogen says that it's not mistaken to think that this one eye of

Vairochana is just one of many eyes of the Buddha and that it's not mistaken to think that the Buddha has only one eye. He says, "Don't be surprised to hear that there are eyes such as these."

One thing I love about Dogen is that his nondualism goes so far that it even negates the dualism of dualism as opposed to nondualism. Even a dualistic point of view is one aspect of the nondualistic universe. So in some sense it's perfectly valid to view things dualistically. He's not saying it's aliens, but …

Dogen next draws our attention again to the line in the poem that says the whole great earth — the universe — is our dharma body.

About this Dogen says, "To seek to know ourself is the inevitable will of the living. But those with Eyes that see themselves are few: buddhas alone know this state. Others, non-Buddhists and the like, vainly consider only what does not exist to be their self. What buddhas call themselves is just the whole earth."

It sounds like a bold claim to say that seeking to know ourselves is the "inevitable will of the living." There certainly seem to be lots of people who have no interest at all in knowing themselves. But that's only true in a very superficial sense.

Seeking to know oneself doesn't just take the form of doing meditation and reading spiritual books. The very fact of being alive is a function of seeking to know oneself. All the activities we do are dedicated to that function.

Our fixation on sex, for example, is a misguided manifestation of trying to know ourselves through exploring other people. We watch dumb reality TV shows in order to know ourselves through learning about the lives of the dumb people on reality TV shows. We are all constantly engaged in this project of trying to understand ourselves on a very deep level, whether or not we know it. It is why we are alive in the first place — because we wanted to know what being alive is. Those who work on knowing themselves directly through meditation and introspection learn a lot more and learn it more quickly and thus are in a position to help others, even if those others often don't really get what it is we're doing.

Dogen then adds, "In sum, in all instances, whether we know or do not know ourselves, there is no whole earth that is other than our self. The matters of such times we should defer to people of yonder times."

This is another classic Dogen-ism. It doesn't matter if we are aware that the whole universe is our true self or not. It is our true self either way.

I love his confidence here. It's like he's saying, "This is the way things are, like it or not. Deal with it."

If we want to know more about who and what we truly are, we can defer to masters of the past — Dogen's "people of yonder times" — who have also talked about the same aspect of reality that Dogen wrote of in his essay.

## 40. I AM MY OWN BAD HAIR DAY
### Buddhas Alone Together with Buddhas, Part 3

IN THE NEXT part of "Buddhas Alone Together with Buddhas," Dogen introduces an exchange between a Zen student and his teacher. The student asks, "When a hundred thousand myriad circumstances converge all at once, what should I do?" In other words, "What do I do when I'm having a bad hair day?"

The teacher responds saying, "Don't try to control them."

Dogen says that this means, "Let what is coming come! In any event, do not stir!" Whatever comes, Dogen says, is the Buddha dharma. This isn't about conditions, he says.

He tells us that these words shouldn't be understood as a rebuke or an admonition. It's not a criticism of the student's desire to do something about the stuff that's coming at him. Dogen understands why the question is being asked. He's probably asked it himself. I think we've all asked it.

This is a difficult lesson he's trying to teach us. I wonder if it might be even harder for us than it was for people of Dogen's time. These days, we're much more steeped in the illusion that we're in control of what happens to us than the people of Dogen's time probably were. Let me give you an easy example. The other day I was out on the patio with my wife and her parents. After the sun went down, some mosquitoes appeared and started biting us. So I went inside, found a citronella candle and some bug spray, brought them out to the patio, lit up the candle and sprayed the spray, and *voilà!* The mosquitoes went away.

That may not sound like much to you. But in Dogen's time that sort of bug-repelling technology did not exist. Maybe they could have smeared themselves with cinnamon-leaf oil or something — if they could find any. But it certainly wasn't as easy as getting a can of spray at the drugstore. Plus, they didn't have things like air-conditioning, or central heating, or running water, or flush toilets, or refrigerators, or electric ovens, or cars, or cell phones, or most of the medicines we take for granted ... the list could go on and on.

Our unprecedented access to such amazing luxuries gives us a sense of control over our environment. Most of the things that we're uncomfortable with in our physical surroundings we can deal with pretty quickly and without much effort. Of course, there still are things we can't deal with so easily, like environmental disasters, or diseases we haven't yet conquered, or the simple fact of how some people can be such jerks sometimes. We can still end up in situations in which we feel a loss of control.

For people of today, the advice not to even try to control things, to let what is coming come, and to "not stir" can sound terribly wrong. Self-styled wise people of today are far more inclined to give precisely the opposite advice. They'll tell you to take charge of your life! Don't just let what's coming come! Do something about it! Take control!

These days even meditation is promoted as a way to take charge of uncomfortable situations and control them. Manage your stress with mindfulness! Make circumstances obey!

But there is a middle way with this. There always is.

Dogen's advice is not for people who are in abusive relationships, for example. I'm sure he wouldn't tell a battered wife to let what is coming come, and do not stir. Nor is he advising people to stoically endure social ills rather than working to improve society. He's not advocating complacency. Rather, he is trying to provide us with an attitude toward that which we cannot control. And this attitude can make a tremendous difference when it comes to dealing with things we can do nothing about, which is pretty much everything.

He wants us to understand that we and the circumstances in which we find ourselves are not two different things that oppose each other. He wants us to see that we ourselves and the world we live in — the circumstances of our lives — are exactly the same thing.

Here's what he says. He begins by quoting an ancient Buddhist master who said, "Mountains, rivers, the earth, and human beings are born together. The buddhas of the three times [past, present, and future] and human beings have always practiced together."

Then he says, "Thus, if we look at the mountains, rivers, and earth while one human being is being born, we do not see this human being now appearing through isolated superimposition upon mountains, rivers, and earth that existed before [this human being] was born."

The world comes into being simultaneously with my coming into being. In *Opening the Hand of Thought*, Kosho Uchiyama says something similar to this but takes it even further. He says, "When I took my first breath, my world was born with me. When I die, my world dies with me. In other words, I wasn't born into a world that was already here before me. I do not live simply as one individual among millions of individuals, and I do not leave everything behind me to live on after me."

In *Each Moment Is the Universe*, Dainin Katagiri puts the same idea like this: "When beings appear, why do you happen to be the particular being that you are now? You don't know exactly why, but you are a being whose life is already supported by the vast network of time and space. When a particular being arises, it is not just one thing that arises — all beings arise simultaneously. One thing can't arise alone because all life is deeply interconnected and nothing has its own independent existence.... When you are born, the whole world is born with you. When you die, the whole world dies with you."

Both Uchiyama Roshi and Katagiri Roshi studied with one of

my teacher's teachers, Kodo Sawaki. In his book *Discovering the True Self* Sawaki Roshi said, "When we are born, our universe is born too. When we die, we take everything of our universe with us."

Now, that is a wild and crazy idea.

Let me see what I can do with it.

I was born on March 5, 1964. The Beatles' first American appearance was on the *Ed Sullivan Show* on February 9, 1964, just under a month before I was born. My parents were married on November 22, 1962. John F. Kennedy was assassinated on the day of their first wedding anniversary, which must have put a damper on whatever celebration they had planned.

All those events, and lots and lots of other things, happened before I was born. Hitler ruled Germany for twelve years and then killed himself. Penicillin was invented. Columbus "discovered" America — at least as far as Europeans were concerned. Dogen lived, wrote a bunch of stuff, and then died. Wooly mammoths went extinct. Fish evolved into amphibians. The solar system coalesced out of interstellar gas and dust. Plenty of things went on!

If I denied that all that stuff, and lots more, happened, I'd be nuttier than those people who try to prove that dinosaurs never existed and that their supposed fossils were planted in the ground by God to test people's faith in the Bible. Furthermore, as I said earlier, there's a decent chance that my writings will outlive me and that some of you might be reading this after I am dead. Heck, Sawaki, Katagiri, and Uchiyama were all dead before I read their prediction that when they died the world would die with them. And Dogen was dead way before they learned that idea from him.

Obviously, then, their statements that the world was born when they were born and would die with them was incorrect. What an insanely arrogant thing to claim! Why would anyone believe such obvious nonsense? And they have the nerve to imply that this bizarre statement applies to me too? What the what?

Dogen knew how absurd what he said sounded. Just after he

says the stuff about the world and the person being born simultaneously, he says, "Just because we have not understood [these words],
we should not disregard them; we should resolve to understand them
without fail. They are words that were actually preached, and so we
should listen to them. Having listened to them, then we may be able
to understand them." Dogen wasn't the first person who said that the
world and the individual are born and die simultaneously. He heard
it from someone else and then confirmed it for himself.

It's back to the matter of trust that I talked about before. Both
my teachers said things that initially made no sense to me. But I knew
they were people I could trust. I knew they weren't telling me these
weird things because they wanted my money or wanted me to join
their cult. They didn't say these things because they were insecure
in their beliefs and were trying to make themselves believe them by
convincing others they were true.

Furthermore, I could tell that my Zen teachers were not crazy.
They seemed to understand things in a radically different way from
the way most people understood them. What's more, they were not
alone in this understanding. The way they understood things was
common among Zen Buddhists, not just now but stretching back
thousands of years.

Plus, there are others outside the Zen tradition who say things
that sound very much like what the Zennies say. In *I Am That*,
Nisargadatta Maharaj says, "All the universe is born with the body
and dies with the body; it has its beginning and end in awareness,
but awareness knows no beginning or end." I've been referring to
the Advaita Vedanta spiritual tradition a lot because that's the one
tradition apart from Zen that I know the most about. But there are
people in other traditions who say similar things.

Therefore, when I hear someone from the Zen tradition say something bizarre like "the world is born and dies with me," I assume
there is a reason they'd say such a nutty thing. I know that they know
how weird it sounds. I don't believe they're just saying stuff like this

for no good reason. Maybe, as Dogen suggests, I ought to listen and try to understand.

So what do I do with this particularly odd assertion?

Well, first I take note that none of the people I'm quoting above make any effort to prove what they're saying is true. Let's see what they say instead.

A few pages after he says the thing about the world being born and dying with you, Katagiri Roshi talks about how the practice of zazen makes these kinds of odd statements found in Buddhist philosophy clear. Then he says, "Now is important because the moment that is right here, right now, is eternal, abiding forever. What does eternal mean? It means that, moment after moment, *right now* appears as all beings; then again: right now; and again: right now. Right now appears forever, that's why now is eternal... this present is not just the present; it's connected with the whole universe. If you see this universe, you realize that you are a part of a dynamic reality that is constantly changing according to the conditions of every moment. Then you understand why human life is important. It is important because, if you take care of right now with wholeheartedness, you create good conditions for the next right now." This is the essence of Buddhist ethics.

As for Uchiyama Roshi, a little bit after he says his thing about the world being born and dying with him, he says, "I can't stress enough how essential it is to look very, very carefully at this universal self that runs through everything in the universe. You live together with your world. Only when you thoroughly understand this will everything in the world settle as the self pervading all things. As Buddhists... we vow to save all sentient beings so that this self can become even more itself." Again, we have another statement emphasizing the ethical side of Buddhist practice — saving all beings. But we are offered nothing in the way of proof that when we are born and when we die the universe is born and dies with us.

Kodo Sawaki also said, "What I call 'me' cannot sustain itself by itself. When we give up this 'me,' it becomes the Self that is the universe." And he said, "Your personal action is the action of the whole universe. You alone act as the universe. That is the meaning of deep Zen practice."

The next thing Dogen says after making his claim about the universe being born and dying with us is, "We do not know the end or the beginning, but we have been born. Neither, indeed, do we know the limits of mountains, rivers, and the earth, but we see them here; and at this place, it is as if they are walking. Do not complain that mountains, rivers, and the earth are not comparable with birth. Illuminate mountains, rivers, and the earth as they have been described, as utterly the same as our being born."

That thing about mountains walking is one of Dogen's pet phrases that he uses a lot. In his translation of *Shobogenzo*, Hubert Nearman interprets it as a reference to humans treading upon the great earth. I think that's one way of looking at it. But I think that Dogen would argue that when humans tread upon the great earth, the great earth also treads upon humans.

Dogen's main point is that mountains, rivers, and the earth are utterly the same as our being alive. We are not living things that inhabit a dead and inert universe. The universe we live in is as much alive as we are. It is as much me as I am. The life we experience here and now is utterly the same life as the life of the universe. The circumstances that come at us all at once are manifestations of ourselves. We are our own bad hair day!

When it comes to being born and dying, the Buddhists have a weird way of understanding what that means too. They have a concept called a kshana, which I've mentioned before. This is the very smallest unit of time possible. Scientists these days have also tried to calculate their own version of a kshana. Theirs is called a zeptosecond, which is a trillionth of a billionth of a second. They say that it takes 247 zeptoseconds for a light particle to cross a hydrogen molecule. But, as Steve Hagen pointed out in a quotation I used a few chapters ago, light isn't really particles and molecules aren't really solid things. So make of the concept of zeptoseconds what you will. In any case, you may recall that the Buddhist *kshana* is so short that there are 6,400,099,180 *kshanas* in a day.

As I said, I do not know how the ancient Buddhists arrived at that figure. My suspicion is that, in spite of the specificity of the number, it's more meant to convey that there are a whole heck of a lot of *kshanas* in a day rather than to insist that there are precisely that number.

Moment to moment — or *kshana* to *kshana* — the world I inhabit and I myself pop into existence and then pop right out of existence again. Dogen is saying that the circumstances that confront me in this world are none other than me. There is no separation. It's exactly like how the world I experience in a dream is nothing more than my awareness of that world. So I must act right now. My life is over before I even get a moment to think about what I've done.

The illusion of time and space makes it seem like we have lifetimes that last several decades and that we interact with things outside ourselves. But the Buddhists say that this is not what happens at all.

In an essay called "Establishing the Bodhi Mind," Dogen says that only a Buddha can perceive a length of time as brief as a *kshana*. The best we can do, he says, is to perceive a *tatkshana*, which is 120 *kshanas*.

His point in that essay, though, isn't to convince us of the length of the smallest perceivable period of time. He wants to let us know what to do with the time that we have, which is way more important.

He says, "If we establish this bodhi-mind for a single kshana, the myriad dharmas will all become promoting conditions." The "bodhi-mind" is the mind of a bodhisattva, one who vows to save all beings. So what he means is that when we make this vow, the circumstances we find ourselves in, instead of being difficulties we have to conquer, will help us do our duty of saving all beings.

Dogen says, "Regardless of our own intentions, and led by past behavior, the cycle of life and death continues without stopping for a single kshana. With the body-mind that is swept like this through life and death, we should establish at once the bodhi-mind which is the will to deliver others before we ourselves attain deliverance. Even if, on the way to establishing the bodhi-mind, we begrudge the body-mind," that is, if we decide not to bother with the whole saving-all-beings thing, "it is born, grows old, becomes sick, and dies; in the end, it is not our own possession."

But there's hope for us yet! Dogen says, "While experiencing the swiftness of this instantaneous arising, vanishing, and flowing, if we arouse one thought of delivering others before we attain deliverance ourselves, the eternal lifetime will manifest itself before us at once." Every master who came before us did this. They all faced the same kind of crap we do — probably much worse crap, in fact — but they rose to the occasion and did their real duty as human beings.

"After establishing the bodhi-mind," Dogen says, "we should steadfastly guard it, never regressing or going astray." We should protect our ethical vows and our commitment to saving others, he says, just like a person who had lost an eye would protect his remaining eye.

Dogen confesses, "I have long feared that I also might regress and lose it." I love that he admits that even he has a tough time with this stuff. He says that lots of people will try to talk you out of your ethical vows. But, he says, "Know [talk] that would turn you against the conduct and vow to deliver others before attaining deliverance yourself as the talk of demons, know it as ... the talk of bad companions. Never follow it at all."

What he's asking of us is hard work, and he is well aware of that. But it's vital work. And there are few who will accept the difficulties involved. If we don't do it, who will? It's really up to you and me.

# 41. OUR ACTIONS ARE THE UNIVERSE
## Buddhas Alone Together with Buddhas, Part 4

IN THE NEXT section of "Yui Butsu Yo Butsu," Dogen begins by reminding us that the buddhas of the three times have already accomplished the truth and perfected realization. Then he asks us, "How are we to understand that this state of buddha is the same as us?"

I find it interesting that he mentions buddhas of the three times, past, present, and future, as having *already* accomplished the truth. Surely the buddhas of the past and present have already done this. But the future buddhas too? As we already saw, Dogen has an interesting view of time. For him, time only *seems* to flow from past to present and into the future. The real nature of time is that now is all that exists, and that it is always now, and that now includes the past and the future.

But as for how to understand that the state of Buddha is the same as ourselves, Dogen begins by saying that we should understand the action of Buddha. Some translators prefer to use the phrase "practice of a Buddha." The word translated as "action" or "practice" means something like "to do." Translating it as "practice" can give the reader a sense that Dogen is referring specifically to religious practices like meditation or ritual. But the word Dogen uses actually has a much broader meaning than that. So *action* or *activity* is a better translation.

The actions of a Buddha, says Dogen, take place in unison with the whole earth and take place together with all beings. Any action that doesn't include everything is not the action of Buddha.

Furthermore, Dogen says, "from the establishment of the mind until the attainment of realization, both realization and practice are inevitably done together with the whole earth and together with all living beings."

The "establishment of the mind" just means the time that we decide to undertake a meditation practice and get serious about following the Buddhist ethical system. Dogen is playing with us here a little bit. He allows that, in conventional terms, establishing the mind comes before realization. But he emphasizes the oneness of practice and realization in the next sentence. Remember that, in Dogen's view, practice and realization are one and the same. We don't practice until we have an experience called realization. The practice itself is realization.

Let's ponder this stuff a bit before moving along. The actions of Buddha take place together with the whole universe and everyone in it. Then how can we say they are the actions of Buddha and not just whatever happens?

Dogen anticipates our difficulties and next says, "You may have doubts about this." You think so, Dogen? This is yet another reason I like this chapter so much. It's directly speaking to the reader in ways other chapters don't. As I said earlier, we really don't know why "Yui Butsu Yo Butsu" was written or for whom. Dogen's most famous piece of writing, "Genjo Koan," started out as a letter to a student. Maybe this chapter also started off as a letter. It has that kind of directness.

Dogen admits that it's hard not to have doubts when it seems like we're talking about something that is unknowable. It's hard to feel you have clarity when it comes to something you can't know! But, he says, the Buddhas of the past have told us that this is how things are. Which is true. This brings up what it means to have faith in Buddhist terms. I have faith that the Buddhist ancestors were trying their best to tell us the truths they learned through intensive practice. This idea that our own being includes the entire universe is a common theme in Buddhism and can be found in plenty of other spiritual traditions as well.

Dogen says that when the Buddhas of the past, present, and future give rise to their intention to practice and to attain realization, we are included in their activity and in their realization. And when we begin our practice, he says, we also do not leave anyone out of it.

To doubt this, Dogen says, is to disparage the Buddhas of the past, present, and future. That's a strong way of putting it. But Dogen tends to state things in pretty strong terms when he feels passionate about them.

Let me see if I can put it a slightly different way. I know I've said this a few times already, but I feel like it's worth repeating. In my own early experience practicing with two Buddhist teachers, it was always a matter of getting certain messages that made perfect sense and that I couldn't doubt, and getting certain other messages that seemed so absurdly grandiose I couldn't help but doubt them.

For example, I could immediately see the value in practicing zazen. I started when I was a teenager beset with worries and concerns, trying to hang on for dear life in a world that seemed to be spinning crazily around me. Zazen gave me a stable place I could return to again and again. Also, the ethical principles of Buddhism seemed clear and worthy of following — even when I couldn't always get them quite right. And as I keep saying, I could tell that my teachers were sincere people who would never deliberately hurt me or steer me wrong.

But then they sometimes threw in some really nutty-sounding ideas. Like the idea that I was the center, and indeed the creator, of the entire universe. Not like in the movie *Bruce Almighty*, in which an ordinary man gets all the powers of God. But in a very real sense nonetheless.

I accepted the things they told me and that I could confirm for myself. But what was I to do with these other, far more grandiose ideas — the ones I could not confirm?

Because I trusted my teachers, I decided to accept the stranger things they said even though I couldn't understand them. I can see what Dogen means here when he describes doubting ideas as a way of disparaging those who share them with us. To doubt my teachers would be sort of like calling them liars when I knew full well they were not.

Dogen gives us a bit of hope in the next few sentences, although it might take some explaining to get at what he means. So let's give it a try.

He says, "When we tranquilly reflect upon this, the principle that our body and mind are behaving exactly like that of the Buddhas of the three temporal worlds, as well as the principle that we are giving rise to the intention to realize Buddhahood, will both be apparent." In that sense, we're just like the Buddhas. We've set our sights on understanding and harmonizing ourselves with the universe. We may not know exactly what that means. But we're willing to give it a try.

I learned a chant at Tassajara with a line that goes, "The Buddhas and ancestors of old were as we; we in the future shall become Buddhas and ancestors." It's part of an essay Dogen wrote called "Voices of the River Valley and Forms of the Mountains" ("Keisei Sanshiki"). In some Zen temples they excerpt a section of this essay for the purpose of chanting it, then retitle this particular section "Eihei Dogen's Words for Arousing the Vow" ("Eihei Koso Hotsuganmon").

You might not think of yourself as someone on the way to becoming a Buddha. But the very fact that you're reading a book like this one is deeply significant. It means you're already going in that direction. I'm not trying to say this is the greatest book you could have chosen. But it's a book about something that most people are not ready to deal with. And you are.

You may not be that deeply committed just yet. You may end up veering off the path at some point. I know I sure did! But you have "entered the stream," as the early Buddhists used to say. From here there is no turning back. No matter what detours you take, you'll always end up right back on the path to Buddhahood. I'm afraid you're stuck with it. But don't despair! That's a good thing. No matter what happens from now on, you are on your way to becoming a Buddha.

Those Buddhas of the past were just like you and me when they started. It's sort of like a band that has to play all the crappy little backyard parties in Pasadena before they get their record deal and become Van Halen. All the great Buddhist masters of the past started off as regular people who were highly dissatisfied with the normal ways of living. They had doubts. They had regrets. They made mistakes. They stumbled and fell. And yet somehow they found their way. In every sense we are exactly like them.

Dogen describes this by saying that "when we reflect quietly, it appears that our body-and-mind has practiced together with all Buddhas of the three worlds [past, present, and future] and has, together with them, aroused the thought of enlightenment."

Then Dogen says, "If we reflect upon and illuminate the moment before and the moment behind this body and mind, the human being under investigation is not I and is not [another] person; in which case, as what stagnant object can we see it, and thereby consider it to be separated from the three times?"

That's a twisty little sentence!

One way of looking at the idea of reflecting on and illuminating "the moment before and the moment behind this body and mind" is to think of it as a fancy way of saying thinking of our own past and future, with the moment before — or in front of — us being the future and the moment behind being the past. Dogen liked to talk about time as a series of discrete moments. He may have envisioned the past and future as almost literally existing in front of and behind us. He believed that action in the present moment affected not only the future but also the past. He didn't think it was all set in stone.

Dogen says that the human being under investigation — that's you or me — is not I and is not another person. This is where it gets a little weird. Well, I guess I should say weirder since it was probably already seeming a little weird.

I know that I'm not another person. Most of us get that part.

But how am I not I? My whole life I have thought of my body and my mind as my self. Some religions are all about the idea that the body is not the self. The self, these religions say, is the mind within the body. Our true identity, they say, is a sort of spiritual spark that is eternally separate from the gross material body.

Buddhism rejects that idea. It says there is no pure spiritual soul dwelling inside this lumpy material body. But then it goes further. You're not your body. But you're not your mind either. That's an important point. The mind comes and goes. Its ever changing. The way you felt yesterday isn't the way you feel today. Tomorrow you might change your mind entirely about something that you're absolutely certain about right now. There is no fixed thing called "mind" that can be identified as "me."

And yet here I am. I'm something. But that something is not body and is not mind.

Another way of translating this same sentence of Dogen's is "we cannot find the boundary of self or others." That's Tanahashi's version. Although I like the Nishijima/Cross version that I quoted above better, I also think the Tanahashi/Brown version rings true. We might think there's a hard boundary between ourselves and everybody and everything else. But in the quiet of meditation, that boundary dissolves.

In any case, Dogen says, "All such thoughts do not belong to us." In fact, none of our thoughts belong to us. Thoughts are just thoughts. They arise, stick around for a while, and vanish. We can try to hold on to them. Some people manage to hang on to certain thoughts by constantly repeating them to themselves. But even if you do that, they eventually change and morph and mutate. And they always go away eventually, no matter how hard you try to hang on to them.

"When the truth is being practiced by the original mind of the buddhas of the three times," Dogen asks us, "how is it possible for anything at all to hinder that moment?" No delusion can get in the way of the truth. I mean, we can get distracted by delusions. But our misunderstandings about reality do not change reality itself in any fundamental way. Reality is still exactly as it is, no matter how deluded we might be about it.

We *are* the truth that the Buddhas of the three times practice. We aren't just part of that truth. We're not just an aspect of it. We are it! This very moment is the truth of the universe.

Dogen ends this part of the essay saying, "The truth, in short, should be called 'beyond knowing and not knowing.'" We can enter into the truth. But we cannot know it. And even not-knowing the truth is impossible.

To say that we know, or even that we don't know, the truth of the universe falls short. Because even our not-knowing is part of the ultimate truth.

## 42. THE DHARMA KING
### Buddhas Alone Together with Buddhas, Part 5

THE NEXT PART of "Buddhas Alone Together with Buddhas" begins with a poem. Unfortunately, it's very difficult to translate it, so all the English versions are different from one another.

The Nishijima/Cross translation goes, "Even the crashing down [of illusions] is nothing different / Fluency is beyond discussion / Mountains, rivers, and the earth / Are just the total revelation of the Dharma King's body."

Tanahashi and Brown give us, "Chopping down is none other than chopping down / Moving about is beyond discussion / Mountains, rivers, and the earth are the entirely revealed body of the Dharma King."

And just in case you weren't confused enough, here's how Hubert Nearman translates it: "Even what we cast aside is nothing other than the Body of the Dharma Lord / That It permeates the three temporal worlds is beyond dispute / The mountains and rivers, along with the great earth itself / Completely reveal the Dharma Body of the Awakened Lord."

I just had a look at the original, and I think I can take a stab at translating it too. To me it reads something like, "Even destroying our illusions is what it is / It doesn't matter how we enter into the practice that takes us there / In any case, mountains, rivers, and the earth are the total revelation of the body of the King of the Dharma."

A lot of times translators get hung up on getting these things just right and yet end up missing the point. Even my beloved teacher

Gudo Nishijima and his brilliant cotranslator Mike Cross seem too intent on giving us a proper translation, in spite of the fact that their version ends up being a bit murky. Hubert Nearman adds some material that simply is not in the original. The Tanahashi/Brown translation speaks a little more to me, but it still isn't quite working.

Fortunately, Dogen weighs in on the meaning of the poem. He says that, no matter what we might think, mountains, rivers, and the earth are already the body of the King of the Dharma. Remember that earlier he had called mountains, rivers and the earth the Dharma Body of the Buddha. Calling them the body of the King of the Dharma is the same concept. The King of the Dharma is Buddha. And his body is the entire universe.

The point he wants to make is, whether or not we know it, that's how things are. That's how they've always been and always will be. Our being aware of it or not doesn't change a thing.

Dogen says, "This idea is like the mountains being on the earth, and like the earth bearing the mountains." I like that line. Dogen is fond of pointing out reciprocal relationships like these. The mountains aren't just on the earth; the earth bears the mountains. When we walk on the earth, the earth itself meets our footsteps. In a sense, the earth walks on us as we walk on the earth.

Then Dogen tells us, "When we understand, the time when we did not understand does not return to impede understanding. At the same time, there is no case of understanding being able to destroy past non-understanding."

That line is intriguing to me. On the one hand, the first part sounds like he is assuring us that once we've got this we're not going to lose it. Yet, if that's what he's saying, what does that next line mean? Why would we worry about whether or not gaining understanding in the present would destroy our past lack of understanding?

Normally, if you learn something you don't unlearn it. I mean, maybe you could get a brain injury that would affect your memory and you could be said to unlearn something you'd already learned.

Or you could learn something and then forget it. For example, I used to be able to play the bass part to the song "You're the One That I Want" from *Grease*, but I can't anymore because I forgot how it goes. But this is clearly not the sort of thing Dogen is talking about.

He's not talking about the usual kind of understanding in which someone tells you, for example, that Will Smith's full name is Willard Carroll Smith and from then on you never forget that his full first name is Willard instead of William and that his middle name is Carroll — of all things.

What Dogen is talking about is a different kind of understanding altogether. It's not that some sort of knowledge has been gained. Rather, a whole different way of looking at things comes into play. And when that happens, you don't say, "Gosh! There it is! Realization! Just as I expected!"

And yet you recognize that this understanding is correct and that the previous way you looked at things was mistaken. It's unexpected. It doesn't derive from your previous way of understanding things. But it's also clearly something that you knew all along because you recognize it as such.

Yet it does not destroy your previous nonunderstanding. So what does that mean?

He's not saying that this revelation somehow retroactively erases your past nonunderstanding. What he's saying is something very different. And it's something I can attest to myself — for whatever my opinion is worth. Here goes.

No matter how deep your realization is, your past nonunderstanding remains. In saying this I'm not trying to claim that I've had the deepest realization ever and can therefore make that judgment call. I'm saying this because not only is it something I've experienced myself, but even guys like Dogen and the Buddha himself take the time to point this out.

Our nonunderstanding of how things really are is part and parcel of our bodies and our minds. In the case of the Buddha, he talked about how the "temptations of Mara" stayed with him his entire life, even after his great awakening. He still felt selfish desires. This is why Dogen talks about dropping off both body and mind. It is the very nature of my mind to misunderstand how things actually are. It is the very nature of my body to get it wrong.

The kind of realization Dogen is talking about isn't a mental realization. Sure, it *affects* the mind. It affects the body as well. But it does not come from the mind. It isn't revealed in such a way that the mind can grasp it and make it its own. I'm using the word *mind* here to refer to the individuated mind, to our sense of being a person separate from other people and things. I'm not talking about the other sense of the word *mind* that Buddhists often use when referring to the Universal Mind.

In my own case, the individuated mind was kind of baffled by whatever revelations it experienced. They didn't fit with the mind's way of putting things together. So while they have left strong impressions on my feeble mind, my mind itself was left pretty much as it had always been, with all its nonunderstanding intact.

This means that the mistaken understanding of things that screwed me up in the past is still a factor to be dealt with and always will be as long as I live. Sometimes this can cause problems. In fact, I'd venture to guess that it always causes problems. Which is why Dogen comments on it.

Those problems might be big and fairly obvious, like a Buddhist master who gets caught doing naughty things and has to be forcibly removed from the sangha. Or it might be smaller and less spectacular, like taking the last piece of cake even though you know your sister will want it when she finally gets home (but that's what she gets for being late).

And yet Dogen has already assured us that "when we understand, the time when we did not understand does not return to impede understanding." The understanding he's referring to here is so far-reaching that nothing can stand in its way. Even if I regress or make mistakes, that understanding remains as solid as ever. I've got no excuses.

Dogen goes on, saying, "Still, both in understanding and in non-understanding, there is the mind of spring and the voice of autumn. The reason we have not understood even them is that, although [spring and autumn] have been preaching at the top of their voices, those voices have not entered our ears — our ears have been idly wandering inside the voices."

Which is a strange thing to say. But let's see what we can do with it. One of Dogen's most famous essays is called "The Insentient Preach the Dharma" ("Mujo Seppo"). In this essay, Dogen points out that nature proclaims the truth to us loudly and clearly, even when we fail to notice it. Here he's saying the same sort of thing.

The voices of spring and autumn haven't entered our ears. We haven't clearly perceived what they've been trying to tell us. We've been idly wandering inside the voices like a guy talking on his cell phone while walking across the street against the light while everyone honks at him. We've been oblivious to the message, even while it was all around us.

"Understanding will take place when," Dogen says, "with the voice already having entered the ears, samadhi becomes evident." I like that he says samadhi becomes evident. As we saw already, samadhi is generally defined as a special state that one achieves in meditation. But Dogen doesn't go by that definition. As we've seen, to him, samadhi is the underlying truth of the universe that is always there but that we usually fail to notice. The time of samadhi becoming evident is called "understanding."

Dogen then tells us that we shouldn't see this as a small thing in relation to the greatness of our nonunderstanding. It's funny he should say that. Because one might be inclined to imagine otherwise, that the revelation of the truth of the universe would be a huge deal.

And it is. But it is also easy to slide back into a state of mind that takes the so-called real world as conceived of by the greater society to be much more genuine and powerful than any little enlightenment experience had by a few oddballs who meditate too much. I've done that myself.

I've often felt like what I had to say about matters like this wasn't of any great importance. Certainly it never made me rich and famous. Not that I wanted to be rich and famous. But you'd think that if I had a clear understanding of something as vast as the essential nature of the universe, surely someone would have at least offered me a reality TV show deal. But alas, I just sit in my little apartment most days, typing away at these books. Sometimes I get invited to go to cool places and give talks. But even then, not a lot of people show up, and honestly, a lot of my audiences just seem puzzled by what I have to say.

I would imagine Dogen and his monks felt kind of the same way. They knew they were in possession of something exceedingly great, something that, if put into wider practice, would profoundly change all of humankind for the better and last hundreds or even thousands of years. And yet, there they were, stuck in some rickety little temple in the mountains, freezing their asses off and subsisting on whatever meager donations the poor farmers of the area could spare them.

Not only that, it would take eight hundred years before the wider public was even aware of the things Dogen wrote! Seriously. Dogen has been known as the founder of Soto Zen in Japan for centuries. Yet his writings were not widely studied until the twentieth century. My god! You can forgive Dogen's monks for not even wanting to try sometimes. Maybe this is why he wrote all that stuff about how great it was to be a monk. It must have been terribly discouraging to be in possession of such a precious understanding and to know that hardly anyone else cared.

Dogen says that what we really are is beyond whatever private ideas we hold about ourselves. And because this is so, he says, the Dharma King is like this. The Dharma King isn't just the Buddha. It is ourselves. Please forgive the use of the gendered word *king*. It's the word the author of the poem that Dogen quotes used. The Dharma King is neither male nor female, nor anything in between, no matter what pronoun I'm forced to use to describe him. The Dharma King is not some fancy spiritual God-like dude up in the sky who sees us as we really are. The Dharma King is us seeing ourselves as we truly are, even as our own doubts and misunderstandings persist — in spite of the fact that we are limitless and all-powerful.

Then Dogen explains the meaning of the phrase "the Body of the Dharma King." He says that the eye is just like the body and that the mind too is the same as the body.

He says, "It may be that both the mind and the body, without the slightest separation, are 'totally revealed.' We understand that in the brightness of light and in the preaching of Dharma, there exists the body of the Dharma King."

The mind and body are not two things but two manifestations of an underlying reality that is neither body nor mind. There is not the slightest difference between body and mind — or between matter and spirit, or form and emptiness — even though we tend to conceive of them as complete opposites.

By expressing this truth — or "preaching the Dharma," in Dogen's words — we reveal the body of the Dharma King. This is tremendously important stuff that Dogen is saying here. He knows it, even if nobody else in his time did.

This stuff is true, but it needs someone to say it or it remains unsaid and unheard. Dogen could have done a lot of other things with his life. When he was young he was groomed to be part of Japanese royalty. He could have had a good career and a life far more comfortable than did most of the people of his day, and certainly far more comfortable than the life of a mountain monk. But he chose instead to pursue something far bigger.

I, for one, am very glad he did.

## 43. WHY BUDDHAS NEED OTHER BUDDHAS
### Buddhas Alone Together with Buddhas, Part 6

BEFORE WE END this discussion of "Buddhas Alone Together with Buddhas," let's go back to the beginning. Why is the phrase that Dogen quotes "Buddhas alone *together with* Buddhas"? What on earth could that possibly mean?

Let's recall that the full quotation from the Lotus Sutra is, "Buddhas alone, together with buddhas, are directly able to perfectly realize that all dharmas are real form. What is called 'all dharmas' is form as it is, nature as it is, body as it is, energy as it is, action as it is, causes as they are, conditions as they are, effects as they are, results as they are, and the ultimate state of equality of substance and detail, as it is."

This quotation from the Lotus Sutra is an important theme that runs throughout the piece. The final paragraph of the essay "Buddha's Alone Together with Buddhas" is where Dogen digs into the part about why the phrase is "alone together with."

Because you'd think that a solitary Buddha would be able to see reality clearly and just sit back and enjoy the show. He or she would not need to be with anyone else. Why, then, the emphasis on "together with"? The writer of the Lotus Sutra could have just said "only a Buddha is able to perfectly realize the truth." But instead the unknown author of the sutra adds "together with Buddhas." Dogen is going to try to explain that to us in the final paragraph of his essay.

The final paragraph of Dogen's "Yui Butsu Yo Butsu" begins, "There is a saying from ancient times that none other than fish know the mind of fish, and none other than birds can follow the traces of birds."

Dogen says that most people think this just means that human beings can't know the minds of other animals like fish or birds. But, he says, regular people miss the much deeper meaning of this old saying.

He says that a better way to understand this old saying is that "fish together with fish always know each other's mind. They are never ignorant [of each other] as human beings are." Of course, his use of "fish together with fish" is a call back to the concept of "Buddhas alone together with Buddhas." He points out that humans are ignorant of each other's minds in ways that fish are not.

By way of example, he says that when fish swim together through the Dragon's Gate or the Nine Rapids of Zhekiang they all know what's going on with each other. They share a common mind. The Dragon's Gate and the Nine Rapids of Zhekiang might not be familiar to us, but we've all seen films of schools of salmon and trout swimming upstream and over waterfalls and rocks and all kinds of stuff in order to spawn. That's what he's talking about.

As for birds, Dogen says that we walking creatures can't even imagine the traces birds can see of each other's movements through the sky. He says that birds can see where other birds have flocked just as clearly as we can see wheel marks or a horse's hoofprints on the ground.

Nowadays science can explain that fish know where to spawn by following scent markers. The way birds know where to fly is a bit more mysterious even now, but some have speculated that they follow the Earth's magnetic fields. I'm no expert on this kind of stuff, so don't listen to me about the particulars.

The point is that these days we have scientific explanations for the movements of fish and birds, and so Dogen's idea that they know each other's minds might sound a bit old-fashioned or even fanciful. But he is not claiming that birds and fish have some kind of special psychic powers. He's not implying that they swim and fly around talking to each other mind to mind about where to go next, like teenagers gossiping on their phones. Even if we went back in a time machine and told Dogen that *act-chew-ally* fish follow scent trails and birds follow the Earth's magnetic fields, I don't think he would alter his claim that they know each other's minds, and furthermore, that they know each other's minds in ways that humans do not know each other's minds. Those scent trails or the ability to follow magnetic fields are part of their knowing each other's minds.

Unlike humans, who offer up theories for discussion and experiment, which must then be verified and accepted and which still might not be convincing to some people, birds and fish smell those scent trails or sense those magnetic fields, and they immediately know what's up without having to debate it. What is known by one fish or bird mind is known by all fish or bird minds. So Dogen is not claiming something magical for birds and fish, and he's not about to claim anything magical for Buddhas either.

About Buddhas, he says that they know each other's minds just like fish and birds know each other's minds. He says, "They suppose how many ages Buddhas have spent in practice, and they know small Buddhas and great Buddhas, even among those who have gone uncounted."

I like that he includes those Buddhas who have gone uncounted. He acknowledges that there are Buddhas who never make themselves known to the wider world, who teach only a few people, or perhaps have just a single student. The world doesn't know they exist, but they're out there doing their thing. And notice that even great Buddhas may be among those who have gone uncounted.

Dogen then adds that if you aren't a Buddha you don't know these things at all. He says that some may ask why those who are not Buddhas can't notice this.

He answers by saying, "Because it is with the Eye of Buddha that those traces can be seen; and those who are not Buddha are not equipped with the Eye of Buddha." So it sounds like he's saying that

Buddhas have some kind of extra special eyeballs with which they can see things that the rest of us can't.

But that's not it. He says that if we can see the traces of a Buddha with our own eyes, that might mean that we are in the presence of a Buddha and might be able to "compare their footprints." In doing so, we can know the length and depth of the traces they've left behind. And, he says, we can "illuminate our own traces." Illuminating our own traces, he says, is called Buddha-Dharma.

Dogen isn't saying we don't have the super-duper Buddha Eye, since he allows that we can see the traces of a Buddha with our own eyes and that we can see our own traces. We can see these things because the whole Earth is our dharma body. Remember that, traditionally, a dharma body is something only a Buddha has. Yet Dogen talks about it as if everyone has it.

There was one passage earlier in the essay that I left out. I'd like to dig into it now because I feel like now we might be ready for it. It's where the ethics of Buddhism really come into the picture.

It goes, "Their 'manifesting the body to save the living' is their 'saving the living to manifest the body.'" *Their* refers to the Buddhas and bodhisattvas. "When we behold their 'saving,' we do not see a trace of 'manifestation,' and when we watch them 'manifesting,' they may be free of concern about 'saving.' We should understand, should preach, and should experience that in this 'saving' the Buddha-Dharma is perfectly realized. We hear and we preach that both 'manifesting' and 'the body' are as one with 'saving.' Here also, [the unity of] 'manifesting the body to save the living' makes it so. When [Buddhas] have substantiated this principle, from the morning of their attaining the truth to the evening of their nirvana, even if they have never preached a word, words of preaching have been let loose all around."

Dogen is riffing on another passage from the Lotus Sutra. The passage goes, "Good son! If living beings in any land must be saved through the body of a Buddha, the bodhisattva of compassion manifests at once the body of a Buddha and preaches for them the Dharma. To those who must be saved through the body of a pratyekabuddha, [the bodhisattva] manifests at once the body of a pratyekabuddha and preaches for them the Dharma. To those who must be saved through the body of a sravaka, [the bodhisattva] manifests at once the body of a sravaka and preaches for them the Dharma." A *pratyekabuddha* is a private or self-enlightened Buddha, one who doesn't necessarily take a vow to save all beings. A *sravaka* is a disciple of a Buddha.

It goes on and on like this for quite a while. Pretty soon we're getting to things like, "To those who must be saved through the body of a rich man, [the bodhisattva] manifests at once the body of a rich man and preaches for them the Dharma. To those who must be saved through the body of a householder, [the bodhisattva] manifests at once the body of a householder and preaches for them the Dharma. To those who must be saved through the body of a government official..." You get the picture. A little further on we get, "To those who must be saved through the body of a child, [the bodhisattva] manifests at once the body of a child and preaches for them the Dharma. To those who must be saved through the body of a god, dragon, yaksha, gandharva, asura, garuda, kimnara, or mahoraga, a human being or a nonhuman being, [the bodhisattva], in every case, manifests at once this [body] and preaches for them the Dharma."

A *yaksha* is a kind of scary-looking guardian deity; a *gandharva* is a celestial musician; an *asura* is a fighting demon; a *garuda* is a kind of bird-god; a *kimnara* is part bird, part human, and part horse; and a *mahoraga* is a sort of snakelike deity. The point is that the bodhisattva of compassion manifests as whatever sort of being is needed by the person in need. This bodhisattva is also known as Avalokiteshvara, Kuan Yin, or Kannon. It's the same bodhisattva that's mentioned in the Heart Sutra.

Dogen says, "Their 'manifesting the body to save the living' is their 'saving the living to manifest the body.'" There is no difference between the bodhisattva of compassion's manifesting a body and her saving living beings. And this doesn't just go for the bodhisattva either. This goes for you and me as well. We are not here to enjoy ourselves and leave a good-looking corpse. We are here for each other. Every encounter we have is a chance to be compassionate and to do something ethical for someone else. We are all manifestations of the bodhisattva of compassion.

Then Dogen says, "When we behold their 'saving,' we do not see a trace of 'manifestation,' and when we watch them 'manifesting,' they may be free of concern about 'salvation.'" Tanahashi/d Brown prefer to translate the word Nishijima and Cross give here as "saving," and *salvation* as "awakening." The point is that your being here in the world is the same as awakening to the truth and is the same as saving living beings.

The way that ethics come into play here is kind of subtle. To save living beings is to help them in all the ways they need to be helped. It is to offer what we have to offer. Sometimes what we have to offer might not be exactly what they want, but it's always exactly what they need. Moment by moment, we appear in the world in response to the needs of others.

The reason you are alive is that someone needs your help.

There's a Latin phrase that's very much like this. "Non nobis solum, sed toti mundo nati" translates as "Not for ourselves alone, but for the whole world were we born." The Roman poet Cicero said this in his treatise *On Duties*. It's also inscribed on the entrance to the Liverpool Institute High School for Boys, where Paul McCartney went to school. I'm sure Dogen would agree with Cicero.

The next line from Dogen is, "We should understand, should preach, and should experience that in this 'saving' the Buddha-Dharma is perfectly realized." Everything we do, and all that we are, is "saving" or, if you prefer, "awakening." The efforts we make to awaken to the truth are the efforts we are making in the service of everyone we encounter, whether or not they recognize it. It doesn't even matter if we recognize it ourselves. Still, we make the effort.

Dogen says, "We hear and we preach that both 'manifesting' and 'the body' are as one with 'saving.'" Our own bodies and our minds as well are not our own bodies and our own minds. They are the universal activity of saving or awakening manifested in physical and psychic form.

The word translated here as "preach" could also be translated as "explain." As Nishijima Roshi told me, "people like explanations."

The Gnostic Christians believed that knowledge could set you free. This is an important tenet in Buddhist philosophy too. Even though lots of people in the Zen tradition have famously advocated throwing away their books and looking directly at reality, they also recognize the importance of clear understanding. When we explain our understanding to others, we explain it to ourselves.

Dogen says, "Here also, [the unity of] 'manifesting the body to save the living' makes it so." Because we are here solely for the purpose of saving each other, we are equipped to do just that. No matter how inadequate we may feel. Whatever we have to offer, in whatever state we're in when we need to offer it, we are always ready and able to do the right thing. Even when we feel like we totally are not.

Finally, Dogen concludes the passage saying, "When [Buddhas] have substantiated this principle, from the morning of their attaining the truth to the evening of their nirvana, even if they have never preached a word, words of preaching have been let loose all around." Whether or not we set out with the intention of preaching or teaching, the very fact of our being alive here and now is the manifestation of compassion and of the energy to bring the truth into the world.

"Buddhas Alone Together with Buddhas" is a short piece that takes us on a long journey. This must have been one of Dogen's later pieces of writing, because it has tremendous depth to it, even though it's so brief. Dogen was good at packing a lot into a short piece of writing.

Why do Buddhas need other Buddhas? If the universe is all just a single living entity, why are there so goshdarned many of us? The fact that there are so many of us is precisely why most regular people would never come to the conclusion that the universe is a single living entity. Obviously it's not! I'm *me*, sitting at a kitchen table writing a book, and you're *you* hanging out in the back of a bookstore trying to decide if you're going to put this book back on the shelf, or buy it, or maybe try to sneak it out of the store without paying for it — don't do that, by the way; it's not ethical.

But the point is that we are two different people. If we weren't, then the whole idea of you reading a book that I wrote makes no sense.

In the essay we've been looking at, Dogen at first seems to be saying that we need to be a Buddha before we can recognize a Buddha, before we can recognize a true master who can help us realize our own Buddhahood. But he's not saying that we need to achieve some special state of realization before we can find a true teacher.

He is saying that we are already endowed with all the realization we'll ever need, including the ability to recognize a true teacher. When we see the traces of Buddhahood in another, it is our own Buddha nature recognizing the Buddha nature of another.

No. Sorry. Let me rephrase that. Buddha nature itself recognizes Buddha nature. The fact that it appears as one person facing another person is an illusion.

When I met my own teachers, I could sense there was something extraordinary about them. This wasn't something everyone else noticed. What made them special wasn't obvious. Not even to me, most of the time. In fact, I had plenty of doubts about both of them. And yet, through it all, I knew I was in the presence of a couple of special people.

As Dogen warns us, "There is no case of understanding being able to destroy past non-understanding." My past nonunderstanding continued to be a factor, even after I'd established a firm understanding of how things were. In fact, that's a big part of why I'm writing this book.

Nevertheless, what I truly am is not involved in my past nonunderstanding. That's just a shadow that crosses over now and then. When I take that shadow to be myself, I make mistakes and falter. But even my mistakes are part of the path.

# 44. NO CHOICE

BEFORE I LET you go, I need to say a few more things about the matter of choice. The best place to start is with the opening lines of an old Chinese poem called "Inscription on Faith in Mind" by Zen Master Sosan.

> The Great Way is not difficult
> Just avoid picking and choosing.

There are a lot of different translations of the first two lines of this poem. I honestly don't know who is responsible for the version above, which is my favorite. D. T. Suzuki's version says, "The Perfect Way knows no difficulties. Except that it refuses to make preference." Philippe Coupey translates it as, "Entering the Way is not difficult, but you must have no love, or hate, or choose, or reject."

In case you care, the Chinese characters are: 至道無難 / 唯嫌揀擇. If you asked me for a literal translation it'd be, "Perfect Way not difficult / Just hate picking choosing."

The poem goes on. "When like and dislike are absent, everything becomes perfectly clear. But if there's the slightest bit of distinction, heaven and earth are infinitely distant."

"To set what you like against what you dislike is a disease of the mind," says the poem. "When you grasp or reject, the truth is hidden."

Later the poem says, "If you stop speaking and thinking, there is nothing you cannot understand." The poem also says, "With one mind there is no arising, then everything is without blame."

In "Eihei Koroku Dharma Hall Discourse number 371," Dogen says, "The third ancestor, Great Teacher [Jianzhi Sengcan, aka Sosan], in 'Inscription on Faith in Mind' said, 'The supreme way is not difficult; only disdain picking and choosing.' Great assembly, have you ever studied the third ancestor's meaning? Tell me, what is the third ancestor's meaning? Passing through three kalpas, without fail we arrive; passing through numberless kalpas, without fail we arrive; without arising from our seat, without fail we arrive; without arising in a single moment, without fail we arrive. Therefore, [the third ancestor] said, 'The supreme way is not difficult.' Simply to disdain picking and choosing is like a garuda not eating anything but dragons."

As you may recall, a garuda is a mythical kind of bird-god that eats nothing but dragons. In their footnotes to their translation of this discourse, Taigen Dan Leighton and Shohaku Okumura write, "Dogen is pointing out a paradox in the Inscription on Faith in Mind. Disdaining or avoiding is a kind of preference, a kind of picking and choosing. But for garudas it is simply natural to eat dragons; for Buddhist practitioners it is simply natural to follow the way."

In "Dharma Hall Discourse number 472," Dogen says:

The third ancestor, Great Teacher [Jianzhi Sengcan], said, "The supreme way is not difficult, simply dislike picking and choosing." Upon hearing this, people who do not understand might say, "All dharmas are without good and bad; every [action] is neither evil nor upright. Simply trust your nature and stroll along. Following conditions, let go of everything. Therefore with all good and bad or evil and upright, do not pick or choose, but just go on your way."

Another may say, "In order to not do this so-called picking or choosing, do not speak using words. This can be done by simply making a circle, holding up a whisk, pounding a monk's staff, throwing down the staff, clapping hands, giving a yell, holding up a sitting cushion, or raising a fist."

Views like this do not depart from the cave of common beings. Suppose someone were to ask me, Eihei, "What is the point of 'simply dislike picking and choosing'?" I would say to him: "A garuda does not eat anything but raw dragons. The Bodhisattva Next in Line [for buddhahood, i.e., Maitreya] is not born except in Tushita Heaven."

Maitreya is the name of the person who the Gautama Buddha supposedly predicted would be the next Buddha after him. Tushita Heaven is one of the many heavenly realms in traditional Buddhist cosmology. It's supposed to be a realm of meditative bliss.

Dogen liked alluding to mythology to make his points. It makes him hard to understand sometimes. Let me see if I can find a way to say the same thing without referencing ancient myths.

We all like to think that we have the power to choose what to do or what not to do. The very fact that the Buddhist precepts exist at all would seem to argue for the idea that we have free will. Otherwise, why would there be a precept, for example, against stealing? If we have no choice of whether to steal or not to steal, why ask us to vow not to steal?

Dogen seems to be arguing that, like the mythical garuda bird, if we are programmed by nature to eat dragons, then we have no choice but to eat dragons. I like that the second time he uses this metaphor he has the garudas not just eating dragons, but eating them raw!

On the other hand, Dogen also criticizes the idea that "avoiding preferences" means to just let go of everything and stroll along on your merry way. And he says that making nonsensical gestures as a way to avoid explaining what this means is a cop-out too.

On the other *other* hand, as the footnote says, "avoiding preferences" is another sort of preference. But I have an answer for that one! I once asked my first Zen teacher about the criticism that having no goal in your zazen practice is a kind of goal — the goal of having no goal. He said that this makes sense semantically. But, he said, in actual practice the "goal of having no goal" — if we want to call it that — is very different from having a goal in the usual sense. Having a preference for avoiding preferences is not the same as other preferences.

Let me back up a little here, though. When Buddhists talk about preferences they're not talking about things like preferring strawberry ice cream over vanilla. They're not talking about how I preferred the sound of the Ibanez Black Eagle bass I used to have over any other bass I ever owned and how much I regret selling it. Those sorts of things are related to the Buddhist view of preference tangentially.

When Buddhists talk about preferences, they're talking about the way we often imagine that our lives could be different from how they actually are. They're talking about the way we imagine that we have any real choice over what life presents us or even much of a choice when it comes to how we respond to what life presents us.

The question I ask myself when it comes to the matter of having preferences is this: Is any action truly my action? The "Inscription of Faith in Mind" also contains the lines, "The doer vanishes along with the deed. The deed disappears when the doer is annihilated. The deed has no function apart from the doer. The doer has no function apart from the deed." Doing and doer are one and the same. You are not an individual who does stuff. Doing stuff happens, but you don't do anything.

Think about it this way. You probably imagine you had a choice when it came to reading this book or not reading it. But did you? The fact that you felt interested enough to get this far into it can be traced to a long line of events in which you had no agency.

But let's take the heat off you and put it on me. I'll ask myself right now why I read *Zen Mind, Beginner's Mind*, the very first book I ever read about Zen.

Well... I was exposed to Hindu religious iconography and beliefs when I was a child because my dad took a job in Nairobi, where there is a large Indian population. I had no choice in moving to Africa when I was a child. The fact that a terrible genetic disorder runs in my family made me very anxious about matters of life and death at an early age, and I certainly had no choice in that. I did choose to sign up for a course at Kent State University called Zen Buddhism, in which the book was required reading. But if the folks who ran KSU hadn't offered that course, I couldn't have chosen it.

If I extrapolate from this I see that my personality is made up of all sorts of things that I had no agency in choosing. Calling it "my personality" doesn't seem right. Who am I to say I own or control this personality?

If I keep in mind how little choice I had in anything about myself, it's hard to feel shame or guilt about what I've done in the past. More significant than that, though, is that if I remember that other people also had little or even no real choice in their actions, it's hard to feel animosity or hatred toward anyone else.

This is not to say that I never feel shame or even hatred. I do. But the understanding that such feelings have no rational basis is very freeing. Of course, the other side is also true. I can't really be proud of myself or my accomplishments either. I can be impressed by the accomplishments of other people, but I can't feel much envy toward them. Or, if I do happen to feel envy, I can be certain that my feelings of envy have no rational basis either.

All sorts of issues pop up when you try to talk about ideas like these. The most simplistic ones are usually along the lines of something like, "Do you mean the Nazis shouldn't be held accountable for their atrocities?"

People always jump to stuff like that. And no, this doesn't mean the Nazis shouldn't be held accountable. Nor does it mean that you or I won't be held accountable for the things we do. That's an entirely different matter.

What it means is that dragons don't need to hate garudas for eating them raw. Maybe the reason Dogen liked to phrase things in terms of myth was to stay out of pointless discussions.

A garuda's job is to eat dragons. Therefore, dragons would do well to avoid hanging out where the garudas hang out. A garuda might say she prefers to eat dragons as opposed to, say, eating Lucky Charms cereal. But she has no real choice in the matter. It's just the way she was created. Eating dragons is her role to play in the mythical ecosystem. Still, whatever karma comes to a garuda for eating a dragon is exactly what it is.

Remember that Dogen didn't think much of the interpretation "All dharmas are without good and bad; every [action] is neither evil nor upright.... Therefore with all good and bad or evil and upright, do not pick or choose, but just go on your way."

This is why part of the Buddhist way is to follow the precepts as best we can. We don't ignore the fact that all actions have consequences, nor do we abdicate responsibility for what we have done. We don't just do whatever we feel like doing. We try to understand what the universe needs us to do and do only that. Since it is very difficult to understand what the universe needs us to do with the thinking mind, we do zazen so that we're more able to follow our deeper intuitive sense.

## 45. THE HUMAN PROJECT

LET ME FINISH this book by telling you about something that I think of as the Human Project.

This is where I am going to deviate a lot from what has usually been considered the proper way of talking about things in the Zen Buddhist tradition. Buddhists in the Zen tradition are strongly discouraged from engaging in speculation. The human mind has limits to what it can know or understand, and some things are outside those limits. We accept those limits and are taught not to speculate about things that no human can possibly know.

Even so, I want to speculate a little bit here.

Ahem.

I think that maybe human beings are a very important part of what the universal mind is trying to do. I suspect that we are kind of a project that the universe is working on.

This is a big change for me. For a lot of my life I thought that human beings were nature's greatest mistake. We just mess everything up. We imagine that we're not part of the natural order — even though we clearly are — and we go around thinking we can improve on nature, but every "improvement" we make ends up causing all sorts of problems. Then we have to fix those problems. And in doing so, we end up making things even worse. It's a huge mess! The world would be better off without us humans. That's what I thought.

But would the world be better without us? Here's one weird

thing I thought of that led to a lot of other thoughts and ended up making me think maybe — just maybe — humans aren't all bad.

A few years ago I was just sitting there thinking about dinosaurs. I often think about dinosaurs. Sixty-five million years ago a giant meteor struck planet Earth and wiped out just about all life on the planet, most notably the dinosaurs. And that wasn't even the first time such a thing had happened — or the worst! There were other mass extinctions before that one that make the one that killed the dinosaurs look like a picnic.

Recalling that, the idea came to me that nowadays there is a life-form on the planet — us — who, at least potentially, could foresee a danger like that and prevent it from destroying everything. Maybe, I thought, nature coughed us up because it got tired of mass extinctions. Maybe we are something Planet Earth created to preserve itself.

The problem is that, instead of preventing a mass extinction, humanity itself could end up causing a mass extinction through the misuse of technology. In fact, some smart people say that we humans are already causing a mass extinction. Which may be true. But I tend to be an optimist. Lots of us are already working on reversing that trend toward destruction. I think we still might make some big mistakes. But I don't think we'll wipe everything out. Your opinion may differ. Mine certainly did for a very long time. If you disagree with my optimism, that's OK. I totally get it.

Anyway, I don't think our only purpose here is to prevent a meteor from destroying the Earth. That was just the train of thought that got me started.

I think the Human Project is something that the Universal Mind engaged in for a reason that only the Universal Mind could ever fully understand. But if I were to speculate, I'd say that it's trying to use the Human Project as a way to reunify itself.

I suspect that even the Universal Mind doesn't quite know where the Human Project is going. However, since ultimately the Universal Mind and the Human Project are one and the same thing,

I think that the Human Project is not in danger of going in any other direction than the direction that the Universal Mind wants it to go. Not ultimately, anyhow. Although the course isn't going to be completely smooth and direct.

The reason it can't be smooth and direct is that, as individuals, we have the ability to go against the Universal Mind to a small degree. The Universal Mind will always win out in the end. But we can temporarily hinder what it wants to do and get in its way. If enough of us get in its way, then things can get messy. Which is what I think may be happening right now.

In order to do the thing the Universal Mind wants, individual human beings had to be smarter than other animals and more capable of individual action. Because we're smart, we can use our smarts to attempt to circumvent what the Universal Mind wants. Which is unfortunate, but probably unavoidable. Still, it's not a big problem as far as the Universal Mind is concerned.

This is because the way we humans can go against what the Universal Mind wants is sort of like the way we can go against gravity for brief periods of time. We can jump up really high, but we always end up back on the ground. We can build an airplane and stay off the ground for hours at a time, but even that airplane has to land eventually. We can build a rocket and leave the planet entirely, but we'll die if we stay away from our home planet too long. It's like that. We can temporarily get in the way of what the Universal Mind wants from us, but it can't last long — at least, "not long" in terms of the Universal Mind's time scale, which is really long.

Anyway, I think this is why so many of us are "awakening the Bodhi Mind," to use Dogen's terms. The Universal Mind wants to sort things out and get the Human Project back on track. Those who awaken to reality, even partially, can help get things moving in the direction the Universal Mind wants things to go.

Reunification of the universe is a long way off. In the meantime, I think human beings have the capacity to create a society that could be truly amazing. If we could just learn to cooperate with each other and stop all the useless fighting we do, I think the possibilities of the Human Project are limitless — literally limitless.

To me, Zen Buddhism is a part of the Human Project. It's one of a number of activities to try to help the Human Project stay on task. It's not the only thing that can save humanity. But it's one of them.

This is why we need to work on not punching ourselves. This is why Buddhist formulas like the Eightfold Path and the precepts are so useful. They help establish a more peaceful society in which some of us can get down to the real work that needs to be done instead of causing each other needless trouble.

But Zen Buddhism is a hard path to take. It doesn't allow you any excuses. The actions you take that cause harm and disturbance to others or to yourself will not be forgiven. That's because there is no one to forgive them. Not even yourself. Doing wrong now to create a better tomorrow is never acceptable.

An undivided heart and an integrated life are required. A clear mind and a clean heart are necessary. The attempt to seek an undisturbed serenity may look selfish to those who fail to comprehend it. It may look like an attempt to remain unperturbed while everyone else goes crazy. But it is the least selfish thing any person can do.

As my friend Rob said, the bodhisattva vow to save all beings is a vow to save all beings... from myself. We have to recognize that we are the very disturbance in the world that we rail against. We are the source of war and terrorism and all the rest of the great challenges humanity faces. When we pretend those things are not part of ourselves and wage battle against them by attacking others whom we characterize as villains, we're only making matters worse.

One reason this is a hard path is that so few really understand it. Even the folks who run the big Zen Buddhist organizations here in the West as well as in Asia mostly fail to comprehend what this path is really about. They entangle themselves in politics and trendy causes because that's so much easier than doing the real work.

Besides, society rewards you when you get involved in society's silliness. Following the real Buddhist path isn't going to get you very many "likes" on social media.

It can be a lonely path too. You might walk this path for days and weeks and months — maybe even years — without encountering a single other person who is taking the same route. It requires tremendous confidence not to give up.

This is why Buddha, dharma, and sangha are important. But as I said, Buddha doesn't have to mean the historical Buddha, dharma doesn't have to always fall under the label of Buddhism, and sangha doesn't have to mean some organization with the word *sangha* in its name. Sometimes, however, you're going to feel like your sangha is nowhere to be found, your dharma is just confusing, and Buddha is no help at all. That's when you have to turn to yourself.

In the Advaita Vedanta tradition they're really into gurus. The Zen tradition also stresses the need for a teacher. But both traditions say that the truest teacher is yourself. In Advaita, they call the inner teacher *sadguru*. Which doesn't mean a guru that's sad. It means an inner guru. The Buddha talked about something similar. He said, "Be a light unto yourself."

Finding your inner guru or light can be tricky. This is why it's good to have a teacher who can help you locate your own inner guide. What I've done when it comes to learning from my teachers is always to try to find a balance between what my teachers have told me and my own gut feelings. Sometimes the balance tips one way, sometimes it tips the other. I trusted my teachers, but it wasn't a blind trust.

Blind trust in a guru or Zen master often goes very wrong. Continually adjusting the balance between what I heard from my teachers and what I understood for myself seems to have worked. Even so, I often wish I'd trusted my teachers more than myself. But I was fortunate enough to have good teachers. Not everyone is as fortunate as I was.

Here's a dialogue between Kobun Chino Roshi and a student that I have found very helpful.

The student says, "For years I preferred to sit by myself, and every time I had to sit with a group, it was always more difficult. I had problems I didn't have by myself."

Kobun answers:

The difficulty wasn't sitting together; the difficulty was yourself! Wanting to be alone is impossible. When you become really alone you notice you are not alone. In other words, we stop our vigorous effort towards ideal purity.

Purity is just a process. After purity, dry simplicity comes, where almost no more life is there, and your sensation is that you are not existing anymore. Still, you are existing there. You flip into the other side of nothing where you discover everybody is waiting for you.

Before that, you are living together like that; day, sun, moon, stars, and food, everything is helping you. But you are all blocked off, a closed system. You just see things from inside toward the outside, and act with incredible systematic logical dynamics, and you think everything is all right.

When noise or a chaotic situation comes, you want to leave that situation to be alone. But there is no such aloneness! It is very important to experience the complete negation of yourself which brings you to the other side of nothing. People experience that in many ways.

You go to the other side of nothing, and you are held by the hand of the absolute. You see yourself as part of the absolute, so you have no more insistence of self as yourself. You can speak of self as no-self upon the absolute. Real existence is only absolute.

*The other side of nothing.*
This funny little phrase sums up a lot of what I've been trying

to talk about in this book. In Zen we often use words like *nothingness* and *emptiness*. Lots of people hear these words and get the impression that Zen is a nihilistic philosophy aimed at realizing a depressingly bleak void. But it's not that. We use these words because what we are aiming at is unlike anything we think we know. The only way to describe it is in negative terms. Whatever you can think of, it isn't anything at all like that. As Dogen said, "No one ever said, 'This is enlightenment — just as I expected!'"

But we're not just concerned with nothing. We're also interested in the other side of nothing. We're here in Somethingland. And in Somethingland, lots of stuff is going on that we have to deal with.

However, in order to really understand what to do in Somethingland, we have to pass through nothing and emerge on the other side. On the other side of nothing everybody is waiting for you. You are held by the hand of the Absolute.

The complete negation of yourself allows you to become completely yourself. I know, it sounds like another one of those "I'm not saying it's aliens, but it's aliens" things. But it's the best way I know of to express what I want to say.

As I said before, each of us is like a puzzle piece and the puzzle is the universe. In order for a puzzle piece to properly complete a puzzle, it has to have a certain size and shape and it has to be just the right colors.

If a puzzle piece had a will like a human being, it might decide that its size, shape, and color were inadequate. A materialistic puzzle piece, might decide it has to be the biggest puzzle piece of them all, the one with the flashiest colors. But if it did that, it couldn't complete the puzzle.

On the other hand, if it were a very spiritually minded puzzle piece, maybe it would decide that it needed to be perfectly round and perfectly clear. But if it did that, it still wouldn't be able to complete the puzzle. In order to complete the puzzle it would have to return to its original size, shape, and color. But maybe, after trying so hard to be a different sort of puzzle piece, it would have a hard time knowing what its original size, shape, and color were. I think that's where a lot of us find ourselves.

When you get to the other side of nothing, you discover that your duty is to be exactly what you are. But having experienced the complete negation of yourself, you notice that you've wasted a lot of effort trying to be something you're not. You've been trying all sorts of ways to alter yourself, but all of them just interfered with your ability to integrate with the rest of the universe. Once you find that perfect fit, nothing you've ever experienced before feels better, and when you start to slip back into old habits and alter yourself again, you notice something is wrong.

You have to die completely.

Zen teachers say this a lot. It's almost a cliché. But you have to give up everything that you believe yourself to be in order to discover what you really are.

Here's another thing Kobun said:

If we experience something, we say it exists. Whether it is truly so or not, we are not sure. When we are dreaming in very deep sleep, we have no sense of, "I am dreaming this." Everything is so real we do not doubt it until someone makes a sound and we wake up. Then we wonder, "Where am I?" waking up from the dream to so-called "reality." Yet, if this "reality" feels fine to you, it's sad to realize it is a dream, and there is nothing to attach and nothing to be attached to.

You think that if you could possess things forever, or be possessed forever, you could sleep peacefully without worrying or thinking. But it doesn't happen. Instead, because of many, many things going on, constant tension is needed to carry this dream on, to keep it from being misty or uncertain, or like a nightmare. And yet, in reality, we have many opportunities to wake up from this dream.

In this dream world, when he tells another his dream, the telling too is just a dream. That's a phrase that I've had stuck in my head for years. For a long time I believed it was from Dogen. But I searched through Dogen's written works and couldn't find anything like that. Then I trolled through the internet for the phrase and came up with nothing. Then I asked a bunch of people who I thought might recognize it, and they didn't know the phrase either. So maybe I'm the one who made it up!

Ultimately, whoever made up that phrase *was* me. Which doesn't mean I should go around claiming credit for every phrase I like. Still... the truth of the matter is that it's all me. But it's all you too. So I guess we have to work things out between us.

To understand that this real world is not the real world at all is kind of sad, as Kobun said. There are lots of things I really like in this world. I like playing with Ziggy Pup. I like reading Dogen. I like listening to King Crimson and watching *Ancient Aliens* on TV. All these activities depend on the existence of a separate "me" who experiences doing them.

Is that why I'm here? Is it because the Universal Mind can't experience itself without splitting itself up into bazillions of pieces? Did something go wrong with this way of the Universal Mind experiencing itself? Is that why we are capable of causing each other such misery? Is that why we need ethics and morals? Is that why we need to understand what we really are, so that we never need or want to cause each other pain?

Maybe it's something like that.

And yet reality is bigger than any dream. It includes all that takes place within the dream, and infinitely more. Nothingness is not nothing. Emptiness is not empty. It's everything, and it's more than everything.

Sometimes I'm asked, "What do you want readers to take away from your books?"

I never know how to answer that question. I hope you enjoyed this book. I hope some of the jokes were funny. I hope you saw yourself in the book. I hope you understand the Buddhist ethical system a little better. I hope you have some idea what nonduality is all about.

Sometimes I even dare to hope that my books will help make a change come about in the world. But I try not to expect very much. As my teacher said, "You can make a little difference." That's all I aim for.

The puzzle piece that is "me" seems to have a compulsion to carry on writing and speaking about this stuff, even though I'm not exactly a bestselling author. I guess Dogen must have felt that way too. I once asked a well-known Dogen scholar how many people he thought actually read Dogen's writings when Dogen was alive. I said, "Do you think it was fifty people?" He said he thought it was far fewer than that.

Still, Dogen kept on writing. I asked Nishijima Roshi why he thought Dogen wrote so much stuff even though so few ever read it. He said he thought Dogen was writing for us, for people centuries in the future who lived in a world so different from his that he could not possibly have imagined it. Did he know for certain that his words would last that long? I doubt it. But he knew it was possible. And so he did the work and he wrote a book for us, even in the face of the very real possibility that all his work and sacrifice might come to nothing.

I'm nowhere near as enlightened as Dogen was. I'm not sure my words are worth preserving for very long. Even so, maybe I can make a little difference.

And so for that reason I will carry on doing what I do as long as I can do it. For the sake of the Human Project I cast these words out there and hope for the best.

I love you.

# APPENDIX
## How to Do Zazen

I'VE TALKED A lot about zazen in this book. You can find dozens of videos on YouTube that show you how it's done, including one by my teacher Gudo Nishijima. But maybe it would be useful for me to explain it a little. Dogen tells you all you really need to know about how to do zazen in a short piece called "Fukan Zazen-gi," which means "Universal Guide to the Standard Method for Zazen Practice." I'll be quoting from the translation in volume one of *Shobogenzo* by my teacher Gudo Nishijima and his student Chodo Cross.

Dogen tells us, "We should learn the backward step of turning light and reflecting. Body and mind will naturally fall away, and the original features will manifest themselves before us."

Here's how he says we can do this. "In general, a quiet room is good for practicing [Za]zen, and food and drink are taken in moderation. Cast aside all involvements. Give the myriad things a rest. Do not think of good and bad. Do not consider right and wrong. Stop the driving movement of mind, will, consciousness. Cease intellectual consideration through images, thoughts, and reflections. Do not aim to become a buddha."

That's the intellectual side of practice. Now for the physical.

"We usually spread a thick mat on the place where we sit, and use a round cushion on top of that. Either sit in the full lotus posture or sit in the half lotus posture. To sit in the full lotus posture, first put the right foot on the left thigh, then put the left foot on the right thigh. To sit in the half lotus posture, just press the left foot onto the right thigh."

You can also put your legs the opposite way around (left foot on right thigh) or in the Burmese posture, which is like a half lotus but without the legs crossed. The main thing is to get both knees down on the ground, or as close to the ground as possible. If this proves too difficult you can place some extra cushions under your knees.

If you absolutely cannot manage to sit on a cushion on the floor, then sitting on a chair is better than not doing zazen at all. But chairs force *their* idea of balance on the body and make it nearly impossible to find your own. If you really, truly must use a chair I'd recommend one of those backless ergonomic kneeling chairs. Or you can put a meditation cushion on a chair, which will help you sit in a more natural way. The point is to find your own balance rather than letting the chair do it for you.

Zazen is a physical practice, not an arbitrary pose you take to work on something mental. Taking yoga classes to loosen up the legs is worth the effort. Zazen is essentially a balance pose, like the Tree Pose in yoga (where you stand on one leg).

Then Dogen tells us to "spread the clothing loosely and make it neat. Then put the right hand above the left foot, and place the left hand on the right palm. The thumbs meet and support each other. Just make the body right and sit up straight. Do not lean to the left, incline to the right, slouch forward, or lean backward. The ears must be aligned with the shoulders, and the nose aligned with the navel. Hold the tongue against the palate, keep the lips and teeth closed, and keep the eyes open. Breathe softly through the nose."

He continues, "When the physical posture is already settled, make one complete exhalation and sway left and right. Sitting immovably in the mountain-still state, *Think about this concrete state beyond thinking. How can the state beyond thinking be thought about? It is different from thinking.* This is just the pivot of Zazen."

This is a reference to a story about a conversation between

Master Yakusan Igen and a monk. The monk asks his master, "What are you thinking in the mountain still state [zazen]?"

The master says, "Thinking the thought of non-thinking." The monk asks how to do that, and the master says, "It's different from thinking." He leaves it at that. If he said any more it would just be more descriptions of thought, which would be counterproductive. Each of us must find our own way to think the concrete state beyond thinking.

Dogen tells us, "This sitting in Zazen is not learning Zen concentration." It's not about getting some great mystical state. "It is simply the peaceful and joyful gate of Dharma."

He's saying that our real state in zazen is the truth itself. It doesn't matter if it feels like what you imagine mystical insights ought to feel like. The state of zazen itself is beyond anything as tawdry as what most of us imagine mystical insights ought to feel like.

Dogen concludes by saying, "If you practice the state like this for a long time, you will surely become the state like this itself. The treasure-house will open naturally, and you will be free to receive and to use [its contents] as you like."

You couldn't wish for a happier ending than that!

Elsewhere in his writings Dogen recommends that his monks do four forty-minute periods of zazen every day. That's a bit much for most of us. Personally I put in about an hour each day — generally forty minutes right after I get up and another twenty before bed. If you can't manage that much, just do however much you can. As long as you do it every day, even five lousy minutes is better than nothing at all.

You can start out right now, today, in your own home. You don't need to go to a Zen center or a temple up in the mountains. But if you do choose to go to those places, there are hundreds around, with more opening up every day.

# ABOUT THE AUTHOR

BRAD WARNER WAS born in Ohio in 1964, grew up in Africa, and lived in Japan for eleven years, where he got ordained as a Zen monk. He now resides in the USA. He started practicing zazen in his late teens and is a dharma heir of Gudo Nishijima Roshi. Brad used to work for a company that made movies about giant radioactive lizards eating Tokyo, and now he writes books like this one.

He has given talks and led Zen meditation retreats in the United States, Canada, England, Scotland, Northern Ireland, Finland, the Netherlands, Germany, France, Poland, Israel, Belgium, Spain, and Japan. His books have been translated into Finnish, Polish, German, French, Spanish, Hebrew, and Greek.

He plays bass in the hardcore punk band Zero Defex (oDFx). He has had major roles in the films *Zombie Bounty Hunter M.D.*, *Shoplifting from American Apparel*, and others. He also directed the film *Cleveland's Screaming*. Plus, he made five albums for Midnight Records under the semi-fictional band name Dimentia 13.

Brad has a dog named Ziggy, who is the cutest dog in the world. Ziggy can be seen on Brad's YouTube channel (youtube.com/hardcorezen), where Brad talks about Zen almost every day. Brad also has a podcast called *The Hardcore Zen Podcast*.